THE PENNSYLVANIA BARN

Creating the North American Landscape

Gregory Conniff
Bonnie Loyd
Edward K. Muller
David Schuyler
Consulting Editors

Published in cooperation with
the Center for American Places,
Harrisonburg, Virginia

THE PENNSYLVANIA BARN

Its Origin, Evolution, and Distribution
in North America

ROBERT F. ENSMINGER

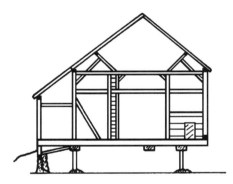

The Johns Hopkins University Press
Baltimore and London

Originally published, 1992
Johns Hopkins Paperbacks edition, 1995

The Johns Hopkins University Press
2715 North Charles Street
Baltimore, Maryland 21218-4319
The Johns Hopkins Press Ltd., London

Photographs are by the author unless otherwise noted. All of the diagrams in the text were prepared by the author and Ken Easterday for this volume. Maps are by the author and Ken Easterday unless otherwise noted.

Library of Congress Cataloging-in-Publication Data

Ensminger, Robert F., 1927–
    The Pennsylvania barn : its origin, evolution, and distribution in North America /
    Robert F. Ensminger.
       p.   cm. — (Creating the North American landscape)
    ISBN 0-8018-4304-9 – ISBN 0-8018-5252-8 (pbk.)
    1. Barns—Pennsylvania—History.   I. Title.   II. Series.
    NA8230.E5   1992
    728′.922′0973—dc20   91-39897

A catalog record for this book is available from the British Library.

To my wife, Rosalin

Without her support, understanding,
companionship, and patience
during all phases of the project,
this book could not have been completed

CONTENTS

ILLUSTRATIONS

Maps

Photographs

Photographs of barns and barn elements may be located by use of the index, where they are listed by type and location.

ACKNOWLEDGMENTS

A claim of sole authorship for a work such as *The Pennsylvania Barn* must be tempered by recognition of the many people who helped. Without them, the project could not have been completed. To the numerous farmers in Canada, the United States, and Europe who freely permitted me access to their farms and barns I express heartfelt thanks. Many people provided information, assistance, and photographs. They are credited in footnotes and in Appendix A.

Many fellow geographers made special contributions. John Fraser Hart, of the University of Minnesota, first suggested to me that I write a book about the Pennsylvania barn. Dr. Hart applied periodic, friendly pressure, which resulted in the initiation of the project. A longtime friend, Joseph Glass, at Millersville University in Pennsylvania, served as an informal consultant and advisor during all phases of the project. Hubert G. H. Wilhelm, of Ohio University, served as field guide, directing me to barns in southeastern Ohio. He also proofread the original document and made valuable suggestions. Glenn Harper, of the Ohio Preservation Office at Bowling Green University, provided valuable data about barns in western Ohio and served as field guide to Adams County, Indiana. Martin Perkins of Old World Wisconsin, in Eagle, Wisconsin, and Charles F. Calkins, of Carroll College in Waukesha, Wisconsin, personally led me to barns in southeastern Wisconsin. Donald B. Kraybill, professor of sociology and director of the Young Center for the Study of Anabaptist and Pietist Groups at Elizabethtown College in Pennsylvania, provided valuable insights into cultural and religious differences between the Amish and the Mennonites. Terry G. Jordan, Walter Prescott Webb Professor of History and Ideas at the University of Texas in Austin, contributed constructive suggestions concerning Walser and Romansch influences on barn evolution in Switzerland.

Emily Yoder Roberts, of Iowa City, Iowa, did field surveys to verify barn counts and provided photographs of Pennsylvania barns in southeastern Iowa. Terry Herschberger, of Middlebury, Indiana, provided photographs of

Pennsylvania barns in Elkhart County, Indiana. Herman Hilty of Bluffton, Ohio, provided information and photographs of barns in western Ohio. Allen G. Noble, professor of geography at Akron University in Ohio, has, over the years, supplied me numerous locations of Pennsylvania barns throughout the Midwest and has verified barn counts in northeastern Ohio. Wayne Price, of the Pioneer America Society, provided photographs and locations of Pennsylvania barns in Illinois and supplied details about their construction and morphology. Alan Keyser, of the Pennsylvania German Society, has been an informal consultant whose suggestions have improved this book.

Kutztown University in Pennsylvania, where I taught for seventeen years, provided facilities and services which were critical to the successful completion of this project. Professors Stephen Justham, Robert Martin, and Richard Crooker provided access to facilities in the Department of Geography. Beverly Williams, the department's secretary, was always available to help in copying the numerous drafts of the manuscript. Student cartographer Ken Easterday deserves special credit. He skillfully produced finished drawings, diagrams, and maps from my notes and designs. Karen De Jarnett, duplicating manager, provided the services of the Kutztown University print shop, which produced copies of the manuscript for proofing and review. Jackie Stark, secretary of the Department of Foreign Languages, deserves special thanks and credit for transcribing my original handwritten manuscript into manageable typed copies. Barbara Kegerreis, interlibrary loan technician for the Rohrbach Library, successfully researched and retrieved obscure but essential publications. On numerous occasions, Curt S. Goldstaub, head catalog librarian (retired), generously provided his expert skills to translate German sources. Raymond A. Phillips, of Allentown, Pennsylvania, also provided written translations of selected German sources.

Several other individuals provided vital specialized help. Norman Hoffman, of the Goschenhoppen Historians in Green Lane, Pennsylvania, provided detailed written translations of German sources that were indispensable to the mapping of Walser migrations. Tom Umholtz, of Valley View, Pennsylvania, provided field locations for numerous early barns in central Pennsylvania. Paul Fink, former superintendent of schools in Allentown, Pennsylvania, did a final proofreading of all documents. Diane Handwerk, of Handwerk Photo Lab in Emmaus, Pennsylvania, supplied the custom photo processing responsible for the many photographs used throughout the text. Christopher Witmer, of Kleinfeltersville, Pennsylvania, deserves special recognition. He is a landscape architect and barn researcher who has investigated the framing technology of Pennsylvania barns. His review of the manuscript and valuable suggestions have enhanced this book. Dale Lehmer and Jim Slabonic of Recycle The Barn People, St. Peters, Pennsylvania, have dismantled and preserved nearly two hundred barns in southeastern Pennsylvania. Many have been reassembled and remodeled for a variety of uses. They provided me the details of the tying-joint articulation for various barns in the area. Phoebe Hopkins, Historic Preservation Director of the Berks County Conservancy, provided survey data showing the locations of significant early barns in Berks County, Pennsylvania. A note of appreciation is reserved for C. Richard Beam, director of the Center for Pennsylvania German Studies, at Millersville University, Millersville, Pennsylvania. He verified the accuracy, spelling, and usage of Pennsylvania-German terms occurring throughout the book. Finally, I wish to acknowledge the special help provided to me by editors George Thompson and Anne Whitmore, of the Johns Hopkins University Press.

INTRODUCTION

The Pennsylvania barn has long been admired as one of the outstanding vernacular farm structures in Canada and the United States. Early accounts by travelers in eastern Pennsylvania indicate that, by the mid-eighteenth century, thriving German farmers were already building large barns, while retaining modest log cabin dwellings—a testimonial to the priority they placed on agriculture. Alfred Shoemaker and Don Yoder document early records and travel accounts in chapters 1 and 2 of Shoemaker's book *The Pennsylvania Barn* (1959). In one of the most revealing of these records, Robert Sutcliff, an English Quaker traveling in Chester County in 1806, writes in some detail about a Pennsylvania barn and explicitly describes a gallery, a six-foot overhang, above the stable doors. He tells of trap doors in the gallery floor through which fodder was thrown down to cattle during the winter months. Keep this description in mind when later we examine forebay bank barns in Europe. He also describes the overhanging gallery's sheltering function, protecting cattle from rain and snow (16).

Yoder can be credited with revealing the earliest known architectural plans for two-level Pennsylvania barns. His article in the spring 1965 edition of *Pennsylvania Folklife* deals with the *Domestic Encyclopedia of 1803–1804*, particularly the part edited by James Mease, who was a physician and scholar in Philadelphia (Yoder 1965, 11–21). Mease describes barns near Philadelphia, including plans for two of them. One, the Miller barn in Chester County, is a two-level "Swiss" barn whose lower-level plan clearly shows a post-supported forebay beyond the front stable wall. The use of the term *bridge* for the means of access to the upper level, plus statements about building the barn "in the hill" and using the lower level for cattle and the upper for storage of grain and for threshing, complete this early description of a Pennsylvania barn (15, 20–21).

The key element in the above descriptions is specific reference to the forebay, an upper-level extension over the basement (lower-level) stable doors. The forebay is the distinctive and diagnostic feature of the Pennsylvania barn. Nearly as important is that access to the upper level, the thresh-ing floor, is afforded by a bridge or bank or by the barn's being built into a hill. The mention of sheaves of grain waiting on the threshing floor is consistent with the location of granary bins in the adjacent forebay. A fore-bay granary can be found in the majority of Pennsylvania barns I have examined. What Yoder's account pictures is a two-level, forebay bank barn. This is probably the earliest definitive description of a Pennsylvania barn.

Yoder also cites the Duffield barn, built in 1789 in the northern part of Philadelphia County, as the first transfer of the two-level barn from the German-speaking culture in adjacent counties to the English-speaking cul-ture near Philadelphia (21). These writings, along with the early records cited by Shoemaker, not only define the basic morphology of the Pennsyl-vania barn, but also establish its Pennsylvania-German development and even suggest Swiss prototypes. Henceforth, I shall refer to this forebay bank barn, which first appeared in southeastern Pennsylvania in the early eigh-teenth century, as the Pennsylvania barn. This designation will be applied to the barn wherever it occurs in Canada and the United States. It will not be used to denote somewhat similar Old World structures, which are its poten-tial prototypes, nor will it be used to designate other barns that occur in Pennsylvania but do not comply with the above criteria.

In the book, I summarize the important literature that deals with these various attributes of the Pennsylvania barn, offer a detailed examination of the barn's origin, evolution, and development, propose a new and more comprehensive classification system for the barn, and chart the diffusion and distribution of the barn. This effort is the culmination of fifteen years of research and fieldwork, covering thousands of miles across North America and Europe. It represents the first scholarly attempt to integrate and update the relevant research about the Pennsylvania barn's origin, development, and diffusion—those aspects that have produced the distinctive agricul-tural landscapes that are characterized, and sometimes dominated, by its presence.

A few books deal almost entirely with Pennsylvania barns. Alfred Shoe-maker's *The Pennsylvania Barn,* published in 1955 by Franklin and Marshall College, in Lancaster, Pennsylvania, was the first book in America devoted to a particular barn type. This pioneering work is amply illustrated and the contributing authors cover various topics, including barn types, barn deco-rations, and an excellent sampling of early references to Pennsylvania barns. Unique is Shoemaker's statistical summary of the barns of 1798, derived from the tax records of that year. This listing by county and township includes a count of the barns by construction materials (i.e., log, stone, frame, or brick), and size. A second printing of the book, by the Pennsylvania Folklife Society, came out in 1959.

The second significant book, *Pennsylvania German Barns,* was published by the Pennsylvania German Folklore Society in 1958 (Dornbusch and Heyl 1958). In it, John Heyl, in collaboration with Charles Dornbusch, produced the first systematic study of Pennsylvania barns based on their morphology.

It contains 150 illustrations and includes detailed analyses of the varied forms of the Pennsylvania barn, resulting in a classification system. Progressing chronologically from simple early barns to larger, more complex later barns, the system establishes an evolutionary process to explain the barn's origin. It is this classification system and Dornbusch and Heyl's hypothesis of the origin of the Pennsylvania barn which I shall revise.

The first scholarly inquiry into the location and distribution of Pennsylvania barns was accomplished by Joseph Glass as part of his Ph.D. thesis in 1971. One result of this work was the first map of the Pennsylvania barn region. Recently, Glass has updated and consolidated his research, in *The Pennsylvania Culture Region: A View from the Barn* (1986). This excellent work is well-illustrated with pictures and maps by Glass. With his permission, some of the maps are included in this text. Another significant contribution by Glass is his examination of the functional advantages of the Pennsylvania barn and its forebay. These things were crucial to the success of the barn after its appearance in Pennsylvania. They fostered broad acceptance, then modification, and, eventually, diffusion of the barn across the continent. For those interested in locating the more obscure articles on farm buildings, including Pennsylvania barns, I call attention to LeRoy Schultz's book, *Barns, Stables, and Outbuildings,* an excellent bibliography published in 1986. It contains more than three thousand entries, of which eighty-four deal with "Pennsylvania-German" barns.

Finally, *Latrobe's View of America, 1795–1820,* is a compilation of selected sketches and watercolor paintings by the famous American architect, engineer, traveler, and naturalist Benjamin Henry Latrobe. One of these paintings is particularly relevant to this study. It clearly shows a stone Sweitzer forebay barn that is in Lancaster County that has a thatched roof, and beside it a central-chimney, continental Germanic farmhouse (Carter, Van Horne, and Brownell 1985, 210–11). The style of both structures indicates that they were built between 1765 and 1785. This painting, done in 1801, is one of the earliest pictorial representations of that magnificent vernacular structure, the Pennsylvania barn.

1

THE ORIGIN OF THE PENNSYLVANIA BARN

In the early eighteenth century, a two-level barn appeared in southeastern Pennsylvania. This barn was larger and more substantial than preceding pioneer farm structures in North America. It was more versatile than the one-level ground barn (*Grundscheier*) being built at the same time. This multipurpose barn could house various livestock in the basement (lower-level) stable, while on the second floor it could store hay and straw and accommodate the threshing of feed grains. These were then stored in the bins of a granary, which was usually located in the forebay. The forebay, or "overshoot," is the second-floor extension, which projects over the front stable wall for a distance that varies from four feet to even twenty or more feet in some barns. The forebay, this extra space, or bay, on the fore side of the barn, is the distinctive and diagnostic feature of the Pennsylvania barn.

Access to the upper level of the barn is created by banking the barn (building it into a hill) or by constructing a gentle ramp or bank leading to the second level, allowing farm machines and wagons to be driven up into the barn. There are numerous two-level barns in Canada and the United States, including many that are banked, that are called *basement barns*. They can be found from New England and upstate New York across the upper Midwest as far as Minnesota. They do not, however, have forebays.

In Pennsylvania, forebay bank barns had become dominant in the southeastern part of the state by the end of the eighteenth century, and they made a distinctive imprint upon that area's landscape. The range of these barns extended farther south and west during the nineteenth century and spread to many states beyond Pennsylvania. Interest in the Pennsylvania barn can be traced back to early nineteenth-century writings, but the first recorded statement about the barn's origin was not made until 1915. In that

Figures 1.1 and 1.2. Bank side (*top*) and forebay side (*bottom*) of the Grosser barn, built in 1793 near Gilbertsville, Montgomery County, Pennsylvania. Throughout this book, the forebay side will be considered the front of the barn while the bank side will be considered the back. (Photo 1989.)

year, Marion Learned, professor of Germanic languages at the University of Pennsylvania, published a paper entitled "The German Barn in America" (Learned 1915, 338–49). He referred to the high Alemannic, or Swiss-German, house as the Pennsylvania barn's probable prototype and suggested that the forebay was a direct survival of the projecting roof and balcony of this house (347). He also pointed out that the very names frequently used for the barn, *Swisser* in English, *Schweizer Scheier* in the Pennsylvania-German dialect, is a strong corroboration of the Swiss connection (348).

Learned's statement falls short of accepting a direct transfer in toto of the forebay barn from Switzerland to North America. He implies some modification: in Pennsylvania, house and barn were separated; the balcony was retained in the barn but was modified and enclosed to become the forebay.

Thomas J. Wertenbaker, writing in 1938, discussed the European roots of American civilization, including his ideas about the origin of the Pennsylvania barn. They parallel Learned's statements. First, said Wertenbaker, "we must seek the ancestry of the Pennsylvania German barn in the wooded highlands of Upper Bavaria, the southern spurs of the Black Forest Mountains, in the Jura Region, and elsewhere in Switzerland. In the Upper Bavarian house, which has the closest affinity of all to the Pennsylvania barn, the residence, barn, and stable are under one roof" (Wertenbaker 1938, 321). Second, "of special interest is the 'Laube' or 'forebay,' an overshoot of the barn floor affording an enclosed gallery above and a protection to the walls, windows, and doors of the stable below" (322).

Wertenbaker felt that the barn part of this highland house had been retained almost unchanged in America, which makes his statement that the forebay may have been an afterthought confusing and inconsistent with his general logic. Nevertheless, his acceptance of a European prototype seems clear, for he details many similarities of morphology between Pennsylvania and Alpine structures. He also enlarges the distributional area of the peasant house prototype, quoting Klaus Thiede and other European folkhousing sources that include the Alps, from central and western Austria to Canton Bern, Switzerland, in the source area (321–25).

One of the strongest statements in support of a direct Swiss prototype for the Pennsylvania barn appears in an obscure booklet, *Hex No!*, by Alfred Shoemaker (1953, 27). In it, he quotes the Reverend Benjamin Bausman, writing in the 24 September 1884 issue of the Lancaster German-language newspaper, the *Volksfreund*. Bausman, traveling in Switzerland at the time, wrote: "In Switzerland, we feel very much at home. There is much to see that reminds one of home. For example, here one sees the original Swiss barns after which all our Pennsylvania Dutch barns were patterned. They have a ground floor for stables and the second story serves as threshing floor and mow space. There is a forebay along the entire length of the barn." This statement is striking in its exact description of a long, eave-side forebay and is the earliest reference to the basic similarity between Swiss and Pennsylvania barns.

Figures 1.3 and 1.4. Black Forest high Alemannic folkhouse (*top*), Vogtsbauern-haus, built in 1570, now located at an open-air museum in Gutach, Germany. This house-barn combination has a large hay storage loft starting above the barn and extending over the residence. (Photo 1975.) Log plank folkhouse (*bottom*), East Tyrol, Austria. The entire back half of this structure is the barn with a forebaylike overhanging loft on both sides. This folkhouse and the Black Forest folkhouse both have overhanging balconies (Lauben) as part of the residence. (Photo 1978.)

More recently, geographer Hubert Wilhelm, writing about Pennsylvania barns in Ohio, stated: "It is more likely that the Pennsylvania-Dutch barn has European antecedents. In the upper Rhine Valley in Switzerland, there are banked forebay barns whose lower stable portion opens toward village streets" (Wilhelm 1974, 159–60). Wilhelm thus suggested the upper Rhine Valley as a potential source area of Pennsylvania barn prototypes.

While the scholars cited all endorse, to varying degrees, the existence of European prototypes for the Pennsylvania barn, the opposing school holds that the barn is an American invention that appeared in Pennsylvania as a result of gradual evolution. Dornbusch and Heyl's *Pennsylvania German Barns* contains the first exposition and defense of this proposition. While Dornbusch's major contribution was the first comprehensive classification of Pennsylvania's barns, Heyl made statements pertaining to their origin. He said that, although the details and methods of construction can be traced to the Old World, the barn has no *direct* precedent in structures of similar use in western Europe or in Britain (Dornbusch and Heyl 1958, x). He cited the common usage in medieval European housing of the overhanging and extended framed bay, plus the abundance of banked structures in Alpine Europe, and concluded that the Germanic settlers in Pennsylvania combined these time-tested forms to accommodate their needs by projecting a new form, the great bank barn of Pennsylvania (xii). These statements explicitly defend the proposition of development and evolution of the Pennsylvania barn in North America and reject the idea of direct transfer of the form from European prototypes.

The main text of Dornbusch and Heyl's book plots the evolution of the Pennsylvania barn by identifying eleven barn types. This system is summarized and reproduced in Appendix B of this book. Appearance of the eleven barn types moves chronologically from the early 1700s to the mid-1800s. The evolution also progresses morphologically from simple ground barns of log construction, to transitional stone ground barns with partial basement stables, to ground barns with protective pentroofs over stable doors, to a two-story bank barn with full pentroof (Type E, in his system). This last form is described as the next logical development of the true bank barn (40). The type that follows it, Type F, has a cantilevered overhanging forebay and is called the Sweitzer barn (80). This evolutionary theory for the Pennsylvania barn's origin implies that the forebay developed from the pentroof. Later types having a forebay supported by extensions of the basement walls or by support posts complete the evolutionary scheme.

This is certainly a logical and attractive approach—that the Pennsylvania barn is a product of evolution and selection forged by the requirements of the Pennsylvania frontier. A closer check of the construction dates of the very barns pictured to illustrate this scheme raises some serious questions about this theory. Most of the Type E (pre-forebay) barns cited date from the late eighteenth century to early nineteenth century, while some of the supposedly successor Type F and Type G barns show earlier construction dates,

Figures 1.5 and 1.6. Bank side of a Dornbusch Type E bank barn near Moselem Springs, Berks County, Pennsylvania (*top*). Front stable wall of the same barn (*bottom*). Flashing line indicating place of roof attachment and beam stumps show that this barn originally had a pentroof protecting the stable doors. Barns like this are common in the southern Lake District of northwestern England. (Photos 1978.)

Figures 1.7 and 1.8. Mid-eighteenth century, double-log-crib ground barn, or Grundscheier, near Fleetwood, Berks County, Pennsylvania (*top*). Cantilever barn near Cades Cove, Tennessee (*bottom*). Overhanging loft barns like the cantilever barn may have been inspired by early forebay ground barns in Pennsylvania. (Photos 1972.)

from the mid-1700s. Furthermore, Heyl stated that the Sweitzer forebay barn was widely distributed in southeastern Pennsylvania by the mid-eighteenth century (xviii), although, in fact, the form prevailed in the *early* eighteenth century (80).

It would seem that the fully developed forebay bank barn appeared nearly as early as the pioneer ground barn and earlier than the first bank barn (Dornbusch Type E), from which it supposedly directly evolved. In fact, the almost simultaneous appearance of both ground barns and forebay barns suggests a familiarity with both forms by early settlers and implies prior knowledge of European prototypes in both cases.

The evolutionary explanation was also embraced by folklife scholar Henry Glassie, who likewise placed the ground barn, or Grundscheier, at the beginning of the progression (Glassie 1966, 12–25). He made a detailed and explicit examination of the Pennsylvania barn in a series of articles beginning in 1965. Glassie recognized that the log double-crib ground barn was known during the earliest period of settlement, and he speculated that a ground barn with overhanging loft must also have appeared then. He stated that this overhanging loft form of barn was carried out of Pennsylvania during the first wave of out-migration, in the second quarter of the eighteenth century, and became established on the eastern and western slopes of the Great Smoky Mountains in North Carolina and Tennessee. Here its evolution continued with the inclusion of additional cribs or with the one-quarter rotation of the roof ridge, resulting in the transverse crib barn, the dominant type of barn in the early upland South (Glassie 1968, 88–93; Kniffen 1965, 563–66).

Glassie then proposed an evolutionary sequence: double-crib ground barn, double-crib ground barn with overhanging loft, two-level barn with unsupported forebay, two-level barn with supported forebay (Glassie 1966, 23). He recognized that many techniques and certain elements of European farm structures known by early settlers had been used in Pennsylvania barns. Specifically, he compared the forebay to the balcony of certain Swiss houses, to the spinning gallery of barns in Lancashire, England, and to the cantilevered balcony of the Bohemian *Umgebindehaus*. But he concluded that the combination of those elements into the Pennsylvania barn was distinctly American (24–25). In 1970, Glassie reiterated this thesis of New World synthesis, stating that even though multilevel banked buildings reminiscent of the Pennsylvania barn can be seen in Switzerland, Germany, and England, precise prototypes can be found nowhere in the Old World (Glassie 1970, 25).

Glassie's evolutionary sequence is certainly logical and also attractive to those who are steeped in the culture and heritage of the Pennsylvania Germans, but any New World evolutionary scheme hinges upon the early development in Pennsylvania of the double-crib barn with overhanging loft. Being the second step in the sequence, it should have survived in larger numbers than the earlier plain double-crib barn. In fact, this is not the case. There are

Figures 1.9 and 1.10. Ramp on bank side of Lake District bank barn in north-western England (*top*). View of the same barn showing pentroof over stable doors (*bottom*). This type of structure is the probable prototype of the Dornbusch Type E barn (see Figures 1.5 and 1.6) of southeastern Pennsylvania. (Photos 1978.)

several hundred—possibly up to one thousand—of the stage one, log double-crib barns still standing in Pennsylvania.[1] Many go unnoticed because they have been disguised by coverings of newer material or remodeling has distorted their original form. Stage two barns with overhanging loft, those which should be more numerous, are relatively rare. I have seen several in Bedford County, Pennsylvania; Glassie has studied them in York and Adams counties (Glassie 1970, 23–34). The survival rates of these two barns should show a strong correlation with their original populations and periods of construction. The fact that this is not the case casts doubt on Glassie's theory of the Pennsylvania barn's origin.

In searching for European sources of structural elements synthesized in the Pennsylvania barn, Glassie and others have suggested the bank barns of the Lake District of northwestern England.[2] In 1978, I visited the Lake District to explore this hypothesis. Barns there are two-level structures with banks or ramps. Stables on the lower level are protected by a pentroof instead of a forebay. They are, therefore, very similar to Dornbusch's Type E barns and could be their prototypes. The fact that this Lake District type of bank barn is most abundant in Chester, Delaware, and Bucks counties, Pennsylvania, adjacent to Philadelphia, supports the idea of its transplantation by people of English stock. I do not believe that English Lake District barns contributed to the initial development of the Pennsylvania barn. In North America they generally date in the latter eighteenth century, *after* the establishment of the forebay barn. In fact, the dates assigned them in England by Brunskill indicate that they appeared in 1730–1740 and did not predominate there until much later (Brunskill 1974, 83–86).

Searching for a European Prototype

So, many scholars reject the idea that the Pennsylvania barn had a direct European prototype and favor the concept of its development in America. How does the record of colonial history, the study of colonial architecture, and evidence provided by the surviving artifacts and folk art stack up? There are numerous examples of the virtual replication of European forms. For example, a visit to the Folk Museum in Innsbruck, Austria, will show a close connection between the tools, fraktur art, wrought iron, wood carving, and decorated furniture found there and corresponding examples in and from Pennsylvania. Evidence of the direct transfer of architectural types is also strong; several types of North American barns came virtually unchanged from Europe. The Grundscheier, which all scholars have recognized as an early barn in Pennsylvania, has been traced by Alan Keyser to the Palatinate, a source region for numerous Pennsylvania-German pioneers (Keyser and Stein 1975, 3). Arthur and Whitney, in *The Barn* (1972), make use of photographs, diagrams, and other documentation to show the continuation of

1. Keyser and Stein 1975, 1–25; statement based on my own fieldwork plus corroboration from similar observation by Alan Keyser, who has spent many years studying barns.
2. Glassie 1970, 25; and conversation with Don Yoder, University of Pennsylvania, in 1976.

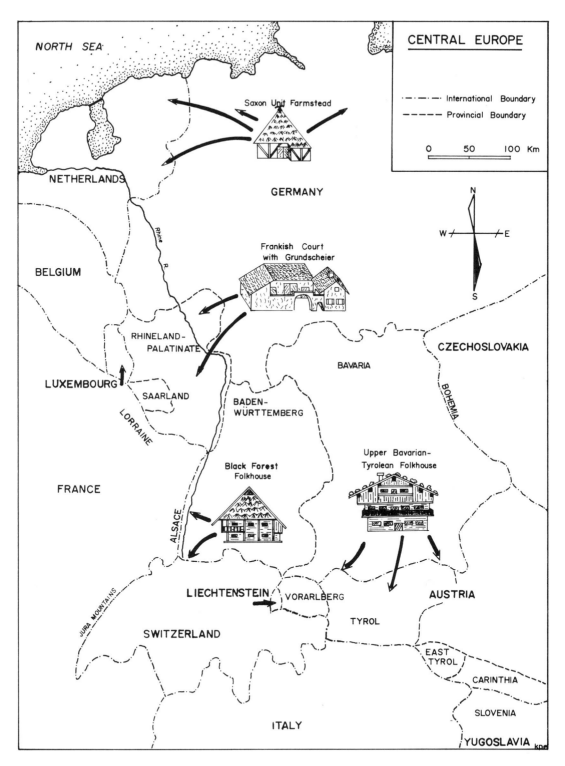

Map 1.1. Central Europe, with general source areas of barn types.

Figure 1.11. Family photograph (circa 1900) taken in eastern Switzerland (precise location unknown). The decorative arched bracket immediately behind the men reinforces a cantilevered beam that supports the forebay.

European forms in America. They examine the English barn and its American counterpart, the Yankee barn; the Breton barn and its French-Canadian extension, the Quebec long barn; and the Saxon unit farmstead and its New World edition, the New York Dutch barn. This last structure is thoroughly analyzed by John Fitchen in his classic study, *The New World Dutch Barn* (1968). He provides detailed architectural analyses and compares the New York barn to its Old World prototypes.

These and other studies chronicle the massive evidence of direct diffusion to America of a broad variety of European material culture forms, including, significantly, the direct transfer of barns from Europe to North America. Strong differences of opinion are expressed in these studies concerning the possibility of a direct European prototype for the Pennsylvania barn. These opinions range from the acceptance of a direct barn prototype, through the theory that European nonbarn structures were revised as barns in Pennsylvania, to the rejection of a direct prototype but the allowance that certain European forms were integrated during the evolutionary process in Pennsylvania.

To solve the problem of the Pennsylvania barn's origin, a survey of European literature, plus fieldwork in Europe, is required. A trip to Europe in 1975 provided me an opportunity to explore the places of origin of the Germanic settlers who arrived in Pennsylvania during the eighteenth century. During this first trip I accomplished a broad overview of Germanic Europe and established a sense of the general location of those barn struc-

Figure 1.12. This Grundscheier, attached to the house in Frankish "courted" arrangement, is south of Heidelberg, Germany. Notice the manure box just beyond the stable door but adjacent to house entrance. (Photo 1978.)

tures that might have contributed to the Pennsylvania barn. The American literature, already summarized, provided only general preparatory information. Several European sources reinforced statements by Learned, Wertenbaker, and Glassie that many European folkhouses contain forebaylike features.[3] But it was an old family photograph showing my wife's grandfather standing beneath the forebay of a barn in his Swiss homeland that really aroused my interest.

My first European survey enabled me to establish the following conclusions. First, the Rhineland-Palatinate, homeland of many Pennsylvania-German settlers, contains no forebay barn prototypes. The Grundscheier is the prevailing form there, frequently occurring in a "courted" arrangement with the dwelling, forming a Frankish, court-type farmstead. Second, a broad Alpine zone of upland folkhouses stretches from the Black Forest and

3. Laedrach 1954; Laedrach and Rubi 1948; Thiede 1955, 103–7; Schäfer 1906, vols. 1 and 2. The first volume of Shäfer's work, subtitled *Atlas*, contains hundreds of detailed drawings and cross sections of farm buildings, as well as layouts, internal morphology, roofing and framing techniques, and photographs of other early structures, many of which no longer survive. It demonstrates that forebaylike features occur on houses and barns throughout Germanic Europe. The second volume, *Text*, contains historic and geographic descriptions and pictures that illustrate the forebay form.

Upper Bavarian regions of Germany, across Switzerland, and into the Tyrol of Austria. These are large banked house-barns with balcony and forebaylike barn extensions. Third, a region of true forebay bank barns, separate from dwellings, occurs in central and eastern Switzerland, extending from Canton Bern to the Rhine.

In 1978, I returned to Alpine Europe to re-examine the forebay barns of Switzerland and to define in greater detail the extent of their distribution. A classic work by the Swiss folklife scholar Richard Weiss provided illustrations of a log forebay barn in Schiers, Prätigau, Canton Graubünden (Weiss 1959, 184). Another work, previously overlooked by American scholars, was much more explicit in providing a detailed description of an early Swiss forebay bank barn, also in Schiers: this 1933 work by Jerosch Brockmann is one of the sources upon which later research by Weiss and other Swiss scholars has built. In it, Brockmann provides an illustration of a Prätigauer *Landenhaus* and includes the following description:

> The stable or "Gaden" is reached from the kitchen door by taking only a few steps. The Stallbrücke or front stable yard is covered by the protruding part of the barn, called the "Vürschutz" [forebay] and contains the "Talina," which runs the entire front length of the barn and serves as a storage area for straw, grain, bags, and fodder. Round logs are sometimes covered with boards which end in decorative arches forming a significant feature of the Prätigau barn. Because of grain processing, the second floor between the two hay mows, or "Heulegi," is divided by a narrow threshing floor, the "Tenn," which is reached by large double doors on the up-slope side of the barn. (Brockmann 1933, 101–7; translated from the German by Robert Ensminger)

Brockmann's description of the Prätigau forebay bank barn would fit any small Pennsylvania barn, but especially those of log construction, which are the earliest types. His illustration shows a cantilevered forebay with a stairway leading from it to the front stable yard—features found in many such barns in Pennsylvania. And his description of a full-length forebay above the front stable area, functioning as a feed storage area, plus two haymows and a threshing floor accessible through large doors on the "up" side completes an almost duplicate picture of a Pennsylvania barn!

The Prätigau region, to which both Weiss and Brockmann refer, has significant populations of early log barns. It follows the valley of the Landquart River, which joins the Rhine just south of Liechtenstein. A dense concentration of several hundred forebay bank barns can be found between the towns of Grüsch and Klosters, a distance of about fifteen miles. Some occur in compact farm villages, but most are found on scattered farmsteads spread from the valley floor to the high meadows and in the tributary valleys. These barns bear a very close correspondence in morphology and internal arrangement to those of early Pennsylvania, and this makes Prätigau a prime candidate as a source region for prototypes of the Pennsylvania barn. My follow-up of Brockmann's early work paid off richly, by providing documentation of these potential prototypes with which to dispute the claims of those

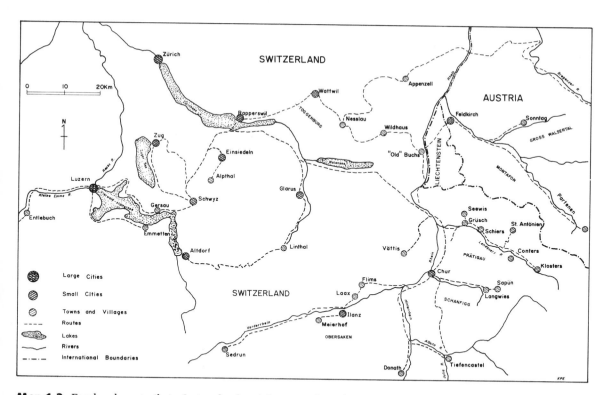

Map 1.2. Forebay barn trails in Switzerland and Austria: selected routes and places.

American scholars who said that there were no forebay bank barns in Europe.

Forebay barns occur extensively beyond Prätigau, from Entlebuch in eastern Bern, in a discontinuous belt across the Swiss cantons of Unterwalden, Uri, Schwyz, Zug, St. Gallen, and Appenzell, and on into Vorarlberg, in western Austria (Ensminger 1980–81, 62–67). Outliers of the forebay barn form are found farther east in Austria, in Zillertal in the Tyrol and in Carinthia, and across the border in Slovenia, in northern Yugoslavia. Slovenia was settled by Germanic peoples in the ninth century. The forebay barns and folkhouses there may represent the southernmost extension of the influence of Alemannic Alpine architecture (61–62).

My investigations up to this point had yielded the following information and conclusions: First, several types of early American barns have direct European prototypes. Second, forebay barns appeared in Pennsylvania in the early eighteenth century, along with other first generation barns. The fully developed cantilevered-forebay bank barn (Sweitzer barn) had been established by the 1750s and was contemporaneous with most of the ground barns from which others say it evolved. Third, the early usage of the term *Sweitzer* for this barn strongly suggests a Swiss origin. Fourth, the log forebay barns of Prätigau are morphologically very similar to the earliest log forebay barns of Pennsylvania. Fifth, early datings for forebay bank barns in

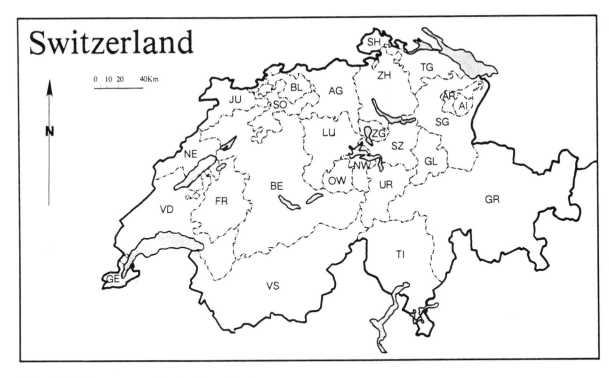

Map 1.3. Swiss cantons. (Map by the author.)

Key to abbreviations:

AG	Aargau	JU	Jura	TG	Thurgau
AI	Inner Rhoden ⎫ Appenzell	LU	Luzern	TI	Ticino
AR	Ausser Rhoden ⎭	NE	Neuchâtel	UR	Uri
BE	Bern	NW	Nidwalden ⎫ Unterwalden	VD	Vaud
BL	Basel Land–Basel-Stadt	OW	Obwalden ⎭	VS	Valais (Wallis)
FR	Fribourg	SG	St. Gallen	ZG	Zürich
GE	Genève	SH	Schaffhausen	ZH	Zug
GL	Glarus	SO	Solothurn		
GR	Graubünden	SZ	Schwyz		

Prätigau prove that the forebay tradition in Switzerland had been established long before settlers migrated from there to Pennsylvania, which virtually guarantees their familiarity with the form. Sixth, the eastern cantons of Switzerland, including Graubünden, did experience out-migration, particularly during the 150-year period following the end of the Thirty Years' War, in 1648. A combination of religious, political, and economic pressures produced a steady drain of surplus population during those times. Oscar Kuhns (1901) and Albert Faust and Gaius Brumbaugh (1968) have documented that many who immigrated to Pennsylvania came from this region. Seventh, the evidence above, coupled with flaws in the various New World evolution-

Figure 1.13. Forebay bank barn near Aschau, Zillertal, Tyrol, Austria. (Photo 1978.)

ary theses, forms a strong case for the theory that the Pennsylvania barn has direct European prototypes and that, although forebays occur on barns over a fairly broad area of Alpine Europe, the log forebay bank barns of Prätigau, Switzerland, provide the best prototype for the Pennsylvania barn.

This solution to the problem of the Pennsylvania barn's origin was met at first with skepticism by some scholars and folk culturists. I had been skeptical myself. I confess that, influenced by my ethnic bias as a Pennsylvania German, I wanted to believe that Pennsylvania's magnificent barn was an expression of my ancestors' creative energy, unleashed by the freedom and stimulation of the Pennsylvania frontier. Thus, when I found no forebay barns during the earlier part of the first European field survey, in Germany, my hope was sustained. When forebay barns did begin to appear, in central Switzerland, I was excited but saddened. My preconceptions were proving to be myths, as I encountered precursor barns by the hundreds. Still resisting, I looked for reasons why these could not be prototypes of the Pennsylvania barn—they were too late to have an impact on early emigrants, or their forebays were mainly for hay storage and lacked granaries like those in Pennsylvania barns. Actually, most early log Pennsylvania barns also had no specific granary partitions in the forebay.

When the log forebay bank barns of Prätigau were surveyed, the weight of the evidence shifted dramatically, and I was forced to accept the strong possibility of a Swiss prototype for the Pennsylvania barn. Fortunately, and coincidentally, support for this new thesis came from an unexpected source. Terry Jordan, a noted cultural geographer and scholar, had also done field research in Alpine Europe in the summer of 1978, while tracing the antecedents of American log architecture. His research necessarily involved the examination of barns across central Europe. He also documented forebay barns in Switzerland, in particular, those in Prätigau. The results are set forth in his article "Alpine Alemannic, and American Log Architecture" (Jordan 1980, 154–80). His conclusions are similar—indeed, virtually identical—to those I have detailed. That two independent researchers, working without consultation, came up almost simultaneously with nearly identical conclusions strengthens the validity of those conclusions.

Jordan reviewed this position and presented additional data in his book *American Log Buildings,* which was published in 1985.[4] In it, he compiled the results of his previous papers and field researches, which covered northern and central Europe, in a comprehensive investigation of log structures in Scandinavia and from the Alps to the Carpathian Mountains. He concluded that the greatest influence on Midland American pioneer log construction was exerted by settlers from the Fenno-Scandinavian area. He documented that bank, forebay, and double-crib barns can all be found in Scandinavia, and he suggested that they could have reinforced similar forms known to other immigrant groups. He stated that settlers from the central European German-Slavic borderland exerted only limited influence on the Midland tradition, but he reiterated his support of an Alpine-Alemannic prototype for the Pennsylvania barn and restated that region's considerable influence on American Midland architecture. He concluded that Pennsylvania's role as a cultural hearth and center of pioneer architectural inventiveness may have been overstated.

In a recent article in *Pennsylvania Folklife,* Jordan brought to light several significant studies from the Swiss literature dealing with forebay bank barns in Switzerland (Jordan, 1987–88, 75–80). One, by folklife scholar Richard Weiss, classifies, describes, and maps barns in Graubünden (Weiss 1943, 30–48, maps). Another, by Simonett and Könz (1968), enlarges upon Weiss's findings with detailed descriptions and illustrations. Both Swiss articles identify additional locations for forebay barns along the upper Rhine River and its tributaries, thus expanding their area of distribution. Both also focus on the Schanfigg district, parallel to Prätigau, as another major location of forebay bank barns. Jordan's excellent research clearly demonstrated that the search for Swiss prototypes for the Pennsylvania barn was far from complete. Using the sources from his report, I undertook follow-up field studies in Switzerland in 1988 to re-examine my original premise that there are direct Swiss prototypes of the Pennsylvania barn.

---

4. Jordan 1985, 100–108, 146–48, 151–53; Jordan and Kaups 1989. In this award-winning book, Jordan and Kaups convincingly detail the predominant influence on the American frontier of the Savo-Karelian Finns who first settled the lower Delaware River valley.

Figures 1.14 and 1.15. Double-log-crib bank barn in southern Norway (*top*). Farm storage building with forebaylike overhanging open gallery (*bottom*), from central Sweden, now relocated to the famous Skansen Outdoor Museum in Stockholm. (Photos 1981.)

Figures 1.16 and 1.17. Forebay bank barn with single log crib and threshing floor (*top*) overlooking Landquart River gap toward Rhine River valley, in Prätigau. Double-log-crib forebay bank barn near St. Antönien, Prätigau (*bottom*). In the latter, the rear doors lead to the threshing floor between the log-crib mows. Stakes used for drying hay in the fields are stored by hanging them under the rear eave of the barn. (Photos 1988.)

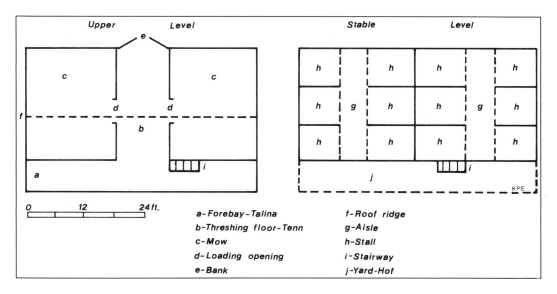

Diagram 1.1. Plan of typical double-log-crib forebay bank barn in Prätigau, Canton Graubünden, Switzerland.

Switzerland Revisited

I returned to Prätigau in June 1988 for a closer look at the barns that Jordan and I had independently singled out as potential prototypes of the Pennsylvania barn. Things had changed little in the ensuing ten years; the hundreds of barns previously described were still in use. Many of these structures are two or three hundred years old and may very well survive their more recent cousins in America, where changes in agriculture and land use have resulted in barns being destroyed at a rapid rate.

The typical Prätigau barn conforms closely to Brockmann's previously quoted description. With log-double-crib mows separated by a threshing or wagon floor, the upper level is virtually identical to the early log Sweitzer barns of Pennsylvania. Both barns have large loading openings, cut out of the log walls adjacent to the threshing floor, that lead to the log crib mows. The top several logs of this "cut out" in the wall are kept intact and serve as tie beams that prevent the crib from collapsing. The removal of log segments to make the openings was necessarily done after the erection of the crib; otherwise, the crib would have collapsed during construction. Log ends exposed by cutting the openings were then stabilized by inserting wood shims or applying vertical frame members over those ends. This identical technology was used in similar barns in Pennsylvania. Figures 1.18 and 1.19 clearly show these and other fundamental characteristics.

The upper level of the Prätigau barn is built against the hillside (that is, it is banked) and has large double doors. The opposite side of the upper level

Figure 1.18. Prätigau forebay bank barn: the forebay walkway, or Talina, (*a* in Diagram 1.1) and trapdoor leading to fodder stairs (*i*). (Photo 1988.)

Figure 1.19. Prätigau forebay bank barn: view from mow to mow (*c* in Diagram 1.1) through loading openings (*d*) on either side of threshing floor (*b*). (Photo 1988.)

Figure 1.20. Prätigau forebay bank barn: under-forebay yard, or Hof, (*j* in Diagram 1.1) showing split stable doors and wooden floor. Forebay support posts are mortised into forebay beams. (Photo 1978.)

projects 4 to 6 feet over the lower front stable wall, enclosing a walkway, or *Talina,* within this forebay. The forebay (*Vorschub* or *Vürschutz*) with Talina is entered directly from the threshing floor, or *Tenn,* and is separated from the hay storage area by the front interior walls of each log crib. The threshing floor is illuminated by a large window in the center of the front forebay wall. Through a trapdoor in the forebay floor the fodder stairs lead down to a small area (*Hof*) in front of the stable and provide for easy transport of hay to the stable doors. The stairway may be centered, or on one side of the forebay. Forebay stairways are also found in some log Sweitzer barns in Pennsylvania and have been used in many later barns in some counties. The barns I have been describing all have a gable roof with the roof ridge parallel to the front stable wall, producing a forebay on the *eave* side of the barn—the standard arrangement in Pennsylvania. Many barns in Switzerland have the roof ridge parallel to the axis of the hill slope with the forebay on the downslope gable end. Hereafter, I shall use the terms *eave-forebay* and *gable-forebay* to designate these barns.

Although settlers arrived with the cultural heritage of their homelands, the melting pot nature of the frontier exposed them to a variety of ideas and techniques that they could select and incorporate into their house- and barn-building practices as they adapted to their new environment. While

Figure 1.21. Prätigau forebay bank barn. Purlins, seen here projecting beyond the gable wall, rest on the logs of the gable-end wall; they support the roof and provide for a protective overhang. (Photo 1988.)

there are many likenesses between the Prätigau barn and its Pennsylvania relative, there are also differences. The Prätigau barn has a more gently sloping roof (15–20 degrees) than do similar barns in Pennsylvania. Stone slab shingles were used, and still survive, on older barns, and, even where newer roofs use tile or wood shingles, stone weights are placed on top to stabilize the roofing material. Both roofing techniques require gentle slopes to prevent these materials from sliding off. In Pennsylvania, early barns nearly always had roof slopes of 40 to 45 degrees, because the commonly used rye straw thatch required rapid drainage (Shoemaker 1959, 47–51; Bucher and Keyser 1982, 1–23). The steeper slope may also reflect a prefer- ence for northern Swiss and Black Forest roofing and framing traditions, which conveniently complemented the availability of Pennsylvania rye straw, or of local red tile during the colonial period.

Prätigau barns, being small, can maintain roof support with purlins, which rest on top of the log gable-end walls, which extend to the roof ridge (see Figure 1.21). Early Pennsylvania barns display various rafter framework plans that use braces resting upon the log crib walls, which end at eave height. The gable wall is then completed by nailing vertical boards to this upper frame. The board-covered gable appeared in Pennsylvania as early as 1686, suggesting Swedish or British influence (Jordan 1985, 138, 147). Roof

Figure 1.22. Early Prätigau forebay bank barn with hewn triangular-block stairway. Forebay beams ar cantilevered into barn and need no additional support. Forebay walls and stable walls are built of logs. (Photo 1988.)

rafters in both Pennsylvania and Prätigau barns join at the peak without inclusion of a ridge board. This incorporation of building practices fr different sources is consistent with pioneer practices of choosing the m appropriate forms to insure survival on the frontier.

The basement stables of Prätigau barns are small and simple. The m common arrangement is to have two separate stable rooms, each served b split door. Each stable contains two rows of three stalls, thus housing cows. These face away from a center aisle, by which food is brought in a manure is removed. The split stable door is very practical, in that the bott half can be kept closed to secure the animals while the upper half rema open, providing light and ventilation. This type of door is used through central Europe. The stable doors open onto the small yard, or Hof, whicl protected by the overhanging forebay. A wooden walkway usually covers floor of the Hof, providing a level location for a water trough. Tools, fa implements, and firewood may also be stored in the Hof. In front of walkway, manure is deposited, often in a wooden board container. T keeps it well beyond the route between the stable doors and the forel stairway, along which hay and straw must frequently be carried.

The functional advantages of this barn, especially its forebay, beco very apparent when one considers the labor required to maintain eve

Figure 1.23. Early Pennsylvania forebay barn, 1747, near Oley, Berks County, Pennsylvania, forebay walls and stable walls of logs. (Photograph from 3 May 1915 issue of the *Reading Eagle*.)

small herd of dairy cows during the long Alpine winter. Little wonder that it relocated so quickly to the Pennsylvania frontier, emerged there as the dominant type, and eventually diffused widely through parts of Midland America. A very early dating (1564) for a surviving forebay barn in Conters, Prätigau, reinforces the conclusion that the forebay barn was well established there long before emigration to Pennsylvania had started (Simonett and Könz 1968, 21).

There are some variations among the eave-forebay bank barns of Prätigau. Barns having two log cribs and no threshing floor or a single crib with threshing floor on one side can be found. Basement stables are usually divided into two rooms. The placement of the door and arrangement of the stalls may vary somewhat. Other variations result from age differences among barns. The earlier ones have fully cantilevered forebays with no other support structures. Their stairways are hewn from triangular blocks of wood (see Figure 1.22). Later barns gain additional forebay support by having posts mortised into the outer ends of the forebay beams (see Figure 1.20). The fodder stairs of these later barns are made of heavy planks. Vertical boards frequently cover the forebay logs and end in decorative scallops. These boards provide insulation from rain and snow—a necessary protection if grains are being stored in the forebay. Log exterior crib walls are left

Figures 1.24 and 1.25. Prätigau all-frame "Victorian" forebay bank barn (*top*), displaying the near attachment of house and barn that is common in Prätigau. Masonry column forebay support posts (*bottom*) occur on several barns in the village of Grüsch, Canton Graubünden, Switzerland. (Photos 1988.)

Figure 1.26. Large gable-forebay bank barn in St. Antönien, Prätigau, built circa 1617. This barn has a ten-foot-deep forebay with stairway leading from it to the Hof. Notice the large covered manure box in front. (Photo 1988.)

unchinked, thus providing necessary air movement through the haymow area. Log stable walls are chinked with mud and moss for insulation. This is only rarely seen in North America, where stone stable walls are the rule.

Some Prätigau log barns have forebays of frame. This almost exactly duplicates the morphology of early Pennsylvania Sweitzer barns, which also combine a framed forebay with log crib haymows. There are only a few examples of full log forebays in North America. It is, therefore, this Prätigau barn with two log cribs and a frame forebay that most closely resembles the original forebay barns of Pennsylvania.

Although most Prätigau barns are not connected to a residence, some are. In other cases the structures are just a few feet apart and, therefore, appear to be joined. Later nineteenth-century Prätigau barns are of all-frame construction, often with Victorian lattice work ventilation openings on the forebay. A few valley barns near Grüsch utilize masonry columns to support the forebay. These variations all fall within the definition of an eave-forebay bank barn. They add, rather than detract, from the reservoir of concepts that were available to emigrants from Graubünden.

Another form of forebay bank barn in Prätigau must be discussed, the gable-forebay barn. I found a fine example high in St. Antönien, in upper Prätigau. This particular barn (Figure 1.26), which dates from 1617, has a ten-foot-deep forebay on the gable end (Simonett and Könz 1968, 21). There are other, much smaller gable-forebay bank barns around St. Antönien and elsewhere in the high meadows and valleys of upper Prätigau.

To the south, in the adjacent, smaller, and more remote Schanfigg dis-

Figure 1.27. Early Alpine barns above Sapün, outer Schanfigg, Graubünden. Accord
ing to Weiss, the Walsers introduced simple bank barns without forebays to the high
tributary valleys of the Upper Rhine River. Similar structures have been documented
in Canton Wallis. The gable forebay (*barn on right*) evolved from the simple cubic
form (*center barn*). (Photo 1988.)

Figure 1.28. Frame forebay ground barn attached to house, Bregenzer Valley, Vorarlberg, Austria. The Walsers settled in this region in the fourteenth century, but barns built before the seventeenth century have not survived. (Photo 1978.)

trict, there can also be found a dense concentration of forebay bank barns. Some are of the eave-forebay Prätigau type, but the majority have the forebay on a gable end, with the bank on the opposite gable end. These barns range in morphology from those with double log cribs, threshing floor, and Talina, as is so common in Prätigau, to a single log crib, without a forebay Talina, over a single stable. Most have a five-foot forebay overhang, which provides room for fodder stairs to the Hof. The example described here is located near the high village of Langwies in the outer Schanfigg.

Above Langwies, at an elevation of 5,000 feet, is the remote village of Sapün. This village is inaccessible by conventional automobile. Hansrüedi Widmer, a local guide and historian, took me there in a four-wheel drive vehicle. Sapün is an early Walser dairy farming village. One house, built of log planks, dates back to the 1580s. Here we inspected an early log eave-forebay barn, possibly from the same period. On the hillside above the village are several other barns with downslope gables (Figure 1.27), including one with a gable forebay. This type may represent an early stage in the evolution of the forebay form of barn. The Walsers, who settled the highest agricultural locations in the Swiss Alps, built many barns like this in their villages in Graubünden.

Richard Weiss pointed out that the Prätigau eave-forebay barn was also

Figure 1.29. Shallow eave forebay on a bank barn with a gable ramp, typical in Obersaxen, Graubünden, Switzerland. (Photo 1988.)

found in the nearby Montafon region (Weiss 1943, 39). This is a logical location, since it is the next valley to the north and parallels Prätigau in adjacent Vorarlberg Province, Austria. My field survey has confirmed the presence of this type of barn there, but I found it in small numbers and scattered locations. More common were small, single-log-crib barns with wood-framed eave forebays, but with access to the bank and loft from the upslope gable side. The forebay tradition extended into a northern tributary valley, Gross Walsertal, in which gable-forebays built of logs reappeared. My field surveys in 1978 in the Bregenzer Valley, north of Gross Walsertal, revealed a significant number of forebay ground barns, which in most cases were attached to the farmhouse. The ones I inspected were wood frame structures and, possibly, had been built later than the log barns described above. Conclusions about this broader distribution of closely connected types of forebay barns are drawn later in this chapter.

Weiss also revealed the presence of eave-forebay bank barns in yet another region of Graubünden, Obersaxen, high above the south side of the Vorderrhein (Fore-Rhine) (44). Max Gschwend provided a date of 1600 for one of these barns, which supplements other early datings for Swiss forebay barns (Gschwend 1965, secs. 36, 36a). Simonett and Könz have also documented these barns (Simonett and Könz 1968, 23). This region consists of farm villages and scattered farmsteads sited on high meadows one thousand

Figures 1.30 and 1.31. Obersaxen barn with shallow, one-meter-deep forebay and ladder to hay hole (*left*). Upper level of Obersaxen barn showing log-crib haymows, threshing floor, and rear ramp doors (*right*). (Photo 1988.)

to fifteen hundred feet above the Vorderrhein. The fairly dense distribution of distinctive log forebay barns that I found there verified the reports of Weiss and Gschwend. Both eave- and gable-forebay barns exist in Obersaxen, but the eave-forebay type predominates. All barns there are oriented with one gable on the upslope side of the hill, with access to the upper-level through doors in this banked gable wall. Most Obersaxen barns are two or three log cribs long. The haymow log cribs are connected by a central passageway that gives access for wagons. That section of the passage closest to the doors stands one to two feet above the level of the mows and serves as a threshing floor. The forebay overhang is usually shallow—about one meter—and is, therefore, able to accommodate only a small hay hole and ladder. I saw one wider forebay, which had a stairway, but none of the barns had the forebay Talina separated from the hayloft, as is the rule in Prätigau. The morphology of most Obersaxen barns does not qualify them for serious consideration as prototypes for the Pennsylvania barn. Rather, they provide additional evidence of the widespread utilization of the forebay form on barns throughout Graubünden.

This broad pattern of forebay usage is described by Simonett and Könz. They include the upper valley of the Hinterrhein (Back-Rhine) and the Albula and Julia river valleys within the range of the forebay bank barn (21).

Figure 1.32. Deep gable forebay on bank barn near Tiefencastel, Albula River Valley, Graubünden, Switzerland. Gable-forebay bank barns are common along the upper Vorderrhein and southern tributaries of the Hinterrhein in Graubünden. (Photo 1988.)

They, as well as Weiss, include the entire valley of the Vorderrhein, above and below Obersaxen, within the region of forebay barns. My own surveys, although confined to the lower and middle stretches of the Vorderrhein and Hinterrhein, confirm their findings. I saw numerous forebay bank barns mixed with other Alpine barn types. The majority have shallow gable forebays, but I saw occasional deep forebays and eave forebays.

Two maps have been prepared for this publication that combine pertinent previously known data on Swiss forebay barns with my most recent field studies. The first one records the broad, general distribution of all forebay barn types, including eave-forebay, gable-forebay, and ground-forebay barns. The second refines this broader pattern by establishing the boundaries of the three types of forebay barns found in Switzerland and western Austria. These types are further subdivided by specific locations and characteristics. To be sure, this attempt to regionalize Swiss barn types is an oversimplification of a complex picture. There are many nonforebay barns within the boundaries I have presented, and they are a majority in at least one of those regions. They have not been considered in this book, however, since they have little bearing on barns in Pennsylvania. This must be kept in mind when interpreting the maps.

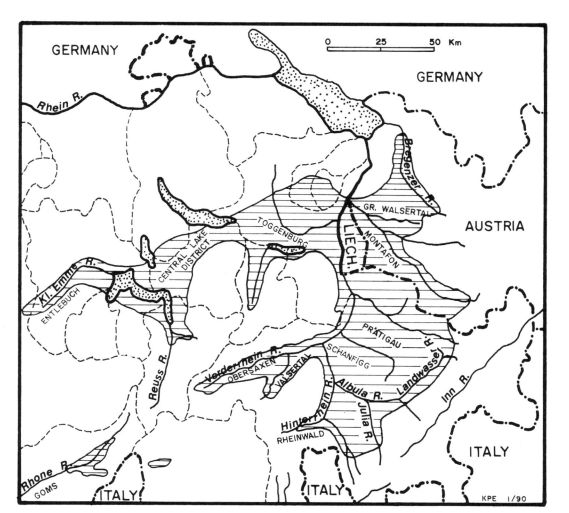

Map 1.4. General areas where Swiss forebay barns can be found.

Forebay barns

Water bodies

.—.—.—.—. International boundaries

– – – – – Provincial boundaries

———— Rivers

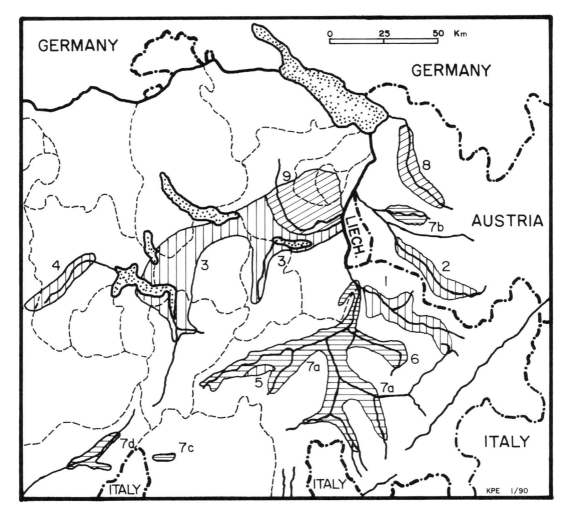

Map 1.5. Distribution of types of Swiss forebay barns.

⬚ (vertical lines)	Predominantly eave-forebay bank barns
⬚ (horizontal lines)	Predominantly gable-forebay bank barns
⬚ (diagonal lines)	Predominantly eave-forebay ground barns

⬚ (dotted)	Water bodies
▬·▬·▬·	International boundaries
-------	Provincial boundaries
▬▬▬	Rivers

Predominantly eave-forebay bank barns

1. *Prätigau.* Multiple-log-crib barns with deep cantilevered or post-supported fore-bay, Talina, and stairway. Some gable-forebay barns.
2. *Montafon, Vorarlberg, Austria.* Small single-log-crib forebay barns with gable ramp. Some Prätigau-type barns with forebay, Talina, and stairway.
3. *Central Lake District.* Barns with deep, post-supported forebays, log and frame construction. Occasional gable ramp, double-decker (three-level), and double-eave-forebay barns. Numerous nonforebay barns.
4. *Entlebuch.* Large deep-forebay log and frame barns, some with forebay support posts. Numerous double-decker barns.
5. *Obersaxen.* Large multiple-log-crib barns with shallow forebays and gable ramps. Some barns with gable forebays.

Predominantly gable-forebay bank barns

6. *Schanfigg.* Single- or multiple-log-crib, deep-gable-forebay barns, most with stairway to forebay. Some Prätigau-type eave-forebay and stairway barns. Both types may or may not have Talina in forebay.
7a. *Upper Rhine River and tributary valleys.* Majority nonforebay barns. Small to medium-sized log barns with shallow gable forebays and gable ramps. Some deep-gable-forebay barns and shallow-eave-forebay barns. Open forebay Talinas with grain-drying scaffolds found mainly in valley of Vorderrhein.
7b. *Gross Walsertal, Vorarlberg, Austria.* Small log barns with gable forebays and ramps.
7c. *Bosco Gurin.* Small log and stone shallow-gable-forebay barns and storehouses.
7d. *Goms, Upper Rhone River and tributary valleys.* Gable-forebay barns and storehouses.

Predominantly eave-forebay ground barns

8. *Bregenzer Valley, Vorarlberg, Austria.* Small front-stable forebay barns usually attached to house.
9. *Toggenburg.* Small frame or frame and log barns with rear overbay above manure door.

Figure 1.33. Large Central Lake District forebay bank barn near Schwyz, Switzerland, featuring arcaded and supported forebay. (Photo 1975.)

As the new maps reveal, the most extensive forebay barn region extends from eastern Bern through the Central Lake District to the Rhine River. I visited this region in 1975 and 1978 and did additional field surveys in 1988. Forebay bank barns are numerous in the lowlands and the higher meadows adjacent to Walensee and Vierwald-stättersee and, especially, on the hillsides surrounding the city of Schwyz. The barns of this region have significant potential as Pennsylvania barn prototypes. The valley barns are large structures, 60 by 100 feet with deep 15-foot forebays. They have four to six posts supporting these forebays. Most are banked on the long side opposite the forebay, but occasional gable ramps are seen. Some barns even have double eave forebays, requiring the ramp to be located at a gable end. Most of these barns have masonry basement walls, split stable doors, and a long asymmetrical roof slope on the forebay side. They strongly resemble the large Sweitzer Pennsylvania barns of the early nineteenth century. Upon closer examination, I discovered that many have log-crib haymows like the early barns of Prätigau. Most, however, have the threshing floor located on one side rather than between the cribs. The forebay support beams do not extend under the log-crib frame but rest instead on top of the front stable wall. The framed forebay and wood siding hide the presence of log cribs within the barns. The roof support systems and the bents of framed exterior barn walls closely resemble the earlier barns in Pennsylvania. Similar morphology is

Figure 1.34. View of log-crib haymow, threshing floor, and frame forebay of a barn near Schwyz, Switzerland. (Photo 1988).

found in adjacent high mountain valleys, except that the barns are smaller.

Barns like those just described reappear as a disjunct outlier in Entlebuch, in the valley of the Kleine Emme River, southwest of Luzern. One barn there is the largest forebay bank barn I have seen in Europe. It is 120 feet long and has a 25-foot-deep forebay. It also is a double-decker, or three-level, barn in which the wagon floors are raised 6 to 8 feet above the lowest level of the haymow floor. This increases storage capacity and permits gravity filling of the lower mow. This unusual barn, which has two access ramps, is pictured in Figure 1.35.

Variations on the forebay barn occur throughout this broad belt, from the Rhine west to the Kleine Emme. They include the occasional connection of house and barn. This type, the unit-farmstead, may represent earlier structures of the region. Gable forebays are also found, but the most unusual discovery was a bank-into-forebay barn located in the old village section of the town of Buchs, just west of the Liechtenstein border. This barn was a double-log-crib barn with loading openings adjacent to the central threshing floor. "Old" Buchs (see Map 1.2) is the site of four or five similar barns. There are several bank-into-forebay barns near Bedminster in upper Bucks County, Pennsylvania. Even if there are no verifiable connections in this case, the existence of yet another variety of forebay barn in both Pennsylvania and Switzerland adds to the evidence supporting the thesis of a Swiss prototype.

The last region to be considered is just to the north of the Central Lake District in the Toggenburg section of St. Gallen. The barns here are small ground barns that have no ramp or full upper level. The so-called forebay on these barns usually takes the form of an alcove or shallow overhang on the rear side of the barn, opposite the main stable doors—a rear overbay. The alcove wall may have windows, stable doors, and even wagon doors facing those on the front side. This would permit hay wagons to be driven in, unloaded up into the loft above the stables, and then driven out on the opposite side. Many of these small barns are of frame construction, but in some the entire stable is enclosed by a log crib. This trait may have evolved from earlier log-crib barns, such as those in Graubünden. The most unusual characteristic of these structures is a small wooden door universally located at floor level under the rear alcove or overbay. Through it manure is removed from the stable area. The overbay provides some shelter for the person transporting the manure to the manure pit, shelter that is especially needed in winter. The same advantage is afforded by the forebays of barns in Graubünden, where manure is also deposited in a pit or box beyond the forebay, and in Pennsylvania, where manure is stored in a pile or pit in the barnyard beyond the forebay. Whatever the reason, there is a 100 percent coincidence of the location of this small door relative to that of the alcove or rear overbay in the ground barns of the Toggenburg. These barns, which could have influenced the development of forebay ground barns in Pennsylvania, deserve more study.

Figure 1.35. Very large (120-foot-long) forebay bank barn in Entlebuch region of Switzerland. This double-ramp barn has three levels and a very deep (25-foot) forebay. Double doors on rear stable wall lead to the feeding alley. (Photo 1978.)

The Walser-Romansch Connection

Richard Weiss was the first person to associate the Prätigau forebay barn with the Walsers, whom he described as a German group originally from Canton Wallis, known for their ability to settle high Alpine valleys (Weiss 1943, 38). Weiss, and later Terry Jordan, stated that etymological evidence pointed to a Romansch rather than Germanic origin for the forebay barn and to the probability that it was adopted by the Walsers after they arrived in Graubünden (Jordan 1987–88, 80). I examine this question in the final section of this chapter.

The Walsers were the descendants of a nomadic Alemannic people who made their home in the Bernese Oberland, after migrating from the north before A.D. 1000. By the end of the twelfth century, they had moved into the high valleys of the Upper Rhone River in Canton Wallis, a region known as the Goms. Their name, *Walser,* comes from the place name, *Canton Wallis.* During the thirteenth century, they spread west into the tributary valleys of the Rhone River and south into the high Alpine valleys of Italy. They also spread east into the valleys of the Hinterrhein and Vorderrhein and their tributaries as far as Davos in the Landwasser Valley. From there, the last wave

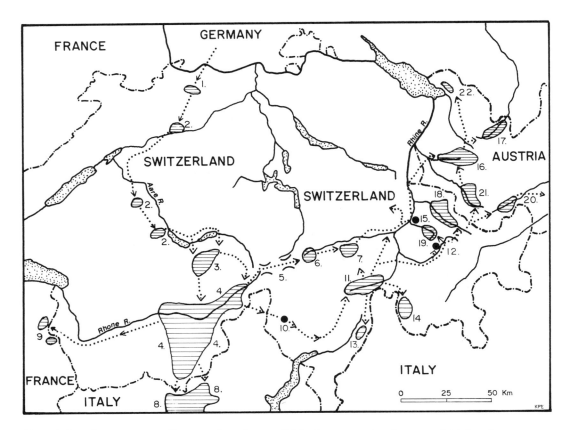

Map 1.6. Walser migration. Dates are based on available documentation; however, initial settlement may have occurred earlier. Many movement streams are inferential since actual routes are unknown.

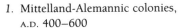

··········>	Migration routes
•	Significant towns or villages
≣	Settlement areas
≍	Mountain passes

▨	Water bodies
·—·—·—	International boundaries
————	Rivers

1. Mittelland-Alemannic colonies, A.D. 400–600
2. Aare Valley homeland, 600–700
3. Berner Oberland, 700–800
4. Goms-Upper Rhone Valley, 900–1100
5. Furkapass and Oberalppass, 1100

6. Surselva, 1100–1200
7. Obersaxen, 1213
8. High Alpine Italian villages, 1200s
9. Haute-Savoie, middle 1200s
10. Bosco Gurin, 1253
11. Rheinwald, 1273
12. Davos, 1284
13. Misox, 1286

14. Avers, late 1200s
15. Chur, 1300
16. Gross Walsertal, early 1300s
17. Klein Walsertal, 1303
18. Prätigau, early 1300s
19. Schanfigg, early 1300s
20. Paznauntal, 1319
21. Montafon, early 1300s
22. Bodensee, middle 1300s

emigrated during the following century, moving first into the Schanfigg and Prätigau valleys and then north and east into Vorarlberg, and even the Tyrol (Baumgartner and Woerdehoff 1988, 39). Map 1.6 shows these movements.[5] Significantly, *this migration pattern correlates very closely with the southern and eastern portion of the Swiss forebay-barn region!*

Both Weiss and Jordan have associated forebay barns with regions of Walser settlement. Most studies show the Walsers to have been the greatest colonizers of the higher Alps. They were cattle breeders and farmers who were able to successfully settle at extremely high altitudes and so could occupy these marginal lands, which had long been under the control of, but not settled by, other Germanic and Romansch peoples. Before arrival of the Walsers, the Romansch possessed title to the high pastures around their valley villages, but they used them only sporadically, as common grazing land. Feudal nobles sponsored the new Walser colonies by providing inducements for settling the higher locations. Walsers were guaranteed personal freedom, the right of inheritance, stable rental agreements, and rights of local self-government. In return, the nobles enlarged the population base of their territories and extended the economic basis of their political and military power. They also received military obligations from the Walsers to fight beyond areas of their own settlement. Thus, a Germanic ethnic group was introduced into the high valleys of Graubünden and came into competition with the Romansch population (Billigmeier 1979, 22).

Walser settlements were made initially on high Alpine pasture lands and upper valley extremities. With great energy, the Walsers extended pasture lands by cutting or burning forested areas. Their settlements were markedly different from those of the Romansch. Walser families constructed log dwellings and barns on the land they were using as individual farmsteads or small family villages. They concentrated on raising cattle and producing milk, cheese, and butter. In contrast, Romansch peasants lived in larger farm villages in valleys and cultivated grains, fruits, and vegetables, as well as grazing animals on outlying pastures (35–37). Climatic changes, in addition to population growth and aggressive colonization by the Walsers, brought them into competition with the Romansch in many areas, and their adaptability gave them a competitive advantage. In Prätigau and the Schanfigg, they gradually replaced earlier Romansch populations (38).

It is in these very valleys that the forebay bank barn achieved its full development—log, double-crib mows with threshing floor, a deep forebay with Talina, and a stairway to the Hof. What started as a small cattle barn and loft evolved into a large, multiple purpose barn, able to accommodate stock,

5. Baumgartner and Woerdehoff 1988, 1, 39; Billigmeier 1979, 31–34; Weiss 1959, 278; Zeller 1972, 44, 137, 141–42; Zinsli 1986, 17–195, 429 n. 90, map inside back cover. Zinsli presents and analyzes a large amount of information on Walser language, family history, and land ownership. He has constructed a complex chronicle of Walser migration and settlement across the Alps, from France, through Switzerland, and into Austria. The easternmost documented Walser settlement is in Sellraintal, Tyrol; however, some scholars suggest penetration even farther east, into Tuxertal, a tributary valley of Zillertal, east of Innsbruck.

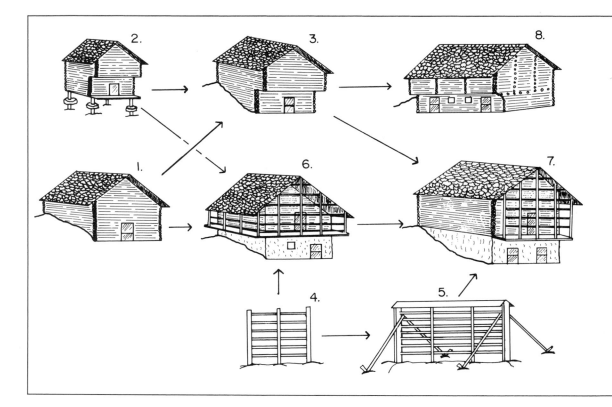

Diagram 1.2. Conjectured development of Swiss forebay bank barns.

1. Basic high Alpine gable bank barn. Berner Oberland and Goms, Wallis to Graubünden.
2. High Alpine granary storehouse with shallow gable forebay, or Vorschub. Goms, Wallis to Graubünden.
3. High Alpine gable bank barn with shallow gable forebay, or Vorschub. Goms, Wallis to Graubünden.
4. Histe, a freestanding grain-drying scaffold. Canton Ticino.
5. Chischner or large, freestanding grain-drying scaffold. Upper and middle Vorderrhein, Graubünden.
6. Barn or house with open grain-drying gallery or Histenlaube. Goms, Wallis, and Italian high Alpine valleys.
7. Gable bank barn with open gable-forebay Talina. Upper and middle Vorderrhein, Graubünden.
8. Gable bank barn with shallow eave forebay, or Vorschub. Obersaxen, Graubünden.
9. Gable bank barn with deep gable forebay supported by stone piers, or Eckpfeilern, but without separate Talina walkway. Upper Vorderrhein and southern tributary valleys of Hinterrhein.
10. Gable bank barn with deep gable forebay, or Vürschutz, separate closed Talina walkway, and fodder stairs. Schanfigg, Graubünden.
11. Eave bank barn with deep eave forebay, or Vürschutz, separate closed Talina walkway, and fodder stairs. Prätigau, Graubünden. This prototype was then carried to southeastern Pennsylvania from where it diffused across the United States and into southern Canada.

migrated from there. He also points out that the place names in Prätigau and the Schanfigg are mostly Romansch names that were later Germanized (Jordan 1987–88, 80). The implication is that the Romansch inhabited even the upper pastures and passed on their names, and their barn technology, to the incoming Walsers.

Actually, the Romansch used the high pastures only as common grazing land. They had provided place names for many such high locations, but there were no permanent settlements there (Billigmeier 1979, 41). Although the Walsers occupied these marginal pastures and adopted and Germanized the existing Romansch names, they did not adopt Romansch barn technology, for no Romansch barns existed at such locations. Rather, the Walsers introduced their own house and barn technology, some of which can be traced back to Wallis. The use of log plank construction for houses and barns and the building of shallow gable forebays on barns and storehouses can be traced back through virtually all Walser settlements along the Vorderrhein and Hinterrhein to the upper Rhone Valley of Canton Wallis. Maps 1.2 and 1.5 illustrate this trail.

The first primitive Walser barns were two-level, single-crib log structures with one gable side facing down the slope and the other gable side banked for access to the mow. Hay was carried out of the upslope door, down the bank, and around the barn to the stable below. This is a basic high Alpine barn. By extending the downslope gable mow one meter over the stable below, a gable forebay was created. This provided the functional advantages of increased hay storage and protection of the stable door—most appropriate to the long, snowy winters in Alpine locations. The original models for such shallow forebays can be found on medieval granary storehouses, which exist in the Goms and elsewhere in the Alps. These early forebay storehouse and barn types the Walsers then brought to numerous high valleys all over Graubünden.

A strong case has been made for the Walsers' being active agents in the development and diffusion of the forebay Alpine barn. The use of the non-Germanic term *Talina* for the walkway within the deep forebay, or Vürschutz, of the Prätigau barn raises serious questions about this thesis. Forebay barn distribution in Graubünden correlates as closely with areas of Romansch influence as with areas of Walser migration and settlement. Jordan stated that the forebay Talina is, in all probability, Raeto-Romansch rather than Germanic in origin (Jordan 1987–88, 80). The problem of a Romansch forebay on a Germanic barn must be resolved.

Augustine Maissen, a professor of Romance languages at the University of North Carolina who is now retired and living in Graubünden, reported in a letter in July 1989 that *Talina* is a pre-Roman Raetic term whose origin is unclear.[7] His Romansch-German dictionary defined *Talina* as a Kornhist or

---

7. The Raetians were an ancient tribe, who migrated possibly from the northern Adriatic coastal regions of Illyria and Venetia. They settled in the Alps between the Inn and Rhine rivers. Their territory, Raetia, was added to the Roman Empire in 15 B.C., and the Romansch language resulted from a latinization of their earlier language.

Figures 1.36 and 1.37. This Romansch Chischner, a large, freestanding grain-drying scaffold (*top*), no longer standing, was located at Curaglia, Graubünden, Switzerland. Romansch Talina, or grain-drying scaffold forming an open forebay (*bottom*), on gable wall of a barn at Sedrun, Graubünden. (Photos from Hunziker 1905, 91, 84.)

Chischner built on to the wall of the barn. Dr. Maissen also referred to the publication, *Das Schweizerhaus,* Vol. 3, *Graubünden,* by Jacob Hunziker (1905), which presents a detailed survey of farms and houses, an analysis of their German and Romansch nomenclature, plus illustrations and photographs, with frequent references to and relevant information about the Talina. It reveals that the Talina resulted from the attachment of a Romansch Chischner, or grain-drying scaffold, to the upper barn wall. The Chischner (*Histe, Kornhist, Getreidehiste, Feldharfe,* or *Trockengestelle,* in German) was a scaffoldlike rack erected in the field to dry grains. It was found at high elevations, where ripening in the fields could not occur. These structures, up to 50 feet long and 30 feet high, were sometimes topped with a narrow, rooflike cap (91).

Hunziker noted that the Talina gradually replaced the freestanding Chischner on farms from the upper to the middle Vorderrhein (84). He specifically stated that the term *Talina* replaced the term *Chischner* when the structure was attached to the barn. He pointed out that the Talina extended several feet beyond the upper gable wall, like a forebay, and protected the front stable wall below (260). His account clearly demonstrates the Talina's emergence in heavily Romansch sections of the upper and middle Vorderrhein. In the neighboring Walser enclave of Obersaxen, the shallow forebay, without Talina, was maintained along with the freestanding Chischner, which is further evidence of the Romansch role in the Talina's proliferation.

Firsthand accounts that reinforce this data have been provided by the following people, who were born and raised in Romansch villages of the Vorderrhein.[8] Henry Arpagus, of Pittsburgh, Pennsylvania, stated that the space in the Talina between the drying scaffold and the barn wall provided a walkway 3 to 4 feet wide that afforded access to the scaffold. Anna Vasti-Quinter, of New York City, recalled from her childhood how lines of people passed grain sheaves into the upper barn and through a door to the Talina walkway, where the grain was hung on the scaffold to dry. The sheaves were held in place by being packed in between the rungs of the scaffold with the heads facing in, which protected the grain against damp weather and hungry birds. The roof extended beyond the Talina, further sheltering the grain. The entire projecting Talina structure in turn provided a cover for the stable doors below. With the attachment of the Talina, a versatile and practical multiple-purpose barn was developed, combining the drying, threshing, and storage of grain, the stabling of cattle, and the storage of hay and straw. Romansch farmers must be given the credit for the extensive construction of this barn and for the application of the term *Talina* to an overhanging walkway and grain-drying scaffold. Separating the walkway from the main upper barn area is the key difference between the Talina forebay and the Vorschub of high Alpine Walser barn. (See Diagram 1.2, nos. 7 and 3.)

8. The Swiss consulate in New York City identified Anna Vasti-Quinter as a local resource person knowledgeable in the traditions of Swiss-Romansch culture. She, in turn, suggested that Henry Arpagus could also provide firsthand information. They related valuable details and insights about Romansch farms and barns which have enhanced this book.

Figure 1.38. Vertical openings in basement door of center structure permit ventilation of the stable of this small bank barn in the village of Wiler in Lötchental, a tributary valley of the upper Rhone River in Canton Wallis, Switzerland. The overhanging galleries of the three barns show varying degrees of closure with horizontal boards between which grain can be packed for drying. These gable galleries (Lauben) are common in Walser regions of Wallis and are forerunners of the closed forebay. (Photograph by Richard Ensminger, 1990, used by his permission.)

The Romansch Talina is but one example of the widespread use in Europe of a cantilevered, overhanging balcony or open gallery on houses and barns. These structures, called *Lauben,* are usually associated with log plank buildings. They occur in northern Europe and across Alpine central Europe as far as Upper Silesia in Poland (Jordan 1985, 145). They may also occur on masonry and half-timbered buildings. The use of freestanding scaffolds to dry hay and grain in the field is also widespread in agriculturally marginal high Alpine valleys. The attachment of the drying scaffold to the Laube, producing an open drying gallery, can be found on buildings in the southern Alps from the French border to the Tyrol (Hunziker 1900, 16, 24, 35, 65, 75, 83; Gephard 1977, 156). For example, Walser farmers in the Goms and high Alpine villages on the Italian side of the Alpine divide developed structures that combined drying galleries with grain storage sheds (*Stadel*), houses, and barns (Zinsli 1986, pls. 35b, 79, 80, 83, 84; Baumgartner and Woerdehoff 1988, 25, 27, 31, 47). The name *Histenlaube,* or drying porch, was applied to similar structures in eastern Graubünden (Simonett and Könz 1968, 64–66). These examples reveal that very similar grain-drying techniques were used in numerous locations by various groups to accommodate high Alpine conditions.

Conclusion

Both Walser and Romansch groups deserve credit for the development of the forebay barn in Switzerland. The Walsers brought high Alpine log barns and storage buildings from Wallis to Graubünden, including ones with a shallow gable forebay, or Vorschub. The Romansch applied the term *Talina* to their version of the forebaylike drying scaffold and walkway, which projected from the upper wall of the barn. In the valley of the upper and middle Vorderrhein, both the Romansch open Talina and the Germanic closed Vorschub can be found, suggesting an intermingling of Walser and Romansch traditions.

A wide gable forebay lacking an open drying scaffold also occurs in this region and represents another assemblage of forebay forms. Barns with this type of forebay are found as well in the valley of the Hinterrhein and its southern tributaries. These deeper forebays sometimes require extra support, which is provided by *Eckpfeilern*. These are masonry piers or extensions of the masonry stable walls (23–24). In spite of the similar terminology, there is probably no connection between these and the *Peilereck* forebay, an extension and alcove on the end wall, which developed around 1800 in eastern Pennsylvania.

The changes that finalized the evolution of the Swiss forebay bank barn occurred in Prätigau and the Schanfigg district, where Walsers displaced the Romansch population (see Diagram 1.2, nos. 10 and 11). The re-emergence of the Romansch term *Talina* and its application to the walkway within the enlarged and enclosed forebay, or Vürschutz, completed the process. In Prätigau and the Schanfigg district, the Talina became a closed multiple-purpose storage area separate from the haymows, where sheaves and bags of grain, as well as tools and firewood, could be kept. The stairway connecting the Talina and threshing floor to the front stable yard provided a convenient and protected route for the movement of hay and straw from the upper mows to the stables. The attachment of such forebays to the eave side of a double-log-crib bank barn produced the classic Prätigau barn. It is difficult to determine exactly who brought about the final synthesis, but it is clear that a blending of both Romansch and Germanic Walser traditions was involved.

The versatile and functional Prätigau forebay bank barn spread west to lower elevations. In the Central Lake District and Entlebuch, it was greatly enlarged to satisfy the requirements of a more extensive agriculture. It also came to America, where its versatility and adaptability were ideally suited to the rapidly developing frontier agriculture.[9] Its establishment in Pennsylvania as the log Sweitzer barn set the stage for continued evolution and diffusion across the United States and Canada.

---

9. Jordan 1989, 489–500. In a letter to me in summer 1990, Jordan suggested that preadaption may apply to the development in Switzerland of those characteristics of forebay bank barns which provided them with a competitive advantage on the Pennsylvania frontier.

2

CLASSIFICATION OF THE PENNSYLVANIA BARN

In the early eighteenth century, European settlers, including skilled Germanic farmers, poured into an area of Pennsylvania beginning north of Philadelphia and extending west beyond the Susquehanna River. There they developed a successful agricultural economy based on the area's rich soils and easy access to urban markets via numerous early roads. This area I shall call the Pennsylvania barn core. It is the region having the densest population of the earliest pre-1800 log and stone Sweitzer Pennsylvania barns today. Although many early barns have not survived, I infer from their present distribution in this core area that an early concentration of the key types occurred here.

This core is surprisingly extensive, reflecting rapid and successful early settlement—for example, Shippensburg, 125 miles west of Philadelphia, in the Cumberland section of the Great Valley, was settled in 1730. The core forms an oblong region extending from the Delaware River, along the Great Valley and the Piedmont, to and beyond the Maryland border. It is difficult to pinpoint any specific hearth zone within this core. I suspect, however, that Lancaster County, Pennsylvania, along with adjacent parts of Berks, Lebanon, Chester, and York counties, could possibly qualify, as virtually every Pennsylvania barn type can be found there. This designation of the core area is admittedly subjective, being based in large part on my observations and extensive field studies.

The core area served as a laboratory for the development of successful agricultural practices and the selection of appropriate farm structures. The Hans Herr house, built in 1719, near Lancaster, is a prime example of a substantial, first-generation, Germanic farmhouse. The nearby Herman barn is typical of early log Sweitzer barns. Both structures indicate that a well-developed agricultural landscape had taken hold very early in south-

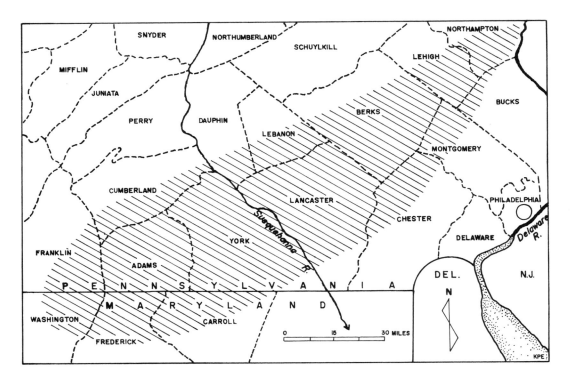

Map 2.1. Pennsylvania barn core region.

eastern Pennsylvania. This core area became a hearth from which farming practices and architectural forms diffused to the south and west across and beyond Pennsylvania.

Both the forebay bank barn and the Grundscheier had been brought by ethnic Germans to the core from European source regions. Expanding agriculture required the development, or adaptation, of appropriate farm structures, especially larger multiple-purpose barns. Pennsylvania farmers were changing from pioneer practices, characterized by grain production, to mixed grain and livestock production (Glass 1986, 12). Populations of livestock increased dramatically (Fletcher 1950, 173–79). During the eighteenth century, the versatile forebay bank barn gradually displaced the smaller Grundscheier. It was then enlarged and modified throughout the nineteenth century. The cumulative result has been the creation in southeastern Pennsylvania of an agricultural landscape dominated by the forebay bank barn—the Pennsylvania barn.

There are significant variations in the details of the design and construction of Pennsylvania barns, for the barn evolved as agriculture changed. It was also influenced by the incorporation of ideas from other structures. It diffused to new locations along with the different agricultural practices to which it was suited. The result of this evolution and diffusion has been a complex and often confusing pattern of barn types, but the barn's fundamental identity, provided by the forebay, has been preserved.

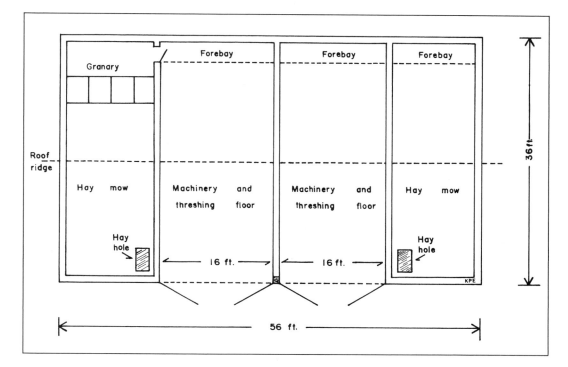

Diagram 2.1. Plan of the upper level of a typical standard Pennsylvania barn, the Hein barn, Lenhartsville, Berks County, Pennsylvania.

The general functional design of the Pennsylvania barn has remained fairly constant through time. It is always banked to provide access to the upper level. This level is used to process and store feed grains, hay, and straw. It contains several sections or bays. Bays entered directly from the bank have large doors and function as threshing or machinery floors; those adjacent to the threshing floors serve as mows for storage of hay and straw.

The upper-level space to the fore of the barn, extending over the stable wall below, is the forebay. Windows in the front wall of the forebay provide light for this area. An opening in this wall, at the front end of the threshing floor, formerly provided draft for hand threshing and winnowing. Through this opening straw can be tossed to the barnyard below. The overhang of the forebay prevents blockage of the stable doors by straw or snow and avoids splash erosion of foundation mortar near ground level during heavy rains. The forebay area may be continuous with the mows, providing additional storage space. Usually, however, it is partitioned from the mows, and houses a granary with bins for various feed grains. In early log-crib barns, a forebay seemingly separate from the cribs is actually framed into them, producing a structural partition between forebay and mows. This partitioned space is the area that in Prätigau barns is the Talina. The fact that in even very early log-crib barns the forebay beams are cantilevered under the mows into the barn frame demonstrates that the forebay was an integral part of the barn design.

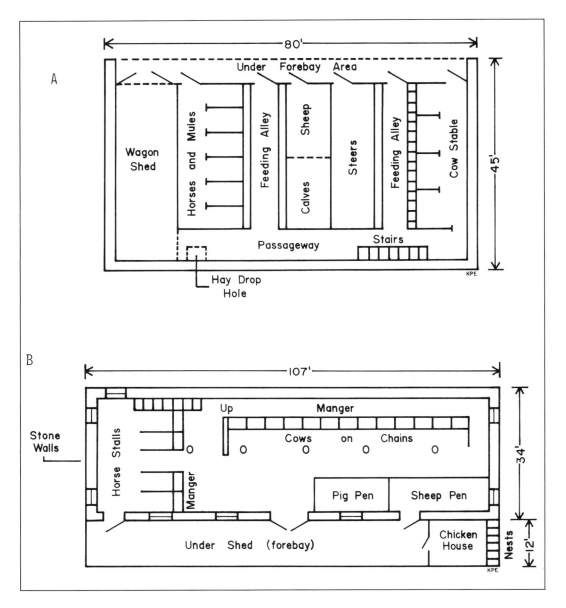

Diagram 2.2. Representative basement stable plans for Pennsylvania barns.

A.) Typical mid-nineteenth-century stable plan provided by Mark Heffner of Lyons, Berks County, Pennsylvania.

B.) Original stable plan for the Herman Schield barn (1908) near Merrill, Lincoln County, Wisconsin. Plan provided by Edmund Schield of Wausau, Wisconsin.

This same morphology is found in barns in Prätigau, which strongly reinforces my contention that the origin of the forebay tradition can be traced to the early log-forebay barns of Switzerland (Ensminger 1980–81, 50–71; Jordan 1980, 167–74).

The lower level of the Pennsylvania barn has always been used to house livestock, including cows, beef cattle, and horses. Farmers learned very quickly that stabling and feeding cattle produced stock superior to cattle raised by the pioneer practice of letting them roam (Fletcher 1950, 82). In many barns, pens for calves and even pigs, sheep, and chickens, can be found. Pen arrangements have varied through time. There may be significant correlations between stable arrangements and various barn types; further research is necessary to explore those possibilities. Access between the stable and the barnyard is through double split doors in the front wall, below the forebay. Gable-end doors in Pennsylvania barns, when they occur, provide access to the feeding alley, or *Fudergang,* which is usually at the rear of the barn and runs between the rows of pens. The most frequent orientation of the barnyard, stable doors, and forebay, is to the south or southeast (Glass 1986, 104–6), which is especially advantageous during cold weather. Locating the granary in the forebay on the warmest and driest side of the barn with fresh air circulation below also makes sense.

Because of the considerable variation that exists in the morphology of Pennsylvania barns, studying them requires a plan of organization and classification. Charles Dornbusch was the first person to deal with this problem. His classification, published in 1958, can be found in Appendix B of this book. It consists of eleven barn types, of which five are forebay barns. The barn population utilized by Dornbusch came exclusively from southeastern Pennsylvania. His system fits fairly well for barns of this region. I feel, however, that a revision is necessary—one that can be applied to a broader range of barn types and locations, many beyond Pennsylvania. His pioneering system does not accommodate many such barns, including some in the Pennsylvania core. A new system should fit all Pennsylvania barns into a comprehensive scheme. It should simplify the basic typology. It should help in understanding the evolution of the Pennsylvania barn and, therefore, reveal how the various types are related.

The forebay is the Pennsylvania barn's diagnostic feature. One can derive a new plan of classification by examining in detail the differences in the specifications of the forebay and the process of its integration into the barn frame. As one examines barns of varying age, size, and construction materials, drastic differences in the size, support, and framing of the barn and forebay emerge. These characteristics, along with the basic construction of the barn, control the angle at which the roof slopes and determine the gable end configuration of the barn. By considering these factors, three basic classes of Pennsylvania barns can be identified into which most types and subtypes can be fitted.

Classes of the Pennsylvania Barn Defined

The following outline lists the major divisions and subdivisions of my classification system; they are further described below.

> Class I. The Sweitzer Pennsylvania Barn, 1730–1850
> > Type A. Log Sweitzer Barn
> > Type B. Classic Sweitzer Barn
> > Type C. Transition Sweitzer Barn
>
> Class II. The Standard Pennsylvania Barn, 1790–1890
> > Type A. Closed-Forebay Standard Barn
> > Type B. Open-Forebay Standard Barn
> > Type C. Posted-Forebay Standard Barn
> > Type D. Multiple-Overhang Standard Barn
> > Type E. Basement Drive-through Standard Barn
> > Type F. Special Forms of the Standard Barn
> > > Type F-1. Gable-Ramp Standard Barn
> > > Type F-2. Gable-Forebay Standard Barn
> > > Type F-3. Stone-Arch-Forebay Standard Barn
> > > Type F-4. Bank-into-Forebay Standard Barn
>
> Class III. The Extended Pennsylvania Barn, 1790–1920
> > Type A. Extended Supported-Forebay Barn
> > > Type A-1. Chester County Stone-Posted-Forebay Barn
> > > Type A-2. Upcountry Posted-Forebay Barn
> > Type B. Front-Shed (Three-Gable) Barn
> > Type C. Rear-Extension Barn
> > > Type C-1. Single- or Double-Outshed Barn
> > > Type C-2. Ramp-Shed Barn
> > Type D. Vertical-Extension ("Double-Decker") Barn

Class I. The Sweitzer Pennsylvania Barn, 1730–1850

General Specifications: The Sweitzer barn, the original Pennsylvania barn, was the earliest to appear in the core area (Dornbusch and Heyl 1958, 79–80). The term *Sweitzer* has been used to identify this early forebay bank barn since the first part of the 1800s (Shoemaker 1959, 6–7). The barn has a forebay of medium depth, 6 to 9 feet, supported only by forebay beams cantilevered into the barn structure. The front roof slope is longer than the rear roof slope because the roof continues unbroken over the forebay. The angle of the slope is steep, 40 to 45 degrees, facilitating rapid drainage from original roofs, which were of thatch, or from wooden shingle roofs. The result is the characteristic asymmetrical gable-end silhouette of the Sweitzer barn. Because of the longer front roof slope, the forebay front wall is low, only two-thirds the height of the real wall. The earliest Sweitzer barns generally have the steepest roofs and the lowest forebay front walls. This creates a striking visual impression that allows for quick identification of this class of barns. Careful inspection of construction materials and internal morphology will reveal several types of Sweitzer barns.

Figures 2.1 and 2.2. Original forebay support post (*left*) on a log forebay bank barn in Prätigau, Graubünden, Switzerland, where it is a frequently used technique. Figure 2.2 (*right*) shows an original forebay support post of the Gephardt barn, Bonneauville, Adams County, Pennsylvania. The use of forebay support posts on log Sweitzer barns is rare in Pennsylvania. (Photos 1988.)

Type A. Log Sweitzer Barn (Dornbusch Type F), 1730–1830

Locations: Southeastern Pennsylvania core area to Virginia, especially the Shenandoah Valley; central and western Pennsylvania through Ohio; and southern Ontario

The log Sweitzer was Pennsylvania's first forebay bank barn and represents a direct connection to its Swiss prototypes in Prätigau. It arrived in the Pennsylvania core area in the early eighteenth century. The Gephardt barn in Adams County has the year 1723 chiseled in the stone stable wall. Even if the date is inaccurate, this is an early barn and has original forebay support posts reinforcing the forebay beams. This technique is rare in Pennsylvania log barns but quite common in the Prätigau prototypes, as we have already seen. The Herman barn in Lancaster County, mentioned previously, is another early example, dating from 1739 (Herman 1978, 24). A stairway into the forebay, seen in this barn, is fairly common in southeastern Pennsylvania and reflects the design of Prätigau forebay barns.

The earliest log Sweitzer barns are small to medium in size. A typical example is 62 by 30 feet, including a 6-foot forebay. The superstructure of

Figure 2.3. Small double-crib log Sweitzer barn with cantilevered, originally unsupported, frame forebay, stone stable walls, and asymmetrical gable configuration. This typical Pennsylvania log Sweitzer barn near Rothsville, Lancaster County, Pennsylvania, is dated 1781. (Photo 1986.)

Figure 2.4. The Old Luckenbill barn, circa 1800, near Friedensburg, Schuylkill County, Pennsylvania, is a log Sweitzer barn with frame forebay showing an original forebay tie beam notched into front log-crib wall. (Photo 1980.)

Figure 2.5. The Schmidt barn, 1809, Black Creek Pioneer Village, Toronto, Ontario, is a large log Sweitzer barn with log stable walls built by a Pennsylvania pioneer. (Photo 1989.)

the barn rests on stone basement walls and consists of two log-crib mows separated by a central threshing floor. The cribs consist of half-squared logs joined at the corners with dovetail or V-notching. Access to the mows was created by cutting out some logs facing the threshing floor, producing large, rectangular loading openings. A frame forebay is supported by a sill resting on beams that cantilever under the heavy log cribs. Most forebay beams extend from the front of the forebay, over the summer beam, and anchor into the rear wall of the barn. The upper part of the forebay frame is supported by tie beams, which are notched into the front log-crib walls.

The inclusion of a forebay on a log barn certainly required extra time and effort when the barn was built and required prior knowledge of and a preference for the forebay form. That it was so often included on log Sweitzer barns clearly illustrates the strength of the forebay tradition and reinforces the case for Swiss prototypes. To complete the barn, vertical boards were attached to the forebay frame and also to the exterior log walls of the mows, covering the log construction.

Although most log Sweitzer barns have stone basement walls, some do have log walls resting on stone sills. This variation is clearly revealed in the Schmidt barn, seen in Figure 2.5. This barn is also an example of a barn that is abnormally long because it includes two threshing floors. The absence of forebay granary bins in many of these barns echoes their absence in the Prätigau prototypes. Their later inclusion may have been a response to changes in practices of feeding stabled stock. Roof rafters are pinned together at the apex, and no ridge board is used. This is typical of virtually all

Figure 2.6. The Isaac Long barn, 1754, near Landis Valley, Lancaster County, Pennsylvania. This early example of a large, fully developed stone classic Sweitzer barn has a steep medieval roof and low forebay front wall. (Photo 1989.)

other American barns. The size of the barn and of its roof determine if purlins are required. If used, they are braced by queen posts, which rest on the top log of the crib walls facing the threshing floor. The substantial nature of the barns just described has insured the survival of many examples, even after two hundred years or more.

Type B. Classic Sweitzer Barn (Dornbusch Type G), 1750–1850

Locations: Southeastern Pennsylvania core area to Maryland; Virginia, especially the Shenandoah Valley; western Pennsylvania; and Ohio

The classic Sweitzer barn appeared in the core area in the middle of the eighteenth century (Dornbusch and Heyl 1958, 98–102). It evolved from the log Sweitzer barn by the replacement of log cribs with masonry walls and hewn interior bents. Having stone construction on three sides plus the front stable wall gives these barns a solid and timeless look. The upper gable walls of the mow area are ventilated with vertical slits in the masonry or rectangular openings with wooden louvers. This type of barn is larger than its log forerunners, sometimes exceeding 100 feet in length. It has large haymows and double-width threshing floors. Additional threshing floors and mows may be found in very large barns.

Heavy bents of hewn oak, mortise-and-tenonned and pinned, provide inner support for barn and roof. A bent is a heavy timber section of the barn framework. Bents were either constructed in place, timber by timber, or prefabricated on the barn floor to be raised and connected to complete the framework. Bents are located on either side of the threshing floor, but

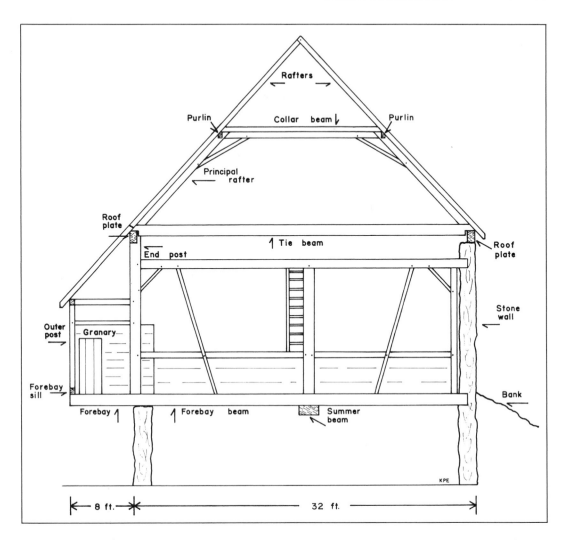

Diagram 2.3. Bent configuration of the Moyer barn, near Blandon, Berks County, Pennsylvania. This is representative of the classic Sweitzer barn using Germanic liegender Stuhl roof truss with truncated principal rafter and braced double collar beam. A barn's threshing floor is the best place from which to observe the characteristic configurations of the bents separating the mows from the threshing floor.

additional ones may be required in larger barns. The typical bent configuration consists of one or two upper cross beams connected to end and inner posts, plus heavy diagonal braces reaching from cross beams, or end posts to floor. In early bents, the end post, top cross, or tie beam and the roof plate are articulated at the top of the post in a complicated mortise-and-tenon tying joint. The evolution of bent configurations is examined in Chapter 3. Mow ladders reaching from the floor to the top beam are incorporated into those bents that stand between the threshing floor and the mows. In large barns, queen posts between tie beams and purlins provide additional support for

Figure 2.7. Forebay bank barn with log-crib haymow and liegender Stuhl roof truss near Schwyz, Central Lake District, Switzerland. (Photo 1988.)

Figure 2.8. Heavy plank stairway from front stable yard into forebay of classic Sweitzer barn. Bertolet-Coker barn, 1787, Oley Valley, Berks County, Pennsylvania. (Photo 1990).

the roof. Most early examples of the classic Sweitzer barn utilize a heavy, truncated principal rafter and braced double collar beam truss instead of queen posts for roof support. This type of frame, called *liegender Stuhl* (lying chair), can be found in sixteenth-century structures, including some barns, in Germany and central Switzerland.[1]

The forebay of the classic Sweitzer barn is 6 to 9 feet deep and is supported by heavy forebay beams under the forebay sill that extend back over the front stable wall, under the heavy timber frame, and on to the rear stable wall. Some forebay beams may reach only to the summer beam. These are extended to the rear barn wall by an adjacent member. The forebay frame, although it extends beyond the barn foundation, is an integral part of the upper barn frame, maintaining the classic asymmetrical silhouette of the Sweitzer barn. In many barns, separate granary rooms were created by walling off one side of the forebay; a door between the two provided access to the front of the threshing floor. Hay drop holes or stairways to the stable below are usually adjacent to the threshing floor, next to the rear wall of the mow (recall the use of hay holes in many Graubünden barns). The forebay

1. Schilli and Richter n.d., 24, 39, 61, 62; Weiss 1959, 75–80; Schäfer 1906, vol. 1, Baden pl. 14, no. 3, Bayern pl. 10, no. 3, Bayern pl. 15, no. 5; vol. 2, 223.

Figure 2.9. Frame Sweitzer barn, circa 1820, Spangsville, Oley Valley, Berks County, Pennsylvania. (Photo 1989.)

stairway, also inherited from Prätigau, is fairly common, particularly in Lancaster County, occurring there in 10 percent of barns.

The Sweitzer tradition was continued during the first half of the nineteenth century, when brick and wood frame began to be used in addition to log and stone. The use of brick construction began in Philadelphia and eastern Maryland and spread across southeastern Pennsylvania to inland cities and rural areas, along with the Georgian-style house, which is built of brick as well as stone. The presence of brick barns in the core, especially in its western reaches, suggests a continued preference for masonry construction as growth continued beyond the earlier stone barn areas. Some brick barns date as early as 1809; the majority, however, were built after 1850, when more farmers were affluent enough to afford them (Shoemaker 1959, 70–87). Brick barns were built in various styles, but those of the Sweitzer class represent the final expression of this tradition in Pennsylvania. Framing and morphology are virtually identical to the stone Sweitzer barn.

The frame Sweitzer barn is also a later development of this type. Early examples of it occur throughout the core, but especially in Lebanon and Lancaster counties. These counties are also the sites of the largest frame Sweitzer barns, as well as of log and stone Sweitzer barns and later types. The frame Sweitzer barn may have developed here, where the traditional Sweitzer form was applied to less expensive timber frame construction in the early nineteenth century. Stable walls continued to be of stone and to sup-

Figure 2.10. Transition Sweitzer barn, circa 1810, near Port Clinton, Schuylkill County, Pennsylvania. Though the forebay beams cantilever beneath a typical Sweitzer upper barn frame, the extended basement end walls, which provide additional support, form a diagnostic closed forebay. (Photo 1990.)

port a superstructure of timber framing and vertical board siding. Frame Sweitzer barns extend west beyond the core into areas where stone and brick barns are rare. Frame construction, the least costly method, predominated in the less affluent areas that were settled later, which explains the westerly extension of this type.

General morphology and framing in this barn are similar to those in stone and brick Sweitzer barns, except that timber frame bents replace masonry end walls as a source of support. End wall bents, plus interior bents, complete the barn frame, which in the past was assembled by "raising the barn." This required partial prefabrication and assembly of the bents, which was done on a floor laid over the basement level. The bents were then stood up, completed, connected, and sided by skilled crews, supervised by a professional barn builder, to finish the barn. In Mennonite and Amish areas, where the practice is followed today, large groups of volunteer workers aid in raising the barn.

Type C. Transition Sweitzer Barn (no Dornbusch classification), 1790–1840

Locations: Southeastern Pennsylvania core area, central Pennsylvania to adjacent Maryland, and northern Virginia

Early examples of this type of Sweitzer barn may be transitional to the

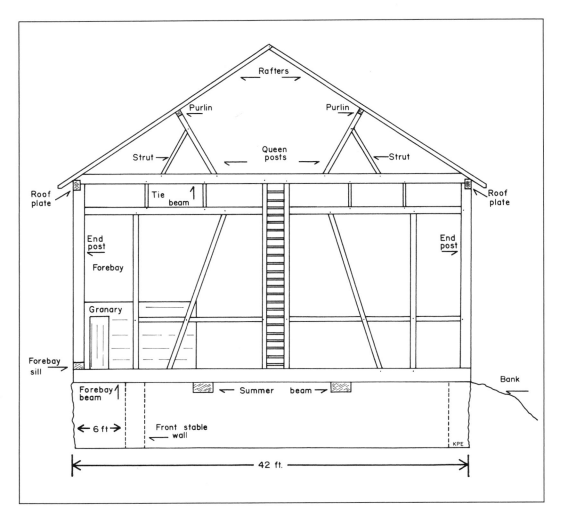

Diagram 2.4. Representative bent configuration of a standard Pennsylvania barn, the Sunday barn, circa 1840, near Kutztown, Berks County, Pennsylvania. This example has a closed forebay.

closed-forebay standard barn; thus the name. These Sweitzer barns have supported forebays. In some cases, support may have been added at a later time; many barns, however, were originally built this way. Except for this support, their basic morphology is similar to other classic Sweitzer barns.

The most common method of providing extra support was to extend one or both basement end walls out under the forebay to support the forebay sill. This "closed-end" Sweitzer occurs throughout the core area but is most prevalent in Lancaster County. Early examples have all-stone gable ends, such as the one pictured in Figure 2.10. As in all Sweitzer barns, the forebay beams cantilever below the barn frame and support the forebay sill. With both gable-end forebay beams and both ends of the forebay sill resting on the extended basement walls, adequate support is guaranteed.

Class II. The Standard Pennsylvania Barn, 1790–1890

General Specifications: The standard Pennsylvania barn is the most numerous and widely distributed class of Pennsylvania barns. Originating in Pennsylvania, it spread south and west, even beyond the Mississippi River, throughout the nineteenth century as the frontier, and farmers, moved west.

This class of barn emerged around 1800 in the core while the classic Sweitzer was still being built there. The major difference between it and the Sweitzer barn is the use of symmetrical bents that include the forebay within the main barn frame, rather than making it an adjacent component of the frame. This permits the roof ridge to be centered over the whole barn structure. The obvious result is to produce a *symmetrical* gable end for the upper, framed part of the barn and a forebay front wall height equal to that of the rear bank wall. The roof slopes are equal in length and have a gentle pitch, generally of 30 to 35 degrees. The symmetrical gable identifies the standard Pennsylvania barn.

The reasons for the emergence of the standard barn are unclear. These barns generally have slightly shallower forebays than the Sweitzers. Forebay beams, which cantilever under the barn frame, are hewn from oak and other hardwoods. A growing scarcity of long, heavy timber for unsupported forebays may have been one factor that encouraged a new design with shorter forebays or extra forebay support. I have found no exact prototypes in Switzerland that could have served as models for this class. I conclude, therefore, that the standard Pennsylvania barn developed in Pennsylvania as a new style, an alternative to the Sweitzer barn. Over time, various types and subtypes of it appeared, whose distinguishing characteristics depend on the depth of the forebay, the method of forebay reinforcement, and other morphological variations. Barns of this class have been constructed of stone, wood, and brick, and all types have been carried beyond Pennsylvania. Forebay granaries, which first appeared in classic Sweitzer barns, are almost universally found in standard barns in all geographical locations.

Type A. Closed-Forebay Standard Barn (Dornbusch Type H), 1790–1890

Locations: Central and southeastern Pennsylvania through central Maryland and west to Illinois, Wisconsin, and Iowa

The closed-forebay standard barn developed in the eastern part of the core area and became the dominant barn in Northampton, Montgomery, Lehigh, and Berks counties. The "closing" of forebay end walls has been documented in the early nineteenth century in Chester County.[2] Most

---

2. Yoder 1965, 11–21. In "The Domestic Encyclopaedia of 1803–1804" Yoder describes the writings of James Mease. Mease provided the earliest known architectural plan of a two-level Pennsylvania barn, the Miller barn in Chester County, Pennsylvania. This plan clearly shows a 10-foot-deep forebay. Significantly, it also reveals a forebay completely closed at one end with a door through the opposite closed end, plus a series of five support posts between the forebay end walls. This barn, having obviously been built before the publication date of 1804, provides proof that both posting and closing of forebays were being practiced around the end of the eighteenth century.

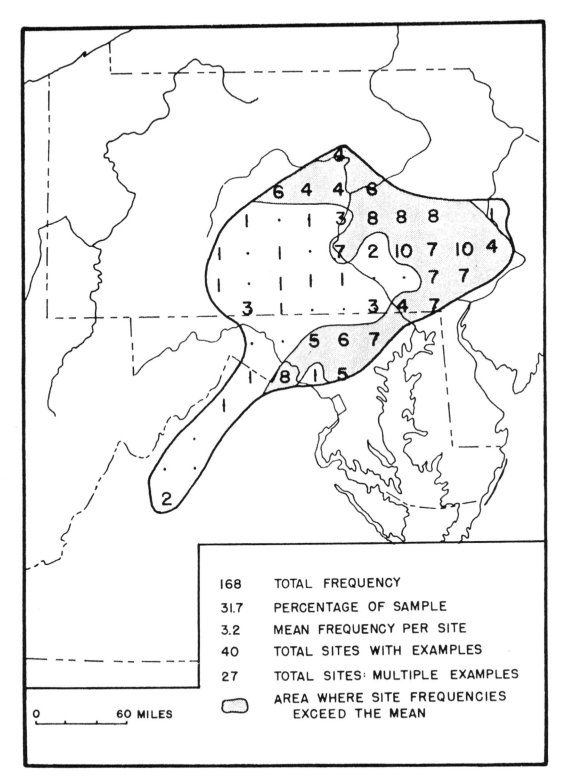

168   TOTAL FREQUENCY

31.7   PERCENTAGE OF SAMPLE

3.2   MEAN FREQUENCY PER SITE

40   TOTAL SITES WITH EXAMPLES

27   TOTAL SITES: MULTIPLE EXAMPLES

AREA WHERE SITE FREQUENCIES EXCEED THE MEAN

0   60 MILES

closed-forebay standard barns cited by Dornbusch and Heyl were built between 1830 and 1860; however, they attribute a few to the late eighteenth century (Dornbusch and Heyl 1958, 153–213).

Many of the barns in the counties just mentioned are of stone construction except for the frame front wall of the forebay. The forebay sill, which rests on top of the forebay beams, is anchored into the stone basement end walls, which extend below the forebay providing additional support. These extended end walls enclose the area in front of the stable. This area, thus recessed, is visible only from the barnyard side of the barn. Forebay depths vary, from 4 to 9 feet in accordance with the size of the barn. However, some large barns can have relatively shallow forebays, which implies that, by this time, style had superseded the functional advantages of the forebay. The forebay stairway, which was transferred from Prätigau to Pennsylvania Sweitzer barns, is found on closed-forebay standard barns occasionally in the eastern core counties. Barn sizes range from medium to large (over 100 feet in length), but some small ones can be found. As in stone Sweitzer barns, upper-level ventilation is provided by vertical slits (loop holes), or rectangular wooden-louvered ventilators. A technique that appeared with this barn was the use of brick to construct the vents on the gable masonry walls of the barn. Various patterns could be used for the vents, but the diamond and sheaf of wheat were most common.

Another practice, common only in the eastern counties of the core region, was to finish the exposed end of the stone gable walls on the forebay side of the barn with large, quoin stones, producing L-shaped edges. The result is a shallow, recessed alcove between the wider, outer wall edge and the front stable wall. This alcove is called a Peilereck, in the Pennsylvania-German dialect. There is some additional strength and protection afforded by this design. In the alcove one may find pegs where harnesses could be hung. Doors were sometimes fitted over the alcove, producing a storage cupboard.

Map 2.2. (*opposite*) Distribution of closed-forebay standard barns in the Pennsylvania barn domain (see p. 147), plotted by Joseph Glass. Glass identified these as "barns with closed ends beneath their forebays." Most types of Pennsylvania barns have not been mapped by scholars because there has been no comprehensive classification system by which to identify them. (Map provided by Joseph Glass, used by his permission.)

Glass superimposed a grid with twenty-mile intervals on a map of his Pennsylvania barn domain. His sampling sites were the 53 intersecting coordinates of the grid. The ten barns closest to each sampling site were surveyed, yielding a data base of 530 barns. The numbers on the map show the count at each site, which Glass called the *site frequency* of the barn type being surveyed. The sum of the numbers from each site provides the *total frequency* of the type. Dividing the total frequency by the data base number (530) yields the *percentage of sample;* dividing the total frequency by the total number of sites (53) yields the *mean frequency per site*. By bounding and shading the area where the site frequencies exceed the mean frequencies, a region of concentration for the specific barn type is defined.

Figure 2.11. Gerlach barn, circa 1840, near Topton, Berks County, Pennsylvania, is a stone closed-forebay standard barn. Gable walls are quoined and widened to an L-shape at the end, creating slight recesses. (Photo 1989.)

Figure 2.12. Recessed alcove behind L-shaped edge of end wall under forebay of closed-forebay standard barn near Seis-holtzville, Berks County, Pennsylvania. The local name for this feature is the *Peilereck,* in the Pennsylvania-German dialect. Its origin is examined in Chapter 3. (Photo 1989.)

Figures 2.13 and 2.14. The transition from closed to open forebays may have begun with the partial opening of one end by the placing of a doorway in one end wall, as seen in the Rothenberg barn (*top*), Oley Valley, Berks County, Pennsylvania. The next step was the elimination of one forebay end wall resulting in the "half-open" forebay of a standard barn, like the one in Figure 2.14 (*bottom*), which is near Lynnport, Lehigh County, Pennsylvania. (Photos 1990.)

Joseph Glass documented that the closed-forebay standard barn is most common in the eastern section of the Pennsylvania barn region that he mapped (Glass 1986, 52). He contends that the closed-forebay type was an early arrival from Europe and was established in those eastern locations (50). In Chapter 3, I analyze the closed forebay of the standard barn, but from the perspective of evolution, not importation. This is the only viable explanation—there are no significant distributions of closed-forebay models in Switzerland that might have been replicated in Pennsylvania.

A transition from closed to open forebays on standard barns is revealed by some barns in the core area that have one end open and one end closed. Occasionally the forebay wall at the closed end will have in it an arched doorway for access to the stable. This characteristic actually can be traced back to some transitional Sweitzers which display identical morphology. In any event, the elimination of first one, then both of the forebay end wall closures occurred as an evolutionary process affecting the standard barn during the early nineteenth century. This resulted in the development of the open-forebay standard barn.

Type B. Open-Forebay Standard Barn (no Dornbusch designation), 1810–1890

Locations: Western part of Pennsylvania core area and central Pennsylvania to Virginia, especially the Shenandoah Valley; western Pennsylvania across Ohio, Indiana, and Illinois to Wisconsin, Iowa, and Nebraska

The elimination of both forebay end walls results in an open forebay, which relies only on cantilevering of the forebay beams for support. Because it is similar to the classic Sweitzer barn in this respect, it is sometimes incorrectly included with this type. The symmetrical bents, consequent symmetrical gable-end silhouette, and forebay placement within the main barn frame are consistent with all standard barns and not Sweitzer barns. The popularity of open-forebay standard barns, especially in the middle of the nineteenth century, places them chronologically in the standard and not the Sweitzer era. Many writers have consistently and incorrectly identified open-forebay standard barns as Sweitzer barns by focusing only on the open cantilevered forebay. I hope this explanation will correct the confusion concerning these "false Sweitzer" standard barns.

Open-forebay standard barns have forebays 6 to 9 feet in depth which are supported by hand-hewn, hardwood forebay beams. All-frame construction is the rule, as is the case with the majority of mid- and later nineteenth-century barns. Perhaps it was the use of frame construction that permitted the utilization of an open forebay for this barn. Frame construction eliminated the need for the support that had been provided by the forebay end walls in stone closed-forebay barns. The popularity of the open-forebay standard barn across the Midwest is consistent with the almost universal use of frame construction west of the Pennsylvania core during the mid-nineteenth century and later.

Figure 2.15. Open-forebay standard barn, circa 1870, located on U.S. Route 11 near Stoughstown, Cumberland County, Pennsylvania. (Photo 1989.)

Type C. Posted-Forebay Standard Barn (no Dornbusch designation), 1840–1910

Locations: Pennsylvania core area to Virginia, especially the Shenandoah Valley; western Pennsylvania and southern Ontario; Ohio to Illinois, Wisconsin, and Iowa

A late phase in the development of the standard Pennsylvania barn occurred when support posts were placed beneath forebay cross beams to provide extra support at the front of the forebay. This permitted a deeper forebay, which was accomplished not by extending the barn frame and forebay but by relocating the stable wall further back under the barn frame, creating an overhang of up to 15 feet. The upper barn layout was not revised by this procedure, but the stable area was reduced. This represented a union of the tradition of supporting the forebay with posts and the traditional balanced bent configuration of standard barns. Although some barns of this type may have been built before 1840, most are contemporaneous with extended supported-forebay barns (to be considered later), which may have influenced them. This influence is revealed in those barns whose forebay beams do not cantilever under the barn frame but rest instead on top of the front stable wall and the forebay cross beam.

Figure 2.16. The Hendrickson barn, in Alsace Township near Reading, Berks County, Pennsylvania, is a posted-forebay standard barn built in 1914. Most barns of this type, which uses four or more posts to reinforce the forebay cross beam, do not require extended end wall support. In some barns, end walls have been extended with frame partitions which close the forebay but do not support it. (Photo 1989.)

Figure 2.17. The Broughter barn, circa 1840, east of Pine Grove, Schuylkill County, Pennsylvania, a multiple-overhang standard barn with 5-foot forebay and 2-foot over-hang on one gable wall. (Photo 1989.)

Many barns of this type in the eastern core counties, where stone construction is common, also have gable walls of stone. Their forebays, however, are always of frame construction and have open forebay end walls (see Figure 2.16). Most later barns of this type are of all-frame construction, except for the basement walls. Wood is usually used for support posts, but cast iron pipe was sometimes substituted in later barns. A variation of this barn has stone forebay-end walls which close the forebay and support the forebay cross beam. Although Peilerecks are sometimes used, one or more original support posts are required to reinforce the cross beam. This "closed form" posted-forebay standard barn has a deeper forebay than the closed-forebay standard barn that it resembles. The use of support posts for either primary or supplementary support always qualifies these as posted-forebay standard barns.

Posted-forebay standard barns also occur from western Pennsylvania to the Mississippi River and across into Iowa. A significant group can be found in Adams County in western Illinois (Price 1987). Another notable concentration of Pennsylvania barns, in Waterloo County, Ontario, is the result of the migration of Mennonite farmers from Lancaster County, Pennsylvania, in the early nineteenth century. Many of these barns in Ontario are posted-forebay standard types and represent the last phase of Pennsylvania barn construction there (Ensminger 1988, 63–72).

Type D. Multiple-Overhang Standard Barn (no Dornbusch designation), 1830–1880

Locations: Scattered locations across Pennsylvania and the Midwest. Major concentration in Shenandoah and Rockingham counties, Virginia; significant clusters in Perry and Fairfield counties, and Allen and Putnam counties, Ohio; several examples near Plainville, Onedaga County, New York

Multiple-overhang barns result when the barn's upper level extends beyond the basement wall on sides other than the front stable, or forebay, side of the barn. "Extra-overhang" barn plans include front and rear double overhang, four-sided overhang, and single gable-side overhang, in addition to the standard forebay. Though the bent configurations differ somewhat from those found in southeastern Pennsylvania barns, their balanced pattern definitely places them within the standard barn class.

In barns with gable overhangs, summer beams extend far enough beyond the gable-end basement walls to support the sill of the gable-end bents. In double-overhang barns, cantilever beams that support the forebay continue under the barn frame and project beyond the rear stable wall, supporting an overhang reaching to the rear ramp. The narrowest overhangs are always on the gable ends and project only 1 1/2 to 2 feet beyond the basement walls. Rear overhangs are wider, 2 to 6 feet, sometimes equaling, but rarely exceeding, the forebay overhang.

A scattering of multiple-overhang barns of various types occurs across Pennsylvania. They are isolated, individual examples that reveal the propensity of barn builders for almost infinite variation in design. One of these is a

Figure 2.18. This multiple-overhang standard barn, built circa 1875 near Orwigsburg, Schuylkill County, Pennsylvania, is unique in having overhangs on three sides as well as a gable ramp. (Photo 1989.)

variant log Sweitzer barn in Northumberland County, which has a cantilevered, framed rear overbay, almost matching the forebay in size. This double-overhang barn, dating about 1825, could be a prototype for the later frame versions occurring across Pennsylvania and the Midwest, several of which are in Green County, Indiana.[3] An article in the 1838 issue of *The Farmers' Cabinet* describes, diagrams, and labels the specifications of a standard forebay barn with rear overhang in Chester County, Pennsylvania ("Chester County Pennsylvania Barn Plan" 1838, 195–97). Besides promoting the double-overhang barn plan, this article reveals its early appearance in the core area, and the importance of the core area in the evolution of barn types.

A significant group of frame double-overhang barns has been identified and studied by Hugh Wilhelm of Ohio University (Wilhelm 1989b, 29–37). Dr. Wilhelm showed me these barns in December 1988. They occur in a line of ten or more, extending twenty miles east-west across Perry and Fairfield counties north of the city of Lancaster, Ohio. At least one double-overhang barn with additional gable overhangs has been reported in the same area. The largest distribution of multiple-overhang barns occurs in the Shenandoah section of the Great Valley in Virginia, including portions of Shenan-

3. Sightings of double-overhang barns in Green County, Indiana, were confirmed by barn scholar Wayne Price, of the Pioneer America Society, in October of 1986.

Figure 2.19. The Schreyeor barn, 1848, north of Lancaster, Fairfield County, Ohio, is a double-overhang barn. (Photo 1989.)

doah, Rockingham, and Augusta counties, Virginia (Glass 1986, 61). This is part of the larger Pennsylvania barn region, projecting southwest from the Pennsylvania core into eastern Tennessee.

The multiple-overhang barns of the Shenandoah differ from those in south-central Ohio in that most are four-sided-overhang barns (Glassie 1966, 16). The forebay overhang is generally 5 feet deep with side and rear overhangs of 1½ to 2 feet. The rear barn ramp sometimes reaches only to the edge of the rear overhang, producing a narrow tunnel between it and the recessed rear basement wall. The basement walls are made of heavy timber frames with wood siding resting on stone foundation walls or sills. The tunnel separates the frame stable wall from contact with the stone and earthen ramp, avoiding rotting and deterioration. Overlapping horizontal board siding is used to enclose the barn frame, rather than the vertical siding used on most frame barns.

This all-frame construction is typical of Pennsylvania barns south of the Potomac River, most of which date from after the Civil War. The majority of earlier barns were destroyed during that conflict (Glass 1986, 55). Prototypes of the four-sided-overhang plan are difficult to find. Early log-crib ground barns with forebaylike overhangs are found in Bedford County, Pennsylvania. Henry Glassie recorded and studied somewhat similar barns in Adams and York counties, Pennsylvania, and to the south, from the

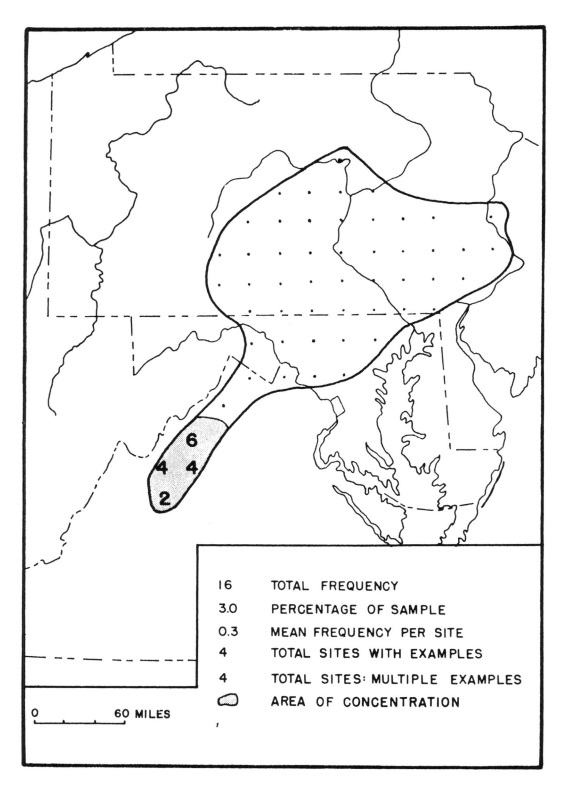

16   TOTAL FREQUENCY

3.0   PERCENTAGE OF SAMPLE

0.3   MEAN FREQUENCY PER SITE

4   TOTAL SITES WITH EXAMPLES

4   TOTAL SITES: MULTIPLE EXAMPLES

          AREA OF CONCENTRATION

0   60 MILES

Figure 2.20. A four-sided-overhang standard barn near Woodstock, Shenandoah County, Virginia. (Photo 1989.)

Virginia–West Virginia border through eastern Kentucky to eastern Tennessee and western North Carolina (Glassie 1965b, 18–19). One pre–Civil War log forebay *bank* barn with three-sided overhang, north of Roanoke, Virginia, was reported by Glassie (1966, 21). It may represent a survivor of a previously broader distribution of similar structures. These could have served as models for the later frame multiple-overhang barns, which were built until the end of the nineteenth century in the Great Valley in Virginia.

Type E. Basement Drive-through Standard Barn (no Dornbusch designation), 1850–1890

Locations: South-central Pennsylvania, particularly Franklin, Fulton, Huntington, and Terry counties; across Maryland to the Shenandoah Valley, scattered locations in Ohio and the Midwest

In addition to the normal function of the lower level of Pennsylvania barns as stables for livestock, some are used for the storage of large machinery. The use of horse-drawn machinery dates from the middle of the nineteenth century. Many older barns were necessarily modified to accommodate its storage. The stable could be remodeled to house machinery or storage sheds could be added to the gable ends of the barn. Eventually, a new

Map 2.3. *(opposite)* Distribution of multiple-overhang standard barns in the Pennsylvania barn domain (see p. 147), plotted by Joseph Glass. Glass identified these as "barns with classic forebays plus gable-end and/or second-floor projections." (Map provided by Joseph Glass, used by his permission.) (See explanatory note at Map 2.2.)

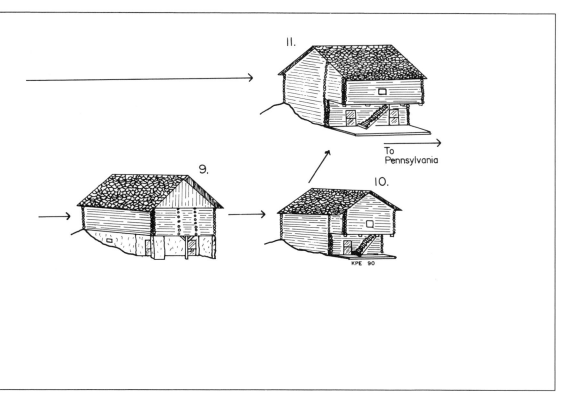

hay, and grains. These changes occurred as the Walsers moved to lower elevations, displacing Romansch farmers and adopting some of their grain-raising techniques. Weiss has suggested that the primitive, highland Alpine barn with shallow gable forebay is a basic type of forebay barn. He also states that it did not in all cases evolve into the Prätigau barn (Weiss 1943, 32–33, 38). Indeed, this simple barn with shallow gable forebay has a broad distribution, reaching west to Wallis, whence the Walsers first came. The gable forebay barn can be found throughout the upper Rhone Valley (see Map 1.5, area 7d). There is considerable documentation of this.[6]

So, who invented the forebay bank barn? Jordan's statement that the Walsers apparently adopted the forebay barn from Romansch farmers after arriving in Graubünden is supported by the chronology of their arrival and Jordan's belief that no forebay structures existed in Wallis when the Walsers

6. Bank barns with gable-forebay drying galleries were documented photographically in July 1990 by my brother, Richard Ensminger, in the village of Wiler in Lötchental, a tributary valley of the Rhone River, in the Walser settlement region of northeastern Wallis. Other sources documenting forebay forms in the Rhone Valley are Baumgartner and Woerdehoff 1988, 43; Phleps 1982, 318–20; Hunziker 1900. Hunziker pictures numerous barns, stables, and storehouses in Wallis, many having gable forebaylike structures and overhanging galleries (Lauben) with open scaffolds (Stangengerüste) for drying grain. Their locations correspond with areas of Walser settlement.

Figures 2.21 and 2.22. A large transition Sweitzer barn (*top*), circa 1825, near Buffalo Springs, Lebanon County, Pennsylvania, provides an early example of a basement drive-through. Figure 2.22 (*bottom*) shows a raised forebay, with a corn crib on the outside gable wall, in a basement drive-through standard barn north of McConnellsburg, Fulton County, Pennsylvania. Some early Sweitzer and standard barns have original wagon bays in the basement, but entry is through a door in the stable wall under the forebay. (Photos 1989.)

Figure 2.23. The Moyer barn, circa 1880, near Blandon, Berks County, Pennsylvania, is a standard barn with upper-level access by a gable ramp. Although it is not visible here, this barn has a normal eave forebay. (Photo 1989.)

basement plan that included a machinery storage bay was adopted. Thus, a wagon entrance in the basement can be found as part of the original design in many barns of the middle and later nineteenth century. They occur in barns throughout Pennsylvania, as well as in some Swiss forebay bank barns.

In some barns, the basement wagon entrance evolved into a convenient drive-through, located on the gable end of the barn and increasing its length by one bay. The precedent for a basement drive-through had been established before 1850, as exemplified by a large transition Sweitzer barn in southern Lebanon County. To the west of the Susquehanna River, particularly in Franklin and Fulton counties, the drive-through became stylized in later standard barns. In these structures, the floor of the forebay, which extends across the entire front of the barn, is raised several feet above the machinery entrance. This extra elevation permits the entrance of larger pieces of machinery than could be accommodated by a normal stable height. The outside gable wall of the drive-through consists of a wooden corn crib, the front end of which is normally flush with the front of the forebay. The barn's versatility is enhanced by having an increased mow volume with the additional upper barn length, increased machinery storage space in the basement, and more feed grain storage in the corn crib just described. Glass documented barns with machinery openings at one end of the forebay (1986, 60). He did not, however, specify if these were exclusively those with a drive-through, which have been singled out here as a specific type.

Type F. Special Forms of the Standard Barn

In addition to the five types of standard barns already discussed, other types can be found. They do not occur in sufficient numbers or distributions to warrant adding more types to the system. They are, however, interesting examples of standard Pennsylvania barns and have been assembled as a special category to complete the picture.

Type F-1. Gable-Ramp Standard Barn (no Dornbusch designation), 1850–1900

Locations: Scattered distribution throughout Pennsylvania core area; occasional occurrence in other Pennsylvania barn regions

Standard barns with upper-level access to one gable end are scattered across southeastern Pennsylvania. There are several in Berks County, and they undoubtedly occur occasionally in all Pennsylvania barn regions. The examples in Berks County are closed-forebay standard barns with the ramp relocated one-quarter way around the barn on a gable side. No stable modification was necessary; the upper-level threshing floor, however, extends lengthwise, paralleling the roof ridge, with the mow areas running parallel to it along the eave walls. Large granary rooms occupy part of the mow area on the forebay side of the barn. This type of ramp location seems to be a way to keep the forebay on the south or southeast side of the barn when such an orientation permits access from the main road on a gable side.

Although many early gable-ramp house-barns occur in Alpine Europe, their later appearance in Pennsylvania indicates no direct connection.

Type F-2. Gable-Forebay Standard Barn (no Dornbusch designation), 1850–1900

Locations: Scattered distribution throughout Pennsylvania core area; occasional occurrence in other Pennsylvania barn regions

Standard barns with gable forebays are most numerous in Berks and Montgomery counties, Pennsylvania. The barn ramp is located on the eave side of the barn, and the threshing floor and mows are arranged in the traditional way. Some modification of the basement is necessary to accommodate the narrower stable and gable-side front wall, which contains the stable doors. Deeper forebays, which can be up to 15 feet, require posting for extra support. Shallow forebays, of less than 7 feet, are unposted and have forebay beams that cantilever under the barn frame.

Reasons for this barn plan are not clear. While gable-forebay bank barns are common in Graubünden, Switzerland, the American examples are late and appear to have no generic connections to those early, Old World examples. For an explanation, one falls back on the standard statements about style alternatives, the choice of individual barn builders, and the great variety of barn styles recognized by farmers. There may be a connection between these barns and the larger population of gable-forebay ground barns occurring throughout the same region. These latter structures have never been studied, thus no leads have been developed.

Figure 2.24. The Stahl barn, near Sanatoga, Montgomery County, Pennsylvania, is a gable-forebay bank barn, circa 1870. (Photo 1989.)

Figure 2.25. Gable-forebay ground barn near Schaefferstown, Lebanon County, Pennsylvania, circa 1860. (Photo 1989.)

Figure 2.26. The Furlong barn, in Bucks County, Pennsylvania, east of County Line Road near Tylersport, is a stone-arch-forebay standard barn which was built in 1810. The ventilating slits, which are narrow on the outside, typically flare much wider on the inside. This design admits a maximum of light and ventilation while providing protection from rain, snow, and strong winds. (Photo 1989.)

Type F-3. Stone-Arch-Forebay Standard Barn (Dornbusch Type K),
1800–1830

Locations: Montgomery County; adjacent parts of Lehigh, Bucks, and Northampton counties, Pennsylvania; adjacent Warren County, New Jersey; and New Castle County, Delaware

In this unusual barn the forebay beams and the heavy stone front wall of the forebay are supported by stone arches and closed forebay end walls. At least nine have been documented in Pennsylvania and one in adjacent Delaware. Two examples with identical forebay morphology occur in adjacent Warren County, New Jersey. Both of these are double-decker barns, which are examined in more detail later in this chapter. Dornbusch recognized and classified these barns as Type K (Dornbusch and Heyl 1958, 245). He assumed, but had not verified, dates in the late eighteenth century for two of the barns; however, dates of 1803 and 1813 occur on two others (246–63). I have examined two near County Line Road, Tylersport, Montgomery County. One, on the Bucks County side of the line, is dated 1810.

These dates, along with the symmetrical gable silhouette, closed forebay, and balanced interior bents, suggest that this barn emerged at about the same time as the closed-forebay standard barn. It fits into the standard barn

Figure 2.27. Rare bank-into-forebay standard barn, circa 1860, in the village of Bedminster, Bucks County, Pennsylvania. (Photo 1989.)

Figure 2.28. This bank-into-forebay barn in the old village section of the town of Buchs, Canton St. Gallen, Switzerland, has a log-crib mow on either side of a central threshing floor. (Photo 1978.)

class chronologically and morphologically. The origin of the barn is unclear. There are no direct prototypes in Europe. The common occurrence in Chester County of somewhat similar stone bank barns may be a clue; these structures, while lacking the forebay, do have stone, arched stable doorways. The occurrence, in Bucks County, of other stone bank barns, with pentroof instead of forebay, suggests a connection to English Lake District bank barns. It seems plausible that these upcountry stone-arch-forebay barns represent a Germanization of an English barn type, occurring at the contact zone between Pennsylvania-German and English cultures in the counties adjacent to Philadelphia. A similar process may have produced the stone-column-supported forebay in Chester County. These possibilities will be examined later, particularly in Chapter 3.

Type F-4. Bank-into-Forebay Standard Barn (no Dornbusch designation), 1850–1890

Locations: Three known to occur in Pennsylvania and one in Missouri

This is the least common type of Pennsylvania barn. Two examples are located close together in upper Bucks County. One of these is in the village of Bedminster. Both are closed-forebay standard barns, with their forebays oriented to the south and at the edge of main roads. The barn ramp connects the road and the threshing floor, whose doors are on the forebay side of the barn. A barn with the same orientation is located just east of State College in Centre County.

Be it coincidence or connection, a small group of bank-into-forebay barns occurs in Switzerland. At least five such barns can be found in the old village section of the town of Buchs, just west of Liechtenstein, in Canton St. Gallen. These are double-log-crib bank barns dating from the early nineteenth century. They occur in a very compact farming village where the only access to either level of the barns is from the village street. Therefore, the forebay and stable doors and the bank must all face the street, on the barn's forebay side. Thus, we find yet another example of similar barn morphology in Pennsylvania and Switzerland.

Class III. The Extended Pennsylvania Barn, 1790–1920

General Specifications: This third class includes a large and significant group of Pennsylvania barns, those which have been enlarged by amending or extending the barn beyond the basic Sweitzer and standard framing limits. The amendments were initially additions to existing barns. The revised designs eventually became formalized and accepted as appropriate barn styles, which then spread across the landscape. They reflect the need for larger barns during the nineteenth century, when agricultural production was increasing rapidly. The agricultural journals of the period frequently reported on the new barn styles, promoting them and thus aiding in their dissemination (Schultz 1986).

The types and subtypes of this class derive from the manner in which the barns were extended. The various possibilities boil down to the following

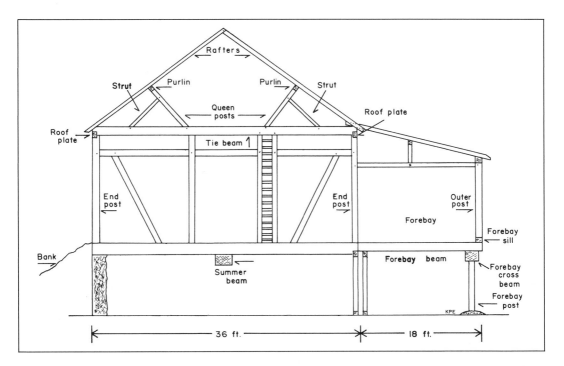

Diagram 2.5. Representative extended supported-forebay bent configuration of an upcountry posted-forebay barn, the author's own barn, circa 1870, Lenhartsville, Berks County, Pennsylvania.

basic methods: extending or amending the forebay, extending the barn's ramp side, and vertically enlarging the barn by adding another level.

Type A. Extended Supported-Forebay Barn (Dornbusch Type J), 1800–1920

This barn type is characterized by a return to the asymmetrical gable end, produced by extending the forebay to 15 feet, 20 feet, or even farther beyond the front stable wall. In so doing, a larger storage area for hay, straw, or grain is created. In early examples of extended barns, forebay depths of up to 15 feet, combined with a long, unbroken front roof slope and low forebay front wall, produced a barn closely resembling the classic Sweitzer. There are, however, significant differences. Sweitzer forebays do not exceed 9 feet and are supported only by cantilevering. The forebay beams of extended supported-forebay barns rest on top of the front stable wall at one end and on a heavy forebay cross beam at the other end. The position of a cross beam *below* the forebay beams is a key diagnostic difference between these and Sweitzer barns. The forebay cross beam is necessarily supported by a row of posts or columns.

In later extended supported-forebay barns, a gentler slope of the roof where it extends over the forebay produces a distinctive "break" in the front roof slope and permits an even deeper forebay, of up to 25 feet, which

Figures 2.29 and 2.30. The Denenberg-Williams barn (*top*), dated 1806, near Phoenixville, Chester County, Pennsylvania. The large forebay straw shed supported by conical stone columns gives this barn the front-heavy look characteristic of extended supported-forebay barns. Figure 2.30 (*bottom*) is a view of the same barn from beneath the forebay, showing the stone column support system and stone-walled barnyard. (Photos 1989.)

increases the storage area even further. These design elements combine to produce a distinctive front-heavy look that, along with the support posts, permits quick identification of this type of barn, which Dornbusch designated as Type J. He did not refine the type further, but I will do so. The details of its evolution are presented in Chapter 3.

Type A-1. Chester County Stone-Posted-Forebay Barn (Dornbusch Type J), 1800–1870

Location: Chester County, Pennsylvania, and adjacent parts of neighboring counties

This earliest form of the extended Pennsylvania barn appeared at the beginning of the nineteenth century in Chester County. The county's early settlement, fertile soils, extensive network of roads, and proximity to both Philadelphia markets and adjacent Germanic regions combined to provide a location ideal for innovation in barn evolution. Bernice Ball, in her book *Barns of Chester County, Pennsylvania* (1974), examines these factors and their resulting impact on barns in the county. She gives Quaker farmers much of the credit for barn enlargement. One way they chose to increase barn size was to add a large Pennsylvania-German forebay to the English Lake District bank barn (Ball 1974, 53, 73, 91, 117). The forebay was necessarily supported by rounded stone columns, possibly of English origin (58, 63, 118).

It is unknown exactly when the practice of using stone support columns to hold up a large extended forebay began. The Denenberg-Williams barn (1806) near Phoenixville, Pennsylvania, is an early example of a barn designed and built from the beginning with stone columns. Other examples clearly show that forebays were added on to existing barns. I suspect that the ones with added-on forebays came first, since forebays were added on to other early barns. The "new style" became formalized around 1800, and stone-column barns were built for the next seventy years. Late barns of this type were constructed of brick and frame. The evolution of the Chester County barn is examined in greater detail in Chapter 3. It does appear that various barn ideas diffused north and west from a Chester County hearth. These include extended forebays with support columns, double-decker (three-level) barns, and the usage of the term *straw shed* or *shed* for large forebays. These terms are used in some other parts of Pennsylvania, and in central Wisconsin *shed* is frequently used to describe forebays of Pennsylvania barns. The examples of these barns found in Wisconsin are examined later in this chapter.

Type A-2. Upcountry Posted-Forebay Barn (Dornbusch Type J), 1825–1920

Locations: All core counties; southwest into Maryland and Virginia, especially the Shenandoah Valley; upper Midwest north to central Wisconsin and west to Iowa

This barn type is very common in the "upcountry" area north and west of Chester County, especially in Montgomery, Lehigh, and Berks counties, which strongly indicates a diffusion out of Chester County of the posted form. The upcountry posted-forebay barn is identical to its Chester County prototype, except that wood posts are substituted for stone columns. As in Chester County, many of the large forebays were added on to earlier barns. Evidence of this will be presented in Chapter 3, where an evolutionary progression for the upcountry posted barn will be proposed.

Most earlier examples of this type of barn are constructed of stone, while those built after 1850 are frame. During the mid-nineteenth century, large numbers of upcountry posted-forebay barns were built, indicating that the style had become formalized and very popular. In the late nineteenth century, Victorian influences affected all structures. Barns with cupolas and decorative trim around the eaves and windows were common. More significant was the addition of a gabled dormer above the forebay. This improved lighting and ventilation in the forebay and provided an opening through which straw could be discarded during mechanized threshing. While very common in Pennsylvania, gabled dormers also occur on barns in the Midwest, particularly in central Wisconsin.

Forebay bank barns are often called "porch barns" in central Wisconsin, where, along with *shed,* the term *porch* is commonly used when referring to the forebay. This usage is certainly logical, given the resemblance of a posted forebay to a porch. The population of forebay bank barns in central Wisconsin, numbering about 150, forms a compact outlier in Lincoln and Marathon counties. They are 1,000 miles from the Pennsylvania core and are disjunct from other Pennsylvania barn areas of the Midwest. Most of the Wisconsin barns were built by local barn builders after 1900 and represent the last concentrated area of Pennsylvania barn construction in Canada and the United States.

These central Wisconsin barns are virtually identical to the upcountry posted-forebay barns of the Pennsylvania core. Some differences are to be noted. The Wisconsin barns always have stone stable-front walls, while many in Pennsylvania are frame. Although the forebay support system, using wooden posts beneath the forebay cross beam to hold up the *uncantilevered* forebay beams, is identical to that in Pennsylvania counterparts, Wisconsin barns have the opposite ends of the forebay beams mortised into a heavy plank sill, resting on the front wall of the stable. This technique is also occasionally found in Pennsylvania, and other states in the Midwest. A heavy frame of hewn or machine-sawn timbers is used, and the bents are arranged in a simpler pattern than is found in Pennsylvania. Central Wisconsin barns, being late examples of the Pennsylvania barn, frequently have gambrel roofs supported by modified roof frames in which longer queen posts support higher purlins. The basement stables follow a center-aisle plan with primary access provided by gable-end doors rather than under-forebay doors. This efficient arrangement permits a larger and more easily serviced dairy herd (Ensminger 1983, 103).

Robert Bastian, writing in 1975, attempted to explain the presence of Pennsylvania barns in central Wisconsin by proposing a parallel but inde-

Figures 2.31 and 2.32. The author's barn (*top*), circa 1870, in Lenhartsville, Berks County, Pennsylvania, is an upcountry posted-forebay barn with 18-foot extended forebay and a gabled dormer that was added later. Figure 2.32 (*bottom*) shows the under-forebay support system for this barn, utilizing wooden posts and braces to support the forebay cross beam and the forebay beams above it. (Photos 1974.)

Figures 2.33 and 2.34. Figure 2.33 (*top*) shows forebay beams mortised into a plank sill resting on the stable front wall of an upcountry posted-forebay barn in Marathon County, Wisconsin. An upcountry posted-forebay barn (*bottom*) west of Wausau in Marathon County, has the large gabled dormer and gambrel roof that are typical of barns built during the early twentieth century. In Wisconsin, forebay bank barns are called "porch barns." (Photos 1982.)

Figure 2.35. Front shed, three-gable barn, circa 1880, north of Middleburg, Snyder County, Pennsylvania. Beams which support the front shed extend under main barn frame, proving that the shed was part of the original design. (Photo 1989.)

pendent evolution. He also suggested a direct connection between these barns and settlers from Pomerania (Bastian 1975, 200–204). I have rejected this thesis and have shown that all Pennsylvania barns in Wisconsin are part of the broader diffusion from Pennsylvania (Ensminger 1983, 98–114). Nevertheless, the term *Pomeranian barn* has found its way into the literature as a name for upcountry posted-forebay barns in the Midwest (Noble 1977, 62–79; 1984, vol. 2, 32). Unawareness of the abundance and cross-country range of many Pennsylvania barn types has encouraged the continued usage of the term *Pomeranian barn*. I suggest that this term *not* be used for upcountry, posted-forebay Pennsylvania barns. The name *Pomeranian* is correctly applied only to the smaller forebay stable that has been documented in southeastern Wisconsin (Calkins and Perkins 1980, 121–25).

Type B. Front-Shed (Three-Gable) Barn (no Dornbusch designation), 1800–1920

Locations: Pennsylvania core, middle Susquehanna Valley, central Ontario, and northeastern quadrant of Ohio

In the front-shed barn, enlargement was accomplished by amending the forebay. The addition of a two-level wing projecting at right angles beyond the forebay resulted in an L plan for the barn and creation of a third gable. This front shed greatly increased the barn's storage capacity, which was needed for the large volume of straw produced by machine threshing. The front shed could store enough straw for bedding the additional cattle housed

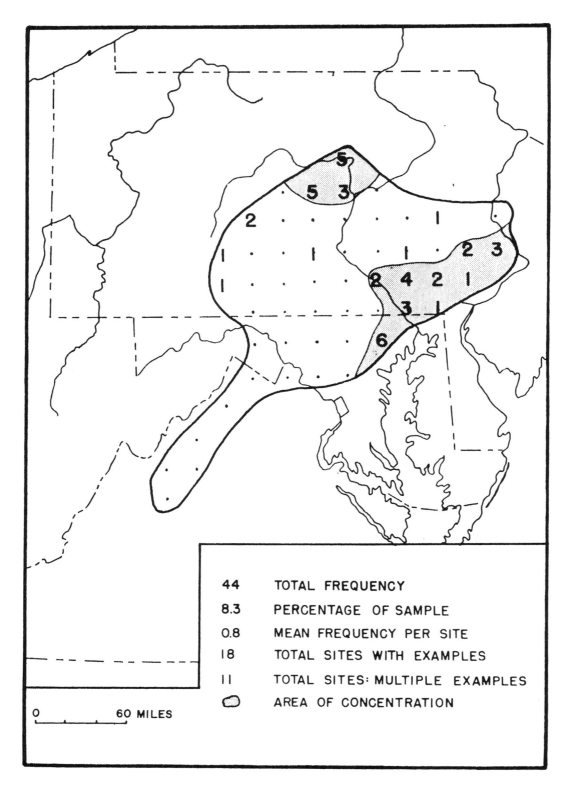

44   TOTAL FREQUENCY

8.3   PERCENTAGE OF SAMPLE

0.8   MEAN FREQUENCY PER SITE

18   TOTAL SITES WITH EXAMPLES

11   TOTAL SITES: MULTIPLE EXAMPLES

⬭   AREA OF CONCENTRATION

0   60 MILES

in the shed's basement level. Very frequently, the sheds were added on to existing barns. Throughout the nineteenth and early twentieth centuries, many barns were originally built with sheds, as the style became formalized (Noble 1984, vol. 2, 42). The front shed, three-gable configuration on a forebay bank barn stands out, providing for easy identification of this type.

Glass was the first person to identify and map the front-shed barn (1986, 63). His map shows two concentrations—central and southeastern Pennsylvania. The latter area has one front-shed barn, near Valley Forge, that is dated 1800 (62). The early occurrence of this type of barn extension close to Philadelphia may indicate that it is a continuation of the kind of barn enlargement initiated by Quaker farmers in Chester County.

The front-shed barns of central Pennsylvania are of all-frame construction and generally date after 1850. The construction of front sheds, whether planned originally or added on later, corresponds to the increase in the size of cattle herds, which occurred later in central than in southeastern Pennsylvania. The same progression occurred in Ontario and the Midwest. In all areas, the front-shed, three-gable barn continued to be built into the early twentieth century.

Type C. Rear-Extension Barn

An asymmetrical gable end can also result from enlarging a barn by extending the rear or ramp side of the barn. Definition of subtypes of rear-extension barns depends on whether there is partial or complete enclosure of the ramp and ramp-side space. The forebay side of the barn is unaffected by rear-extension enlargement.

Type C-1. Single or Double-Outshed Barn (no Dornbusch designation), 1790–1860

Locations: Lancaster County, Pennsylvania, through western core counties in Pennsylvania to northern Maryland; scattered locations in the Midwest

Outshed rear-extension Pennsylvania barns in significantly large number pepper the rural landscape of the western core, particularly along the Great Valley, from Lebanon through Franklin counties, and across the state line into Washington County, Maryland. This strongly localized barn type is characterized by having one or two shedlike rear extensions beside or on either side of the barn ramp. These outsheds are in most cases part of the original barn structure, not later additions. Evidence of this is that the basement walls continue beneath the outsheds. Also, the upper barn frame for these extensions is integrated into the main barn frame. There are later additions on some barns which imitate this plan, but these are easily detected by examination of the basement and frame.

Map 2.4. *(opposite)* Distribution of front-shed, or three-gable, barns in the Pennsylvania barn domain (see p. 147), plotted by Joseph Glass. Glass identified these as "barns originally constructed in an 'ell' shape." (Map provided by Joseph Glass, used by his permission.) (See explanatory note at Map 2.2.)

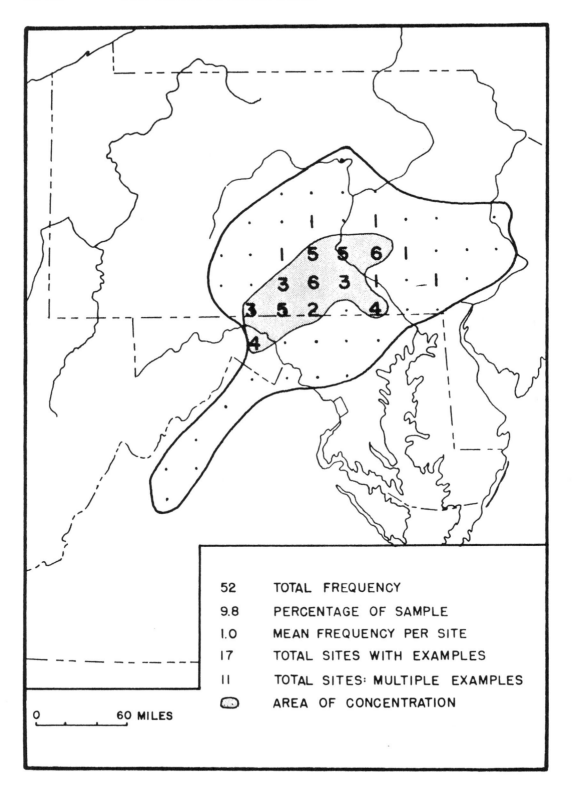

52   TOTAL FREQUENCY
9.8   PERCENTAGE OF SAMPLE
1.0   MEAN FREQUENCY PER SITE
17   TOTAL SITES WITH EXAMPLES
11   TOTAL SITES: MULTIPLE EXAMPLES
⬭   AREA OF CONCENTRATION

0   60 MILES

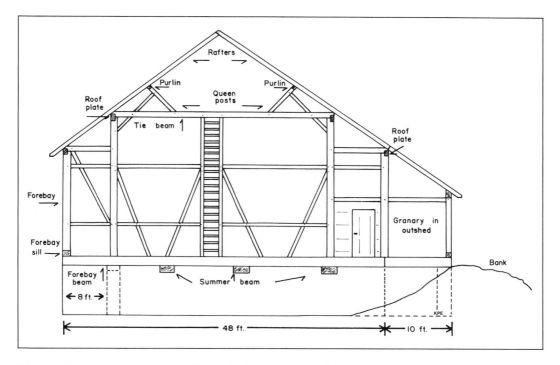

Diagram 2.6. Representative double-outshed rear-extension bent configuration, the Moyer barn, circa 1860, east of Jonestown, Lebanon County, Pennsylvania.

Glass studied these structures and produced a map, presented here as Map 2.5. He called the type "barns originally constructed with rear granary extensions" (1986, 62–66, map on 67). In almost all cases, the extensions function as granaries, which have been relocated from the forebay, thus making even more storage area available there for hay and straw. Access to the granary bins in the outsheds is both from the rear of the threshing floor, inside the barn, and by exterior doors on the upper rear of the gable walls of the barn (see Figure 2.37). The asymmetry of the gable end plus the external granary doors permit quick identification of this type of barn.

Various names have been applied to the rear extensions. Brunskill identified "outshuts" on both houses and bank barns in the Lake District of northwestern England (1974, 59–65, 82–86). Estyn Evans described "outshots," which provide extra space for beds in stone cabins in Northern Ireland (1974, 61, 63). After considering the various terms, I have settled on the word *outshed*. It is simple, descriptive, and close to the English words *outshut* and *outshot,* from which it derives. It also applies exclusively to barns

Map 2.5. *(opposite).* Distribution of single- and double-outshed barns in the Pennsylvania barn domain (see p. 147), plotted by Joseph Glass. Glass identified these as "barns originally constructed with rear granary extensions." (Map provided by Joseph Glass, used by his permission.) (See explanatory note at Map 2.2.)

Figure 2.36. Stone Sweitzer barn, circa 1810, south of Carlisle, Cumberland County, Pennsylvania, has double outshed. (Photo 1988.)

in North America and anticipates the final stage in rear-extension barn evolution, the full-ramp-shed barn.

The great majority of outshed barns are of the double-outshed variety. Some early examples with a single outshed, in Lancaster County suggest the evolutionary process of the type, which will be examined in Chapter 3. The primary differences among barns of this type derive from the ages of the barns and the resultant configurations of their bents and ramp sides. The earliest examples developed from the inclusion of outsheds on Sweitzer barns. These are usually all-stone models with 15-foot shed depths that shift the weight of the asymmetry from the front, with a 9-foot forebay, to the rear side. Mid-nineteenth century models developed from the addition of outsheds to standard barns made of brick and frame. Other examples seem to fuse Sweitzer and standard bent patterns into a new type, which involves framing and covering part of the upper barn ramp between the outsheds. This "partial-ramp-shed" barn is transitional to the full ramp enclosure, which is the subsequent subtype.

Many outshed barns are "brickenders." A higher frequency of brick-end barns occurs in the western end of the Pennsylvania barn core than anywhere else in North America. The majority of these are double-outshed barns which are similar in form to those made of stone and frame. Of special interest are the unique gable-end decorations produced by laying the bricks

Figure 2.37. Single-outshed Sweitzer barn, the Heisey barn, circa 1810, south of Silver Springs, Lancaster County, Pennsylvania. The rear gable-wall door leads to the outshed granary. It permitted transfer of grain directly into wagons. (Photo 1989.)

in a pattern that leaves brick-end-sized openings arranged in decorative designs. These openings, besides being attractive, are functional, providing light and ventilation. The decorative patterns range from simple diamonds and sheaves of wheat, to initials, dates, and even a man on a mule. Alfred Shoemaker's *The Pennsylvania Barn* includes an entire chapter, with numerous photographs, on brickenders. The majority of brick-end Pennsylvania barns were built after 1850, but one in Lancaster County has a decorative brickwork date of 1816 (Shoemaker 1959, 70–87).

The origin of this brickwork technique is clearly English (Brunskill 1987, 101–3). I have seen similar work on brick farm buildings in central England. Glassie pointed out occurrences of it in England that date from as early as the fifteenth century, and he has proposed that it was transplanted from there to the Tidewater region of Virginia (1966, 23). Construction in the lower Delaware Valley was also dominated by English building techniques, including a form of decorative brickwork that was used on some eighteenth-century houses (Wertenbaker 1938, 236–39). During the colonial period, Scotch-Irish pioneers moved west from Philadelphia, New Castle, Delaware, and other tidewater ports. Their early settlements were located in Chester County, Pennsylvania, and the upper Chesapeake region of Maryland; but many moved to the Pennsylvania frontier west of the

Figures 2.38 and 2.39. Two barns owned by Lester Angle, near Mercersburg, Franklin County, Pennsylvania, have decorative ventilation openings in their brick gable walls. The barn in the exterior view (*top*) is a double-outshed standard barn, circa 1850. The interior view is of a barn built circa 1835. (Photos 1989.)

Figure 2.40. The Litweiler barn, circa 1860, west of Bern, Adams County, Indiana. The ramp shed was added on to the rear barn wall about 1885. (Photo 1988.)

Susquehanna River, in what is now the western section of the Pennsylvania barn core (Jordan and Kaups 1989, 61, 80–82, 232–34). This migration could explain the inclusion of English traits, such as decorative brickwork and, possibly, even the outshed, on the Pennsylvania-German barns of that area. The brick-end barns of south-central Pennsylvania display the diversity, complexity, and beauty found in the broad range of vernacular structures falling within the scope of the Pennsylvania barn.

Type C-2. Ramp-Shed Barn (no Dornbusch designation), 1850–1900

Locations: Entire Pennsylvania core; northwestern Ohio and Adams County in eastern Indiana

The final way of extending the rear side of the barn that constitutes a definite type of barn is the complete ramp shed. Many standard and extended supported-forebay barns in the eastern core counties were amended by the later addition of a rear shed that enclosed the entire rear wall area of the barn, including the ramp. This provided a large additional storage area. Few barns in the eastern region were planned and built in this manner from the beginning. It was in the western core, where most outshed barns are found, that formalization of the full ramp shed occurred. This happened in two stages. First, the double outsheds were retracted and shortened. Then, the area between them was enclosed, eliminating the outshed form and creating the ramp-shed form.

A significant group of Pennsylvania barns, in the Mennonite area of Adams County in eastern Indiana, has been examined by Glenn Harper and Leslie Smith (1988, 73–81). Of the approximately one hundred barns that

Figure 2.41. Storage tunnel under ramp shed, which was part of the original construction plan of the Shetler barn, dated 1889, northwest of Bern, Adams County, Indiana. (Photo 1988.)

they plotted, one-third have full ramp sheds. Glenn Harper showed me these barns in July 1988. A close examination revealed that many were early barns, circa 1860, which had been amended by the addition of ramp sheds. Barns of this type built after 1880 were originally constructed with the ramp shed. This is revealed by the consistent use throughout of sawn timbers and boards and wire nails. The ramp shed usually forms a bridge over the space behind the rear stable wall, creating a tunnel-like storage area.

Similar barns have been located by Harper in the Amish-Mennonite settlement area of Fulton County in northwestern Ohio. He is currently researching this area, and we await further information. A photograph and description of a ramp-shed barn are presented in *Out of the Wilderness* (Greiser and Beck 1960, ch. 5). This book states that forebay bank barns were being constructed in Fulton County during the 1850s. Since the settlers in Adams County and Fulton County had no direct contacts with the Pennsylvania core, the appearance of ramp-shed barns there could be an example of parallel but independent development.

Type D. Vertical-Extension ("Double-Decker") Barn (Dornbusch Type L is a double-decker barn without forebay), 1800–1880

Locations: Chester and Lancaster counties, Pennsylvania; scattered locations elsewhere in Pennsylvania and in the Midwest; Warren County, New Jersey

Quaker farmers are credited with the barn enlargement that resulted in the double-decker barn, as they are with creation of the Chester County stone posted-forebay barn (Ball 1974, 53). Adding a third level produced

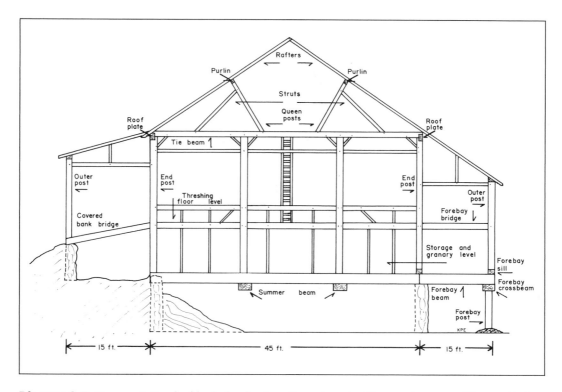

Diagram 2.7. Representative double-decker bent configuration, the Clemmer barn near Clayton, Berks County, Pennsylvania, dated 1857.

what is called the double-decker barn, which consists of a two-level loft and the basement stable. Access to the upper level of the loft is by an extended ramp or bridge. A threshing bridge then reaches across the upper level to the front forebay wall, providing access to the forebay straw shed. The advantages of this design are manifold: extra capacity for hay storage in a deeper loft area; easier gravity filling by unloading hay downward from the threshing bridge; large, protected granary below the threshing bridge; and increased capacity of forebay straw shed. The lower level of this huge storage loft could be reached by stairways and ladders from the threshing bridge, or directly through doors below the exterior ramp bridge. On some barns, a ramp on the barn's gable side provided access to the upper level.

Although Quaker farmers have been credited with the early development of the double-decker barn in Chester County, the form is common in farm structures in Germany, Switzerland, and Austria. I have seen this morphology in sixteenth-century house-barns in the Black Forest, in eighteenth-century structures in Emmental, Switzerland, and the Tyrol in Austria, and in large separate barns in central Switzerland. I know of no examples in the British Isles, including the English Lake District. There are many American variations of the double-decker form, and they do not fall conveniently into a set classification scheme.

Figures 2.42 and 2.43.
The Hugh Hodges barn
(*above*) near Coburn,
Centre County, Pennsyl-
vania, was built in 1832.
The seam in the vertical
siding on the gable wall
and forebay front wall
reveals the position of the
two lofts in this double-
decker barn. The bridge
(*right*) above the door to
the lower loft reaches to
the level of the upper loft.
(Photo 1989.)

Figure 2.44. The De-Long barn, dated 1804, in Bowers, Berks County, Pennsylvania, shows an exterior door to a root cellar under the barn bank. In many barns, the only access to the root cellar is from inside the barn through the rear of the stable. (Photo 1989.)

The Root Cellar

Before concluding the discussion of classification and morphology of the Pennsylvania barn, one final barn form must be examined. Root cellars were occasionally built into Pennsylvania barns, beginning in the late eighteenth century and continuing through the nineteenth century. They served as storage areas for turnips, fodder beets, and even pumpkins, all of which were used to feed cattle. Photographs by Shoemaker of the root cellar in the Breiner barn (1848), Lancaster County, Pennsylvania, are among the several references to this feature (Shoemaker 1959, 36–37; Long 1972b, 156, 163, 345; Bertland 1974, 25). Most of the details reported here were provided by Alan Keyser and derive from his research and fieldwork.[4]

A root cellar's primary function was to prevent fodder and root crops from freezing in winter by protecting them in a storage room in the ground, *below* the frost level. Root cellars could also be used in summer because the cool temperatures below ground level helped prevent spoilage. Root cellars

---

4. Alan Keyser, scholar, author, and friend, has spent many years studying Pennsylvania-German culture. His firsthand knowledge of crops, tools, and barns has been extremely helpful in numerous aspects of the preparation of this book.

were constructed of stone masonry, even the ceiling, which was supported by vaulting. The ideal location was under the bank or ramp behind the barn. In some barns, a door in the rear stable wall provided direct access; in other barns, the door was located outside the barn and on one side of the rear bank. Alan Keyser reported one alternative location for the cellar, citing the Issac Long barn (1754) near Lancaster. A cellar was excavated 5 feet below the floor of the basement stable and roofed with heavy planks. In some rear-extension barns, the basement alcoves below the outshed granaries form separate storage rooms for turnips, potatoes, apples, and the like. They are not completely below ground level and do not qualify as true root cellars. The use of silos, beginning in the late 1800s, provided for the storage of silage to feed larger herds of cattle, rendering the root cellar obsolete. Since root cellars were part of the original morphology of many Pennsylvania barns, their examination here serves to complete the record.

3

THE EVOLUTION OF THE PENNSYLVANIA BARN

Cultural evolution and change, while not responsible for the initial appearance of the Pennsylvania barn in the New World, is very important in understanding the emerging diversity of Pennsylvania barns. Changes in farm size and agricultural practices required changes in the size and form of barns. The resulting evolution of barns can be followed by examining progressive changes in their form, construction, and bent typology.

Factors Influencing Barn Evolution

In working structures such as barns, form derives from function, and practical considerations exert a powerful influence. Barns must be efficient and convenient. These necessities, combined with an awareness of traditional European barn forms, resulted in the relocation to the Pennsylvania frontier of two Germanic barn types—the Grundscheier and the forebay bank barn. Both were multiple-purpose structures suited to pioneer agriculture as practiced by Germanic and Swiss farmers in Pennsylvania. Even though the cultivation of wheat and other grains dominated Pennsylvania agriculture during the colonial period, Pennsylvania Germans were exponents of livestock husbandry from the beginning. They tilled intensively and built comfortable barns for the livestock. Stabling cattle permitted control of breeding and allowed for careful feeding and maintenance. The manure in turn was used to foster soil fertility (Fletcher 1950, 50).

As these practices were expanded and more land was cleared, production increased, and some surplus products were available for market. The needs of this expanding agriculture resulted first in the selection of the log Sweitzer barn over the smaller Grundscheier. As larger barns became necessary, the classic Sweitzer barn emerged, becoming the dominant farm structure by the late eighteenth century.

By the middle of the eighteenth century, most settlements in the Pennsylvania core were already connected to each other and to Philadelphia by roads (Long 1989, 20). Major inland towns, such as Lancaster, York, and Reading, were accessible by Conestoga wagon, whereby Pennsylvania-German farmers hauled their surplus to market (Fletcher 1950, 259–63). Philadelphia's market opened in 1710, and the inland towns soon followed suit (273–79). Thus, by 1800, commercial farming was replacing self-sufficient, pioneer agriculture in southeastern Pennsylvania. The half-century from 1790 to 1840 was the golden age of Pennsylvania agriculture. New agricultural practices resulted in larger yields and more prosperous farming (319–20).

It was during this period that increases in barn size and changes in barn form were most likely to occur. In spite of such changes, the basic morphology of the Pennsylvania barn has remained constant for two hundred years. Its very size and versatility rendered it immune to drastic revision until the middle of the twentieth century. For example, the threshing floor of a Sweitzer barn, on which wheat was hand-flailed and winnowed during the eighteenth century, was large enough to house the modern harvesting and combining machinery of the twentieth century.

Changes in the Pennsylvania barn's morphology resulted from the need for increased storage and stabling capacity. This was first accomplished by lengthening the barn, without modifying its form, by the addition of extra threshing floors and mows on the upper level, and by the corresponding enlargement of the basement stable. The very large classic Sweitzer barns of Lancaster County that exemplify this practice were already being built by the middle of the eighteenth century (see Figure 2.6).

The first strategy used by Chester County farmers to enlarge the English Lake District bank barn was to modify its two-level design by adding a third level, originating the Quaker double-decker barn. An alternative approach entailed modifying the barn by extending its width to the front. This strategy's appearance is illustrated in the Chester County stone-posted-forebay barn, the first example of this type of modification. Its development was in direct response to changes in agriculture that occurred in the country following the Revolution. By this time, soil fertility on the older farms around Philadelphia had become very poor, after generations of continuous grain cultivation. Agricultural societies began to promote soil conservation practices, which included the use of gypsum and lime, along with crop rotations involving grains and red clover. The production of clover and grass allowed farmers to keep more livestock and have more manure for the land (124–27). The resulting displacement of grain farming by livestock farming began about 1790. It made Chester and Delaware counties, Pennsylvania, the center of beef cattle grazing in America by 1820 (159). During this period, drovers moved large herds of cattle from the South and Midwest to Chester and adjacent counties, for fattening and marketing in Philadelphia. They were fed for about a year, pastured during the summer and stall-fed throughout the winter (179–81).

The demands of stabling and winter feeding large herds of livestock provided the stimulus for barn modification in southeastern Pennsylvania. The development of the stone-posted-forebay straw shed in Chester County was one result. Early development of the front-shed or three-gable barn in this same area was based on similar requirements. This method of barn enlargement not only provided for additional volumes of hay and straw, but the basement level of the extended shed could be used to stable additional livestock or house wagons and farm implements. When livestock farming moved farther inland as road and railroad access improved, both of these front-extension barn types diffused into the upcountry areas of the Pennsylvania core. Rail accessibility, plus the development of dairying in the mid-nineteenth century, helped spread the popularity of large front-extension Pennsylvania barns beyond the core.

The development of rear-extension or outshed barns is not as easily explained. Their appearance in Lancaster County may be related to that county's bountiful crops of grass and grain and its eventual emergence as the center of both grain production and stall-fed beef production in the state (181). As mixed grain and livestock farming became the mode in fertile Lancaster and the core counties to the west of there, the displacement of the ox by the horse for motive power also occurred. While oxen were fed mainly hay, horses required oats and other grains as well. The increases in feed grain storage demanded by this style of agriculture led to the development of the single- and double-outshed barn. Large outshed granaries shifted this function away from the forebay, which then could be used for additional hay and straw storage, a barn enlargement strategy suited to the needs of the mixed farming economy of the region.

Changing and expanding agriculture does not explain the emergence of the standard Pennsylvania barn. In fact, its generally shallower forebay would have reduced the storage capacity of the upper level. The smaller dimensions of many standard barns may have been compatible with the smaller size of many farms in the rolling Piedmont uplands of outer Montgomery and Bucks counties, where these barns first appeared. In these areas, with their adjacent English influences, the shallow, almost functionless forebay of early standard barns may reflect a style concession to the Swiss-Germanic forebay, which was so dominant just to the north and west. The early closed-forebay standard barn may represent another example of the fusion of English and Pennsylvania-German barn forms. The stone construction, balanced gable, and shallow roof slope all conform closely to the morphology of the English Lake District bank barns, which were common closer to Philadelphia. The creation of an overhang by recessing the front stable wall and replacing stone with frame for the forebay front wall provided an easy modification to achieve the popular forebay style.

The change to gable and roof-line symmetry in the standard barn may also reflect the need for order and balance perceived by the Pennsylvania-

Figure 3.1. Early log forebay barn (circa 1780) ten miles west of Gettysburg in Adams County, Pennsylvania. This barn combines the Prätigau-like balanced gables and log basement walls, the frame forebay of the Swiss Lake District, and the steep roof slope of northern Switzerland and the Black Forest. (Photo by Henry J. Kauffman, used by his permission.)

German farmer, especially after he adopted the symmetrical Georgian farmhouse. The fact that the roof slope angle (30 degrees) of the standard barn conforms closely to that of the Georgian farmhouse provides cause for such speculation. Whatever the reasons for its development, the standard Pennsylvania barn became the most abundant and widespread of all classes.

A detailed look at selected examples will clarify these evolutionary processes. The transitions examined here are the most significant ones in the development of the various classes of the Pennsylvania barn.

From Switzerland to Pennsylvania

The early log Sweitzer barn of Pennsylvania compares closely in size and form to the double-log-crib eave-forebay bank barn of Prätigau, Canton Graubünden, Switzerland. Early changes differentiate the Pennsylvania models from the Swiss originals. Roof slopes steepened, from 18 degrees to more than 40 degrees. This was in response to the use of straw thatch rather than stone slab roof covering, and it indicated a preference for northern Swiss and Black Forest roof-framing traditions. Some early Pennsylvania log barns had log forebays and balanced gables like most barns in Prätigau. The

Gephardt barn, dated 1723, in Adams County, Pennsylvania, has Prätigau-like forebay support posts. Another Adams County barn combines a balanced gable silhouette, log stable walls, and a frame forebay (Kauffman 1954, 60). These examples relate directly to Swiss prototypes in Prätigau. The great majority of log Sweitzer barns in Canada and the United States exhibit an asymmetrical gable silhouette, resulting from a longer front roof slope that extends over a frame forebay supported only by cantilevering— the diagnostic Sweitzer characteristics. This morphology is similar to that of Swiss Lake District forebay barns, which, in addition, utilize forebay support posts.

It is quite possible that early log Sweitzer barns in Pennsylvania were adapted from a variety of Swiss forebay barn types. For example, if one were to combine the steep northern Swiss and Black Forest thatched roof, the Prätigau double-log-crib eave-forebay bank barn, and the Swiss Lake District frame forebay, a Pennsylvania log Sweitzer barn would be the result. Practical considerations were certainly involved. Prätigau barns utilize log gable walls that reach to the roof ridge and support purlins and rafters. In the Pennsylvania log Sweitzer, the roof is supported mainly by rafters, rather than by the end walls. Purlins with various support systems may be used to reinforce rafters, which rest atop front and rear log crib walls, which in turn transfer considerable roof weight to the foundation below. This design defers stress from the lighter framed forebay, which is supported only by cantilevering. The front roof slope can then be continued over the forebay, and the asymmetrical Sweitzer gable is created. This design became standardized in the log Sweitzer barn in early Pennsylvania.

From Log Sweitzer to Classic Sweitzer Barns

The evolution from log Sweitzers to the classic Sweitzer barn began with the use of timber frame bents in place of logs for inner mow partitions. The late eighteenth-century "transition" Sweitzer barns that illustrate this progression occur throughout the Pennsylvania core region. Some examples have log walls on three sides of the crib, which is completed with a timber frame bent on the threshing floor side. Others add frame partitions for inner forebay walls, resulting in half-log-frame cribs. The Laverne Barrett barn, circa 1785, near Womelsdorf in Berks County, has a crib of three log walls with a timber frame bent on the threshing floor side to enclose the east mow. The west section of the barn is of stone construction with a timber frame bent on the threshing floor side. This unusual combination of log and stone construction was in the original design, and it represents an intermediate stage in the transition from log to stone Sweitzer barns.

The use of stone masonry construction for early classic Sweitzer barns marks the change from the uncertain frontier agriculture to a successful, stable agricultural economy. Stone was appropriate for building larger barns. There are various precedents for such construction. Stone structures are common in parts of the Palatine homeland of many Pennsylvania Ger-

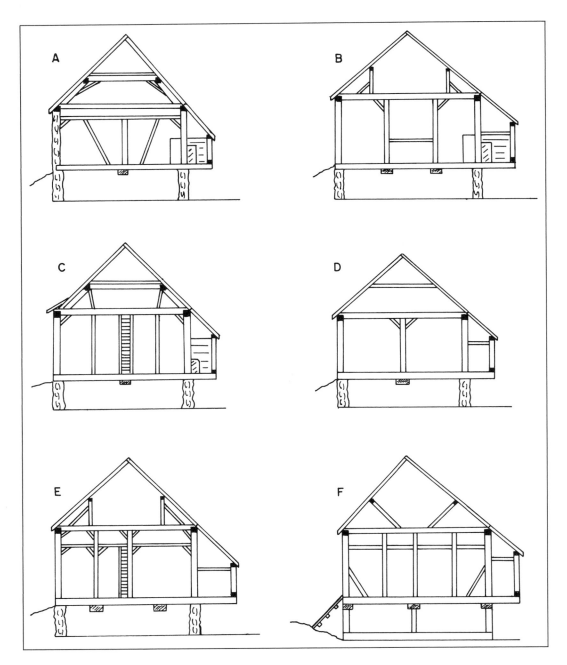

Diagram 3.1. Comparative bent typology of classic Sweitzer barns in Pennsylvania.

A. Moyer barn, circa 1780, Blandon, Berks County; stone construction.
B. Loeb barn, circa 1785, Gablesville, Berks County; stone construction.
C. Grosser barn, dated 1793, Gilbertsville, Montgomery County; stone construction.
D. Gift barn, circa 1800, Earl Township, Berks County; stone construction.
E. Reedman barn, circa 1810, Oley Valley, Berks County; stone construction.
F. Lepro barn, circa 1830, Almont, Centre County; frame construction.

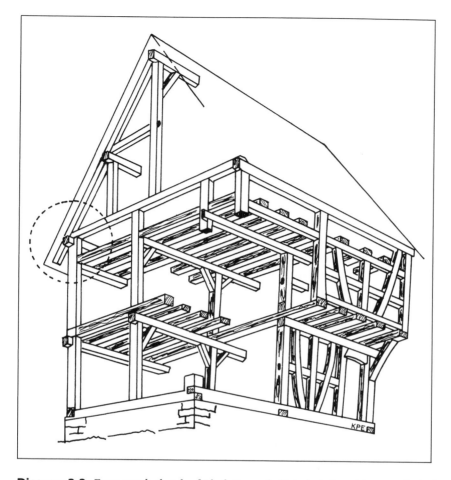

Diagram 3.2. Framework sketch of Black Forest half-timbered speicher in which the tie beam is over the roof plate and end post. It can be inferred from this example that a mortise-and-tenon arrangement like that used in southeastern Pennsylvania barns is used to lock the joint.

mans, and the Herr house, built in 1719 near Lancaster, is an early example of the Germanic stone building tradition.

The change to stone may also have been influenced by English building practices in Chester and Bucks counties. The prototype bank barns of the English Lake District utilize stone work similar to that found in the Pennsylvania barn, including quoined corners and ventilating slits. The Pennsylvania-German farmers also gave in to the influence of popular style: they replaced their pioneer cabins or Germanic central-chimney houses with larger and more stylish Georgian stone houses, expressing their successful conversion from Germanic peasants to landed citizens. When it came to practical matters, they retained the versatile and functional Sweitzer barn form, although they began to build barns that were much larger and constructed of stone, the material of choice in the core during the late eighteenth century.

The use of stone was the culmination of the differentiation process that produced the classic Sweitzer barn. Hand-hewn timber frame bents and stone walls replaced log crib walls in this and other barns. A sampling of classic Sweitzer bent configurations is provided in Diagram 3.1. Although they show considerable variation in pattern, there is one consistent element—the tie beam always fastens *over* the roof plate in a complex tying joint that locks into the end post. Bents like this were constructed in several ways. For example, in early classic Sweitzer barns, the stone front stable wall continues up to the roof as an interior stone partition between the mows and the frame forebay. Front and rear stone walls provide support for the roof plates and gable-end tie beams, which were lifted into place member by member. Timber frame bents on either side of the threshing floor provide support for the barn and roof between the stone gable walls. Classic Sweitzer bents consist of end and inner posts plus braces and cross beams. They include the tie beam–over–roof plate and post joint. As frame replaced stone for upper barn walls, end bents were needed to complete the barn frame.

In constructing the barn frame, flooring was laid on top of the basement level; then timbers for the lower part of the end bent—posts, beams, and braces—were carried up to this floor, assembled there, and raised. The remaining bents were likewise assembled and raised in succession, braced, and connected with girts. Long planks were then laid against the uppermost girts at the rear of the frame. These served as ramps or skids on which the upper frame members could be slid to their proper height. Next, the roof plates were worked up the skids by teams of workers standing on a temporary board scaffold inside the upper frame. The workers, pulling on ropes and pushing with pikes, lifted the plates section by section and fitted them into the outer plate tenons on top of the end posts (see Diagram 3.3). This stabilized the bents in their final vertical position. Tie beams, after being moved up the same skids, were rotated by workers at the top of the scaffold, then lifted and fitted into the inner tenons of the end posts, locking over the roof plates and securing the barn frame. The roof framework and rafters could then be put in place and the barn completed with roofing and siding.

The details of this procedure were related to me by Charles A. Speicher of Womelsdorf, Pennsylvania, in April 1989. Charles was a foreman in charge of building numerous barns in the Berks County area. Between 1922 and 1957, he built thirty-two barns and helped with twenty-two more. At age 87, Charles was alert, vigorous, and enjoyed discussing barn building. He said that in half a day, the frame could be completed and the roof started. He also revealed that the use of gin poles and other mechanical devices to lift heavy beams was slow and cumbersome compared to an efficient and well-supervised crew. Charles Speicher is one of the few living Pennsylvania-German barn builders who can accurately describe the details of the earlier barn-building process as it was practiced in eastern Pennsylvania.

Many people assume that raising completely assembled bents was the

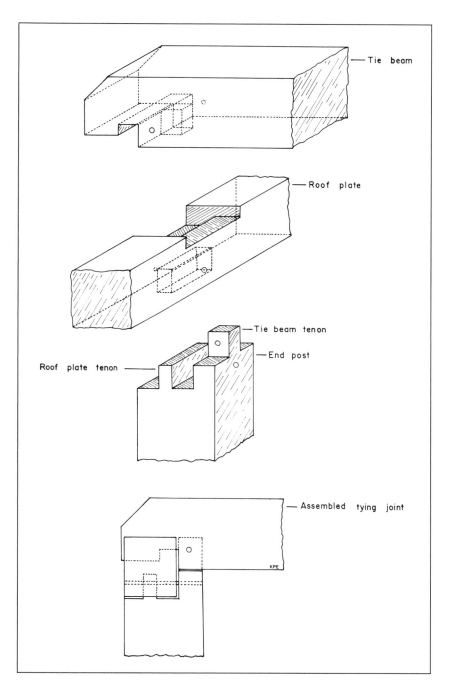

Diagram 3.3. Assembly of tie beam–over–plate and post joint. Commonly used in Pennsylvania barns.

Figures 3.2 and 3.3. Charles Speicher (*top*) of Womelsdorf, Pennsylvania, an old-time Pennsylvania-German barn builder, was 87 years old in 1989. He is shown holding the homemade templet he called his "inspector," which he used to gauge the sizes of mortises and tenons before barn frames were assembled. Figure 3.3 shows a barn being built in 1933 north of Reading in Berks County, Pennsylvania, by Charles Speicher and crew. Notice the planks laid diagonally against the upper girts to serve as skids on which roof plates and tie beams were raised into place. (Photos used by permission of Charles Speicher.)

Figures 3.4 and 3.5. The tie beam–over–plate and post joint is almost universally used in barns built before 1860 in southeastern Pennsylvania. The example in Figure 3.4 (*left*) is in the Hein barn, circa 1850, Lenhartsville, Berks County, Pennsylvania. Figure 3.5 (*right*) shows a Germanic liegender Stuhl roof truss in the Bertolet cabin, circa 1735, Oley Valley, Berks County, Pennsylvania. Compare with examples shown in Diagram 2.3 and Figure 2.7. (Photos 1989 and 1988.)

only way to construct a barn frame. It certainly was faster, but it could be carried out only after H-bents came into use. In H-bents, tie beams were connected to end posts *below* the roof plate. H-bents could be completely prefabricated on the upper floor of the barn, then raised and connected with the roof plates to finish the barn frame.

The great majority of Pennsylvania barns in the eastern core have the earlier bent configuration, joining the tie beam over the roof plate and end post, a type of joinery that was used from the time of earliest settlement until the late nineteenth century. Some builders, like Charles Speicher, continued the practice well into the twentieth century. Later barns in Pennsylvania and most beyond used the H-bent and other modified standard bents. The tie beam–over–roof plate frame is European in origin. I observed it in early Black Forest timber frame houses and early northern Swiss barns. It was used in early Pennsylvania houses as well as barns, along with Germanic roof frameworks, such as the liegender Stuhl. Some of these same structures also employed the medieval "kick-in-the-roof" style of roof, in which the slope of the roof changes where it extends beyond the outer walls.

Henry Glassie pointed out that tie beam–over–plate and post framing was used in colonial New England and can be traced from there back to the thirteenth century in southeastern England. In these English examples, the tops of the posts were usually flared for extra support (Glassie 1975, 15–16). Brunskill also documented the flared-post frame in England and detailed its tying joint, which is very similar to that used in Pennsylvania barns (1971, 75). It appears that a similar joinery was used over a broad area of medieval Europe. This broad usage was confirmed in discussions with Jack Sobon, a timber-framing expert from Massachusetts. A survey of the literature dealing with European vernacular architecture will reveal the almost universal positioning of the tie beam over the plate and post in early half-timbered and timber-frame structures from the Alps to England, and it is frequently combined with the liegender Stuhl roof framework in Germanic Europe.[1] John Heyl also documented the use of the flared-top post in early Pennsylvania barns, which my own observations confirm. He stated that this type of joinery was used across Europe in medieval half-timbered buildings (Dornbusch and Heyl 1958, 294–95). An examination of the Sheffey barn, near Limerick in Montgomery County, Pennsylvania, reveals use of the same tying joint. This circa 1760 Grundscheier shows the very early use of this joinery in Pennsylvania. The examples and references cited here strongly support the continental Germanic and Swiss origins of the framing and roof support systems used in Pennsylvania structures.

Although Sweitzer barns were less numerous than later types, their bent patterns show considerable variation, suggesting experimentation by barn builders. Smaller barns had simpler bents, which required only a single tie beam. Many earlier barns used the liegender Stuhl roof framework. Some barns used a purlin system supported by queen posts set vertically, as is usually the case in Europe. The queen posts in most Pennsylvania barns were set at an angle—canted—and frequently reinforced with angled struts. By the early nineteenth century, most bents used a double connection that included a cross beam several feet below the tie beam, plus interior posts and heavy diagonal braces, to provide extra support for the greater spans of the larger barns then being built. This elaborate bent pattern carried over from Sweitzer to standard barns and continued until the latter part of the nineteenth century, when simpler H-bents became popular.

The brick Sweitzer barn emerged when brick was substituted for stone masonry early in the nineteenth century. The development of the all-frame Sweitzer barn followed a similar sequence. The existence of half-log-frame Sweitzer barns suggests an alternative progression. Many of these structures in Lebanon and Berks counties date from the late eighteenth century and indicate that the transition to frame had an early start. The Bailor barn, in Snyder County, shown in Figures 3.6 and 3.7, exemplifies the transition from log to frame Sweitzer barns, which occurred in central Pennsylvania west of the stone barn region.

1. Phleps 1942, 191; Gephard 1977, 57, 64; Weiss 1959, 75–92; Schäfer 1906, vol. 1, Baden pl. 14, no. 5; Bayern pl. 15, no. 5; vol. 2, 223.

Figures 3.6 and 3.7. The Bailor barn (*top*), circa 1810, Mount Pleasant Mills, Snyder County, Pennsylvania, appears from the outside to be an all-frame Sweitzer barn. An interior view (*bottom*) reveals half-log-frame construction. Timber frame inner bents and front mow walls are combined with log rear mow and gable walls using interconnected vertical posts. This transitional technology, known as posting or corner posting, occurs occasionally throughout southeastern and central Pennsylvania. (Photos 1989.)

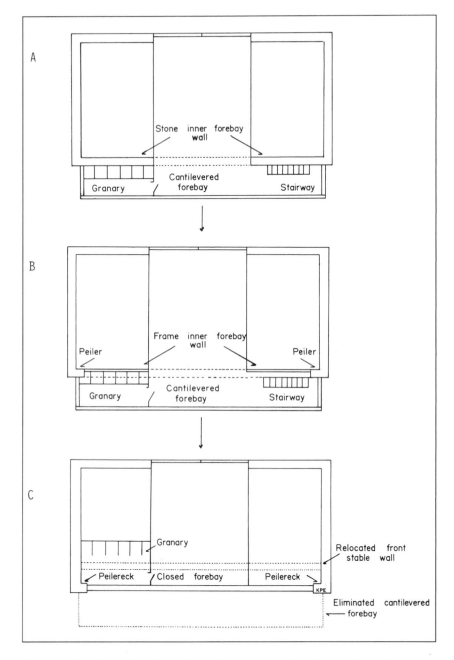

Diagram 3.4. Upper-level wall plans showing stages in evolution from classic Sweitzer barn to closed-forebay standard barn with Peilerecks.

A. Early classic Sweitzer barn with stone inner (rear) forebay wall supporting front roof plate.
B. Later classic Sweitzer barn with frame inner (rear) forebay wall and Peiler supporting front roof plate.
C. Closed-forebay standard barn with Peilerecks adjacent to front stable wall.

From Sweitzer to Closed-Forebay Standard Barn

The standard Pennsylvania barn is the most numerous and widespread of any barn class, and its development is significant. The closed-forebay standard barn was the first type of this class to emerge. Most of those in the eastern core are of stone construction, and many date back to the early nineteenth century. Since the classic Sweitzer was still very popular when the closed-forebay standard barn first appeared, it follows that one could have evolved from the other.

The first impulse is to credit a progression from classic Sweitzer to closed-forebay transition Sweitzer to closed-forebay standard barn. While possible, this would have required an extension of the entire barn frame forward over extended basement end walls and an elimination of the Sweitzer forebay frame to produce a standard symmetrical gable-end.

Several unusual double-log crib closed-forebay standard barns have been reported by Alan Keyser and William Stein in northern Berks and Lehigh counties. These structures, which were not dated, are no longer standing. They are the only barns of this type known to me. If early, they could have provided an alternative sequence in the evolution of standard barns. The most likely explanation is that they were later examples in which log construction, which was continued into the nineteenth century in outlying areas, was applied to the popular standard barn form.

The Clarence Sattazahn barn, near Womelsdorf in Berks County, built circa 1810, is an example of a closed-forebay standard barn, with log walls for the back and gable-end sections of each mow. The partial-log construction does suggest that an alternative progression from log Sweitzer barn to partial-log standard barn to frame standard barn was possible.

There is another solution, which will better relate to the morphology of the classic Sweitzer barn. When framing replaced the stone inner, or rear, forebay wall of the Sweitzer barn, stone reinforcing piers were retained at the front corner of each gable wall. These extended from the top of the stone front stable wall to the roof, producing an L-shaped pier, or Peiler (see Diagram 3.4). The inside projections of the Peilers supported the ends of the roof plate, plus each gable-wall tie beam.

The change from Sweitzer barn to closed-forebay standard barn could be accomplished by eliminating the entire forebay, producing a balanced gable silhouette without modifying the main barn frame. The fact that the main bents of later Sweitzer barns are identical in pattern to those of early closed-forebay standard barns supports this contention. The use of liegender Stuhl roof supports in some early closed-forebay standard barns also reveals a connection to Sweitzer framing. Relocating the front stable wall 5 to 6 feet back under the barn frame preserved the forebay form and also supported the forebay beams. By retaining the stone gable wall and extending its L-shaped Peilers to the ground, the "closing" of the forebay was accomplished. Moreover, a small alcove was created between the lower part of the Peilers and the stable walls. This alcove, or Peilereck (pier corner or pillar corner), as it is called in Berks County, is pictured in Figure 2.12. It is usually found in the earliest closed-forebay standard barns of the eastern core counties in Pennsylvania.

The evolutionary sequence just presented is credible and logical. It connects the early stone closed-forebay standard barn directly to the stone classic Sweitzer barn by way of the Peilereck—a functional form in both structures. The closed-forebay standard barn continued to evolve through the nineteenth century, producing the various types and subtypes classified in Chapter 2.

Bent Configurations of Standard Pennsylvania Barns

The bent configurations shown in Diagram 3.5 are representative of the differences through time and from place to place in the framing of standard barns. The differences are in the arrangement of posts, braces, and cross beams and in the manner and location of the tie-beam connection. In spite of these differences, these configurations maintain the diagnostic balanced-gable silhouette of the standard barn.

In general terms, the ten examples progress from early to late nineteenth century, from double- to single-tie-beam connections, and from complex to simple tying-joint articulation. Examples *A* and *B* utilize the traditional, complex tie beam–over–plate and post tying joint, plus an upper cross beam. The 1914 date for the Hendrickson barn (*B*) shows the persistence of this early and traditional technology into the twentieth century. It is this type of bent and frame that required several stages of raising and erection to complete.

Examples *C* and *D,* located on the Eastern Shore in Maryland and in western Ohio, respectively, show changes occurring beyond the Pennsylvania core. While the double connection of tie beam and upper cross beam is retained, the tie beam is connected by mortising it into the inner side of the end post *below* the roof plate, the significant difference that permitted prefabrication of the entire bent, including the tie beam. These bents could then be raised as completed units and connected by roof plates, eliminating the final tie beam phase. This type of frame, while giving up some strength, gained in speed of assembly and efficiency of raising.

Examples *E, F,* and *G* show considerable modification of the bent configuration. Inner posts have been extended to the roof, and tie beams reaching from end post to end post have been eliminated. This post-to-purlin design appeared in the mid-nineteenth century in divergent locations, mainly beyond the Pennsylvania core. Multiple-overhang barns in Ohio (*E*) and Virginia (*F*) show its uses. An early form of the post-to-purlin configuration, which retains the tie beam–to–end post connection, is shown in a Chester County double-overhang barn plan documented in 1838 ("Chester County Pennsylvania Barn Plan" 1838, 195–97). This example suggests an evolutionary process beginning fairly early in the Pennsylvania core. The same configuration also occurs in western Pennsylvania (*G*) and in New York

Figure 3.8. Interior view of forebay of stone Sweitzer barn, circa 1800, south of Leesport, Berks County, Pennsylvania. The function of the L-shaped stone Peiler as support for the main front roof plate and the gable wall tie beam is clearly shown. (Photo 1988.)

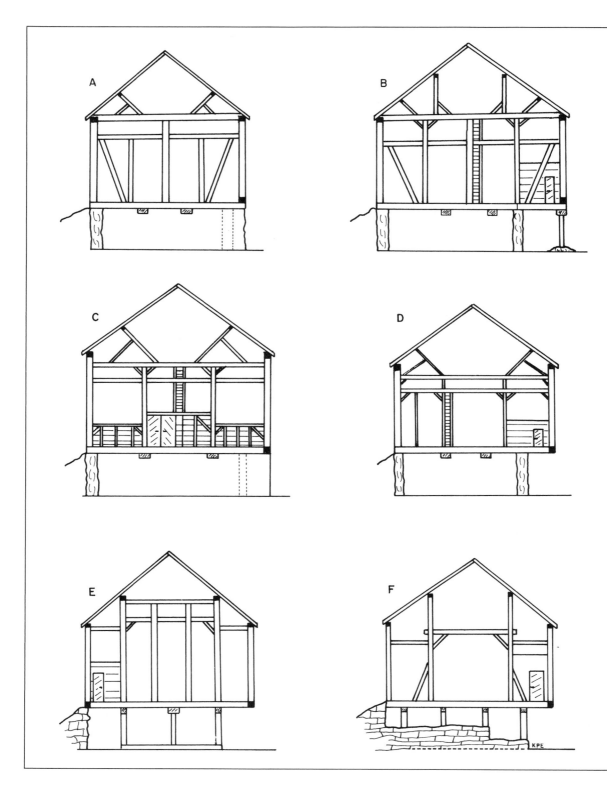

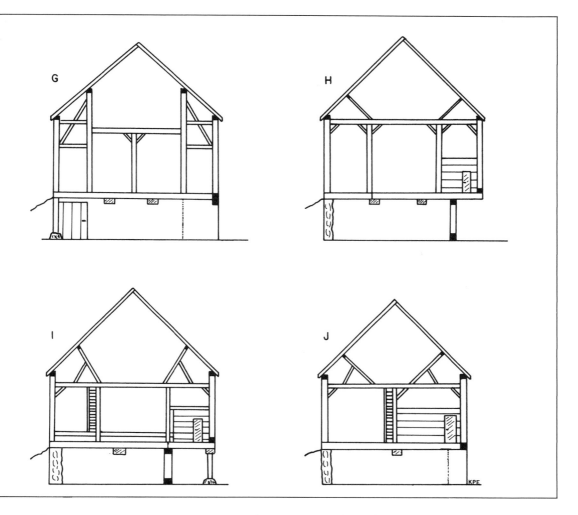

Diagram 3.5. Comparative bent typology of standard Pennsylvania barns.

A. Miller barn, dated 1819, a closed-forebay standard barn near Blandon, Berks County, Pennsylvania.

B. Hendrickson barn, dated 1914, a posted-forebay standard barn in Alsace Township, Berks County, Pennsylvania.

C. Willis Redden barn, circa 1870, a closed-forebay standard barn near Ruthsville, Queen Annes County, Maryland.

D. Thompson barn, circa 1860, an open-forebay standard barn near Springfield, Clark County, Ohio.

E. Schreyeor barn, circa 1848, a double-overhang standard barn north of Lancaster, Fairfield County, Ohio.

F. Multiple-overhang standard barn, circa 1875, southwest of Woodstock, Shenandoah County, Virginia.

G. Posted-closed-forebay standard barn, circa 1870, north of Washington, Washington County, Pennsylvania.

H. Hawbaker barn, 1860, open-forebay standard barn west of Bern, Adams County, Indiana.

I. Rudolph barn (old Hoopes estate), circa 1875, a posted-forebay standard barn south of Honey Brook, Chester County, Pennsylvania.

J. Martin barn, circa 1890, a closed-forebay standard barn north of Milwaukee, Washington County, Wisconsin.

State. Henry Glassie pointed out that the general form of this bent can be found in medieval aisled buildings in Germany, Holland, France, and England (Glassie 1974, 211). Any direct historic connections reaching back to these sources would be questionable at best. The popularity of this form of bent in the latter half of the nineteenth century is related directly to the use of the hay track and fork, a mechanical device that was rigged under the roof ridge and used to transport hay the length of the barn to the mow sections. The post-to-purlin bent eliminated queen posts and struts, which would have interfered with this movement. It retained cross beams, but they were connected to the inner posts far enough below the purlins that they did not impede the movement of the hay fork along the track. In some earlier barns, these various roof support members were removed, or relocated, to clear the space when hay tracks were eventually installed. The post-to-purlin design was endorsed by engineers, because it could be modified during planning to accommodate a hay track (211–12). The Ohio example (*E*), dated 1848, uses a double connection between the inner posts, suggesting a transitional phase to the new design.

Examples *H, I,* and *J* complete the standard bent progression. All three exhibit relatively simple bent configurations with similar roof support frameworks, consisting of queen posts and struts. In all three cases, a single tie beam is mortised into the end posts 6 inches to 2 feet *below* the roof plates, resulting in the simple H-bent. This bent is widely distributed and is used in a variety of barn types. It occurs in later barns in and adjacent to the Pennsylvania core and is found in many mid- and late nineteenth-century Pennsylvania barns in Waterloo County, Ontario, and across the Midwest, from Indiana to Wisconsin. Glassie documented its use in Otsego County, New York, in banked basement barns (207–12). It occurs in basement barns across the upper Midwest as far as eastern Minnesota, suggesting a westward diffusion of the northern, or "Yankee," barn-framing tradition. The frequent use of the same H-bent on many Pennsylvania barns in the middle Susquehanna Valley, beginning in the 1850s, challenges the Yankee origin of this tradition. The most likely explanation for the emergence and diffusion of the H-bent is its economy of construction and erection. Barn builders may have independently, and almost simultaneously, adopted this efficient bent in a number of locations in the eastern United States. Its diffusion from several potential source regions would account for its widespread appearance beyond the Pennsylvania core in barns built in the late nineteenth century.

The Evolution of the Extended Supported-Forebay Pennsylvania Barn

The extended supported-forebay barn developed along three somewhat different tracks. One, a continuation of the progression from classic Sweitzer, sees the closed-forebay transitional Sweitzer barn developing into an extended barn with a forebay that was closed and supported with posts. The Miller barn, built around 1810 south of Claussville in Lehigh County, Penn-

Figures 3.9 and 3.10.
The Miller barn (*above*),
circa 1810, near Clauss-
ville, Lehigh County,
Pennsylvania, is an early
Sweitzer-like extended
post-supported-forebay
barn. The under-forebay
view of this barn (*left*)
reveals that the forebay
cross beam embedded in
the Peiler provides addi-
tional support *under* the
forebay beams, qualifying
this structure as an ex-
tended Pennsylvania barn.
(Photo 1989.)

Figure 3.11. The Bender barn, circa 1790, south West Chester, Chester County, Pennsylvania, shows evidence of a later added-on forebay. A crude recess on the lower right corner is aligned with the remnant of a conical stone column where the added-on forebay beam was anchored and supported. The rough edges of the upper front wall opening, at the upper left of the picture, indicate that it was later enlarged to provide easier access to the added-on forebay from the upper level of the barn. (Photo 1988.)

sylvania, is a good example. In spite of its Sweitzer-like long, unbroken roof slope and asymmetrical gable, it is an early type of extended forebay. Several features prove this. The 10-foot forebay, which reaches just beyond the limits of effective support by cantilevering only, is supported by a cross beam, which is anchored into the end walls of the closed forebay and supported by two posts. Even though the forebay beams cantilever halfway back under the barn frame to the summer beam, the additional support techniques qualify this as an extended supported-forebay barn. It also has Peilerecks on the forebay and walls, evidence of the ties between the classic Sweitzer barn and later types. Similar barns can be found throughout the eastern core counties.

The earliest developmental track for the extended supported-forebay barn originated in Chester County, where English Quaker farmers adopted the forebay and applied it to other barns. In the late eighteenth century, the shift in focus of the region's agriculture from grains to stabled livestock greatly increased the need for hay and straw storage. The English Lake District bank barn was already in use in the counties adjacent to Philadelphia, but the storage capacity of these barns had to be increased dramatically. The first way to achieve this was to extend the design of barns vertically, creating three-level, double-decker, bank barns. When even more capacity was needed, large forebay straw sheds were added to existing two- and three-level bank barns.

Quaker farmers were familiar with the forebay bank barn, which was already common in the adjacent upcountry Pennsylvania-German counties. It was logical and practical for them to adopt and enlarge the forebay and apply it to their barns. The Zook barn, near Malvern in Chester County, was only twenty-five miles from the center of Philadelphia. It was a typical log Sweitzer barn, built around 1740, and indicated a very early penetration of the English areas of Pennsylvania by upcountry Germanic traits. It was the earliest barn on record to be amended by the addition of a large forebay straw shed.

Adding a large forebay straw shed to existing barns was the initial step in the evolution of the extended supported-forebay barn. The use of a forebay cross beam and support columns was necessary to accommodate the weight of a large forebay addition. Although the Zook barn has not survived, early photographs reveal its original log Sweitzer morphology (Ball 1974, 30–31, 66). One of the photos shows a later forebay, extending beyond the original structures and supported by conical stone columns.

Conical stone forebay-support columns are the trademark of Chester County barns. Although occasionally occurring in adjacent counties, they are closely identified with early Quaker farms and suggest English building practices. The use of lime stucco with a spattering of fine pebbles to finish the surface of the columns is credited to the influence of English settlers (116). The use of similar rendering to improve and protect stone surfaces in English structures has been reported by Brunskill (1971, 39). Stone columns provide the forebay support for several barns in Prätigau, Switzerland. These columns are cylindrical, not conical, and occur on nineteenth century barns, which would not have influenced building practices in Pennsylvania. Even though wooden-post-supported forebay barns are also common in Switzerland, posting was rarely used in the early Sweitzer barns of Pennsylvania. The posting tradition for barns of Chester County must, therefore, be English. The use of conical columns in storage sheds in the English Lake District has been documented by Brunskill.[2] The occurrence of Lake District bank barns and the use of whitewashed conical stone support columns by Quaker farmers in English Chester County provide strong evidence in support of an English origin for these forms.

An excellent example of a stone-column-supported forebay straw shed added on to a double-decker bank barn is provided by the Bender barn, just south of West Chester, Pennsylvania (Figure 3.11). The original small door in the upper front wall was enlarged to provide adequate access to the added-

2. Brunskill 1974, 99–101. This same reference also documents the occurrence of square stone support piers in the English Lake counties. Although not as distinctive as conical stone columns, they, too, are used in Chester County as forebay supports; Brunskill 1987, 68, 71–72, 92.

Figures 3.12 and 3.13. Supplemental framing on the outside of the front stable wall (*above*) supports the forebay beams of the forebay added on to the Cornwell barn, dated 1804, near Phoenixville, Chester County, Pennsylvania. In the Denenberg-Williams barn (*right*), dated 1806, also near Phoenixville, the forebay beams extend through upper stable wall and beneath the barn frame. This indicates that the forebay was part of the original design of this stone-posted-forebay barn. (Photos 1988 and 1989.)

Figure 3.14. Under-forebay view of the Leiby barn, circa 1840, south of Lenharts-ville, Berks County, Pennsylvania. Long added-on beams extend beyond ends of original cantilevered forebay beams and rest on post-supported forebay cross beam, which holds up the added-on forebay straw shed. (Photo 1989.)

on forebay. Stone columns 24 feet from the front wall indicate the size of the forebay straw shed. Front wall corner stones were removed, leaving crude recesses into which the two outer forebay beams were anchored. This evidence indicates modification of the original structure to accommodate the addition of the forebay.

A comparison of the Cornwell barn (Figure 3.12), dated 1804, and the Denenberg-Williams barn (Figure 3.13), dated 1806, shows the difference between a barn with an added-on forebay straw shed and a barn initially conceived and built with this feature. The under-forebay stable walls reveal differences in forebay support. The Cornwell barn has a support frame that was installed outside the stone stable wall to support the inner forebay beams of the added-on forebay. This barn was originally a two-level English Lake District bank barn without forebay. The upper front wall, now within the forebay, has the original wood louvered ventilators. These indicate that it was originally an outside wall. The forebay beams of the Denenberg-Williams barn extend through the upper stable wall and continue under the barn frame. This characteristic is consistent with a barn that included the forebay straw shed in the original plan.

The examples just presented provide evidence that the Chester County stone-posted forebay started as an added-on feature, which became formalized around 1800. The resulting new type, the extended supported-forebay barn, has conical stone columns and was constructed throughout Chester County for the next seventy years. It also diffused west and north to

Figure 3.15. The Leiby barn, circa 1840, south of Lenhartsville, Berks County, Pennsylvania, showing early barn decoration (hex sign) and window on what was originally the forebay front wall, before it was enclosed by addition of a straw shed. (Photo 1989.)

adjacent counties, where wood replaced stone for forebay support posts.

The third line of development of the extended supported-forebay barn resulted in the appearance of the upcountry posted-forebay barn. In adjacent Berks and Montgomery counties and nearby Lehigh County, the closed-forebay standard barn was popular and abundant during the early nineteenth century. The growing need for increased hay and straw storage caused farmers in these counties to imitate the Chester County example by enlarging the forebays of their barns and adding support posts. The evolution of this morphology in the upcountry differed from its development in Chester County, in that added-on forebay straw sheds were applied to closed-forebay standard barns instead of to English barns.

The Leiby barn, south of Lenhartsville in Berks County clearly shows this modification (see Figure 3.14). Under-forebay support beams for the added-on forebay, and remnants of the original forebay-support elements can be seen. The Peilereck support of the original forebay sill and beams is still intact. Additional forebay beams rest on top of the front stable wall and extend 12 feet beyond the Peilereck to a forebay cross beam supported by wooden posts. The forebay addition was then framed upon this added-on

Figures 3.16 and 3.17.
The Kline barn (*left*),
dated 1816, Warren
County, New Jersey, is a
double-decker stone-arch-
forebay barn. The longer
vertical openings in the
front wall are doors into
the loft levels. An ex-
tended rear ramp (*below*)
provides access to the
upper-most level from the
rear and covers the storage
tunnel and the root cellar,
entered by a small door in
the ramp wall. (Photo
1989.)

Figure 3.18. The Miller barn, dated 1819, near Molltown, Berks County, Pennsylvania. Germanic masonry arches (in brick or stone) for stable doors are common in central Berks County. (Photo 1990.)

support system. Many barns in this area were similarly modified, converting standard barns into upcountry posted-forebay barns.

The most telling evidence of conversion of the Leiby barn is a barn decoration (hex sign) and a window on the inner forebay wall. Both features occur only on exterior walls of barns. This proves that this present interior wall was originally the outer side to the forebay front wall of a standard barn before the addition of the forebay.

By the middle of the nineteenth century, the upcountry posted-forebay plan was formalized. Many barns were then built according to this plan; however, the Peilereck, no longer functional, was eliminated. The popularity of this type of barn continued into the twentieth century, and its occurrence in the Shenandoah Valley in Virginia, and west to Wisconsin indicates diffusion of the style far beyond Pennsylvania.

Chester County's role in barn innovation accounts for the extended forebay, stone-column supports, and three-level barns. The English connections of this county may also account, in part, for the stone-arch-forebay standard barn (examined in Chapter 2). The stone arch is frequently used

Figure 3.19. In the DeHaven barn, circa 1790, near Hampton, Adams County, Pennsylvania, stone outsheds were part of the original barn plan. Interior access to the granary in the outshed is through a small door behind the log crib. (Photo 1988.)

for stable doors in both English bank barns and Quaker double-decker barns in Chester County (Ball 1974, vi, 75–76, 122, 124, 126, 129, 159). The adoption of this arch form for forebay support may provide yet another example of the fusion of English and Germanic traditions in the contact zones of Montgomery, Bucks, and adjacent counties in Pennsylvania. The combination of the stone-arch forebay with the Quaker double-decker barn is demonstrated by two barns in Warren County, New Jersey, just across the Delaware River from Pennsylvania. One of these, the Kline barn, is dated 1816 (Bertland 1974, 18, 24–25). This date is consistent with other stone-arch-forebay barns in Pennsylvania and also with the stone-column forebay supports of Chester County. Brunskill also documented the use of stone arch openings on farm buildings in England (1971, 148–49; 1987, 92–94). The arched masonry (brick and stone) doors and windows found on some Pennsylvania-German houses and barns in Berks County are continental in origin (see Figure 3.18). Although they may have influenced the development of the stone-arch forebay, the evidence presented more strongly suggests English origins.

Figure 3.20. Outsheds are sometimes found on forebay bank barns in Switzerland, as in this example in Grüsch, in the Prätigau region of Canton Graubünden. Note also the masonry forebay support column. (Photo 1988.)

Figure 3.21. Double-outshed standard barn north of Shippensburg, Cumberland County, Pennsylvania. Shallow, retracted outsheds and hoodlike rear roof extension anticipate the full ramp enclosure and resulting ramp shed form. (Photo 1988.)

Figure 3.22. The double-tie-beam bent that first appeared in eighteenth-century classic Sweitzer barns in Berks County and is common in the western part of the barn core, is shown in a brick double-outshed barn near Mt. Holly, Cumberland County, Pennsylvania. (Photo 1989.)

The Evolution of Rear-Extension Pennsylvania Barns

The first rear-extension barns were built in the central core counties in the late 1700s. The DeHaven barn, built circa 1790 near Hampton, in Adams County, Pennsylvania, is a log Sweitzer barn with stone double outshed extensions. Behind each log crib there is an inside entrance to the out-shed granary (see Figure 3.19). The basement stable includes the under-outshed space, proving that the barn was originally built according to this plan. The Heisey barn (see Figure 2.37), west of Lancaster, is a single-outshed stone Sweitzer barn, built about 1810. The nearby Getz barn is a double-outshed stone Sweitzer barn, built in 1814. The dates of these three barns with outsheds as part of their original designs indicate that an outshed plan was used to build early barns. Interestingly, added-on outsheds did not appear until later.

The precise origin of this style has not been determined. The importance of producing feed grain for beef and dairy cattle in Lancaster and the western core counties in Pennsylvania could have inspired a design with increased storage capacity; double-outshed granaries would have satisfied this require-ment. Rear-outshed extensions do occur occasionally on forebay barns in Switzerland and on Lake District bank barns in England (Brunskill 1974,

Figures 3.23, 3.24, and 3.25. This series plots the development of the ramp shed barn in Adams County, Indiana. Figure 3.23 (*top*) shows the Lehman barn, circa 1860, a typical mid-nineteenth-century midwestern open-forebay standard barn before modification. Figure 3.24 (*bottom*) illustrates the partial-ramp-shed bank bridge that represents the transition to full-ramp-shed form. The Litweiler barn (Figure 3.25, *opposite*) north of Berne, Indiana, has a full ramp shed, which was added in the 1880s. (Photos 1988.)

83–85). Granaries are not usually included in those outsheds.[3] It is possible that the form of English Lake District outsheds could have diffused to Pennsylvania; however, their function as granaries is undoubtedly an American invention. Barns with this morphology became the predominant type in the western core counties in Pennsylvania by the middle 1800s, and outsheds in various later forms have been added on to many barns throughout Pennsylvania.

The bents shown in Diagram 3.6 illustrate an evolutionary progression in the form of rear-extension barns. The three earliest examples show a combination of rear-extension morphology with Sweitzer bents. The last five examples show rear-extension morphology combined with the later standard bents. In examples *A, C, D,* and *F,* the addition of Sweitzer-like forebay framing *behind* the main bent frame results in a shallow ramp shed, which encloses the upper bank between the outsheds, providing interior access to them. On these barns, the outsheds extend beyond the ramp shed and flank the lower barn bank. This combination of ramp shed and outshed

3. Ronald Brunskill, in a phone conversation in June 1989, stated that the outshuts (outsheds) found on some bank barns in the English Lake District are part of the initial barn construction. This is revealed by the inclusion of their lower level in the original stable foundation. He also explained that upper-level access to the outshuts is provided only by doors to the barn bank, and not directly from the threshing floor, as is the case in Pennsylvania. He pointed out that the upper levels of these outshuts serve multiple functions. They could be used to house young cattle but also sometimes as temporary "corn holes," where oats, barley, or rye could be stored. This usage usually occurred on small farms, which lacked the granary capacity typically found in the upper level of the cartshed or other farm buildings. Brunskill felt that the specialized granary function of the Pennsylvania outshed had no direct connection to the outshuts described above. The absence of outsheds on the early Lake District–type bank barns of Chester County provides another reason to question any direct connections between the Pennsylvania outshed and English sources.

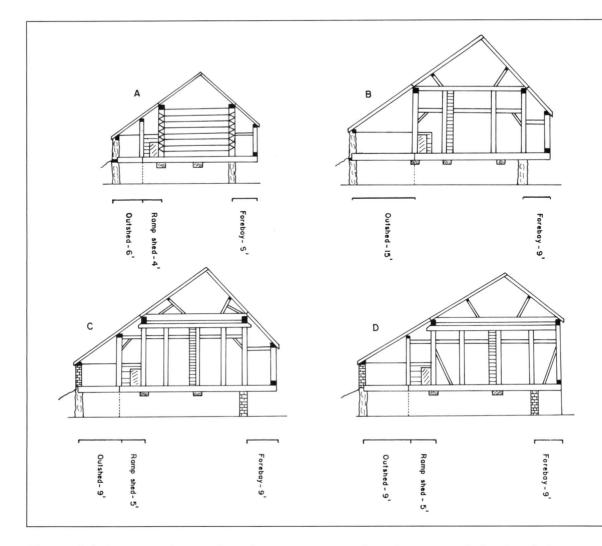

Diagram 3.6. Comparative bent typology of rear-extension Pennsylvania barns. Ramp-shed and outshed extensions cause the gable-end rear asymmetry that characterizes rear-extension barns.

A. Log Sweitzer barn with stone double-outshed extension. DeHaven barn, circa 1790, near Hampton, Adams County, Pennsylvania.
B. Stone Sweitzer barn with double-outshed extension. Old Getz barn dated 1814, west of Lancaster, Pennsylvania.
C. Brick Sweitzer barn with ramp shed plus double-outshed extension. Lester Angle barn, circa 1835, near Mercersburg, Franklin County, Pennsylvania.
D. Brick closed-forebay standard barn with ramp shed plus double-outshed extension. Lester Angle barn near Mercersburg, Franklin County, Pennsylvania, circa 1850.

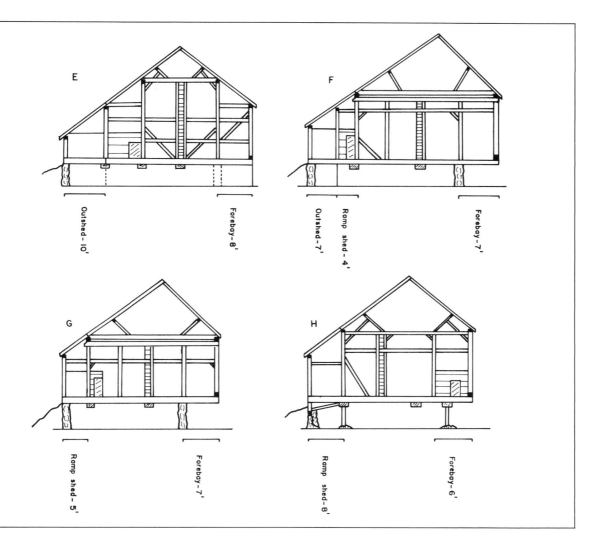

E. Frame standard barn (modified standard bent) with double-outshed extension. Moyer barn, circa 1860, east of Jonestown, Lebanon County, Pennsylvania.

F. Frame standard barn with ramp shed plus shallow double-outshed extension, circa 1870, north of Shippensburg, Cumberland County, Pennsylvania.

G. Frame standard barn with ramp-shed extension, circa 1885, north of Shippensburg, Cumberland County, Pennsylvania.

H. Frame standard barn with ramp-shed extension over storage tunnel. Shetler barn, dated 1889, Adams County, Indiana.

extensions produces the gable asymmetry that is usually a characteristic of rear-extension barns.

The final phase in the evolution of rear-extension barns in the western core in Pennsylvania occurred when the outsheds were eliminated. The remaining ramp shed then extended along the entire rear barn wall. This ramp shed, however shallow, when combined with a late standard barn frame, usually resulted in modest rear asymmetry.

The Moyer barn in Lebanon County uses a single-tie-beam, post-to-purlin standard bent for the main barn frame. Its outsheds connect directly to this frame without an intervening ramp shed section, as is common in many rear-extension barns of the central core counties in Pennsylvania. Another practice, differentiating western and central from eastern core counties in Pennsylvania, is the use of a double-tie-beam arrangement for the main section of the bent. In bents like this, the upper tie beam was locked over the roof plate in traditional fashion after the main section had been raised. The double-tie-beam insured a very strong bent, well suited to support the large barns of the central and western core counties, whose more complex framing included forebay and rear-extension elements.

In Adams County, Indiana, a simple evolutionary progression produced ramp-shed barns largely independently of direct Pennsylvania influence. The earliest forebay barns here, circa 1860, were open-forebay standard barns, which still predominate numerically in Adams County. The evolution to ramp-shed structures included a transitional stage that featured a large covered bridge, or partial ramp shed, over the middle of the rear bank and tunnel. A similar barn with an original partial ramp shed has been documented by Daniel Troth near Bluffton, in Allen County, Ohio. Its presence may indicate that the progression to ramp-shed barn started in western Ohio and then diffused into Adams County, Indiana. The evolution was completed when the ramp shed was enlarged to cover the entire rear barn wall, bank, and storage tunnel below. Proof that the first complete ramp sheds in the county were added on to earlier barns is revealed by differences in the age of nails and boards between the barn and its added-on structure. Figure 3.26 is a view of the back frame of the Litweiler barn, as seen from within the ramp shed. The shaped rafter ends indicate that this was originally the outside rear eave of the barn roof. Rafters added later to extend the ramp shed are clearly visible. The rear end post also retains an original forged iron pintel, on which a strap hinge for the large threshing floor door was hung, which provides additional proof that this was originally an outside wall. This evidence indicates that evolutionary processes resulted in the formalization of the ramp shed barn in Adams County by the 1880s.

Figure 3.26. Interior of ramp shed of Litweiler barn (see Figure 3.25). Shaped rafter ends and hinge pintel on vertical post indicate an original outside wall. Adz marks on hand-hewn original barn frame beams and roof plate contrast with appearance of the sawn timbers and rafters of added-on ramp shed. (Photo 1988.)

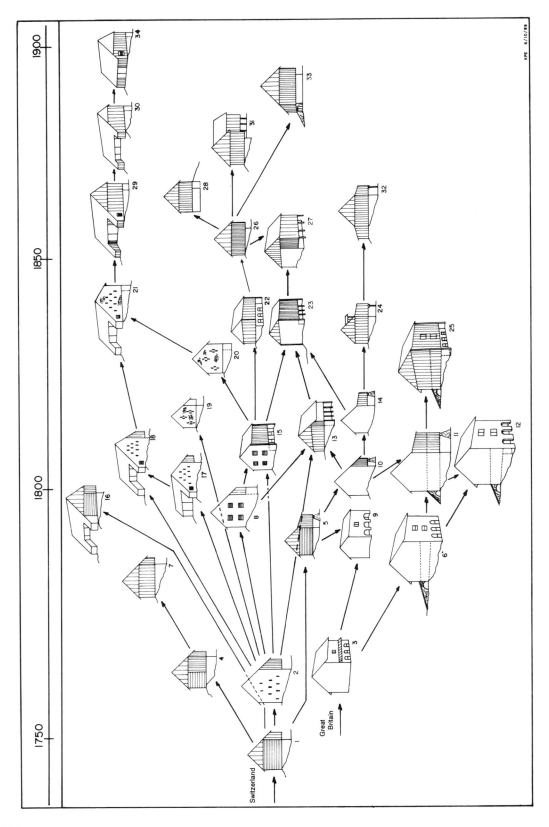

Diagram 3.7. Conjectured evolution of Pennsylvania barns.

1. Log Sweitzer barn
2. Stone classic Sweitzer barn
3. English Lake District bank barn
4. Half-log-frame transition Sweitzer barn
5. Log Sweitzer barn with added-on stone-posted forebay
6. Chester County double-decker bank barn
7. Frame classic Sweitzer barn
8. Transition closed-forebay Sweitzer barn
9. Stone-arch-forebay standard barn
10. Chester County stone-posted-forebay barn (early form)
11. Chester County stone-posted-forebay double-decker barn
12. Stone-arch-forebay double-decker barn
13. Extended supported-forebay barn (early form)
14. Chester County stone-posted-forebay barn
15. Closed-forebay standard barn
16. Log-stone double-outshed Sweitzer barn
17. Stone single-outshed Sweitzer barn
18. Stone double-outshed Sweitzer barn
19. Brick classic Sweitzer barn
20. Brick closed-forebay standard barn
21. Brick double-outshed standard barn
22. Half-open-forebay standard barn
23. Posted-closed-forebay standard barn
24. Upcountry posted-forebay barn
25. Double-decker standard barn
26. Open-forebay standard barn
27. Posted-open-forebay standard barn
28. Bank-into-forebay standard barn
29. Frame double-outshed standard barn
30. Ramp-shed double-outshed standard barn
31. Front-shed (three-gable) extended barn
32. Ramp shed added on to upcountry posted-forebay barn
33. Ohio-Indiana ramp-shed barn
34. Ramp-shed barn (western core)

Conclusion

Since only a few basic barn types were imported directly from Europe, the multiplicity of recognizable barn styles is proof of evolutionary change. Diagram 3.7 summarizes and illustrates the evolution of this complex set of barn structures constituted of Pennsylvania and related barns. It shows how modification and synthesis produced this varied assemblage of structures. It reveals that the largest number of new barn types appeared between 1790 and 1840, during the golden age of Pennsylvania agriculture. The diagram and the descriptions of barn classes and types in Chapter 2 indicate that Pennsylvania barn evolution was completed by 1900. Construction of standard and extended barns continued until the mid-twentieth century. Many barns were built or rebuilt with traditional framing, but using commercial rather than hand-hewn timbers. Some are still being constructed in this manner in Amish and Mennonite communities, an example of the power of tradition within these groups.[4] The evidence presented above is offered in support of my theory of the origin and evolutionary development of the classes and types of the Pennsylvania barn.

4. Weyer 1988; discussions with barn builder Charles Speicher and barn researcher Christopher Witmer about barn building practices in this century; discussions with Joseph Glass, who has attended Amish barn raisings in Lancaster County and who has interviewed Amish barn builders from that area.

4

DIFFUSION AND DISTRIBUTION OF THE PENNSYLVANIA BARN

The density of Pennsylvania barns across North America varies considerably. The most concentrated area is the Pennsylvania barn core (see Maps 4.1 and 2.1). It is the result of early and intense settlement. The agricultural landscape created by the early settlers has persisted in spite of increased urbanization and rural residential development in recent years. Beyond the core is an area plotted by Joseph Glass, who accomplished the first mapping of the distribution of Pennsylvania barns through many years of intensive fieldwork. With Dr. Glass's permission, the area he established as the "Pennsylvania barn region" I have designated as the "domain"—the area of dense and continuous occurrence—of Pennsylvania barns. In the domain, non-Pennsylvania barns are a small minority of the total of barn structures, and the region is, therefore, dominated and defined by the overwhelming number of Pennsylvania barns. The domain covers the entire southeastern quarter of Pennsylvania, extends into nearby parts of New Jersey, Maryland, and West Virginia, and projects southwest along the Great Valley into western Virginia. Pennsylvania barns have also spread far beyond the core and domain. The limits of this further diffusion delineate the third region, the least intense distribution of these barns, which I call the sphere. It contains scattered examples and small clusters of Pennsylvania barns. It also includes disjunct islands of larger and more intense groupings of Pennsylvania barns mixed in with other barn types. In some of these disjunct islands, Pennsylvania barns may be in the majority over one or more counties, replicating the Pennsylvania landscape far from Pennsylvania's borders.

The data for Map 4.1 come from several sources: my extensive field surveys; all the scholarly books, articles, and papers known to me that deal with Pennsylvania barns; occasional newspaper and magazine articles on Pennsylvania barns; and sightings reported directly to me by qualified ob-

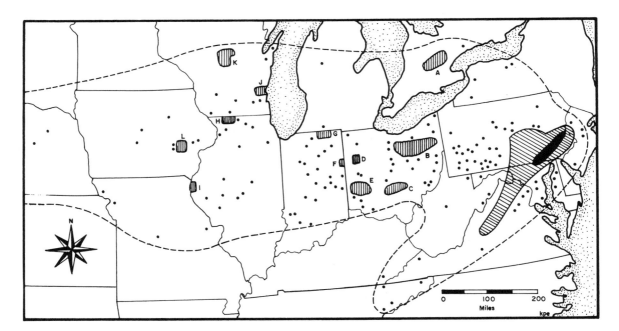

Map 4.1. Distribution and diffusion of the Pennsylvania barn.

 Core: most intense concentration of Pennsylvania barns with most frequent occurrence of log and stone Sweitzer barns built before 1800 (Ensminger)

 Domain: dense and continuous distribution of Pennsylvania barns (documented by Glass 1971 and 1986)

 Sphere: scattered and disjunct distributions of Pennsylvania barns (Ensminger)

 One or more Pennsylvania barns recorded within the sphere

 Major Pennsylvania barn regions within the sphere: minimum of 75 barns per region. (In five regions, based on complete field survey; in seven regions, based on estimate: derived from partial field surveys)

Major regions within the sphere:

A. Waterloo County, Ontario
B. Northeastern quadrant of Ohio, Columbiana to Richland counties
C. Fairfield and Perry counties, Ohio
D. Putnam County/Allen County, Ohio, border
E. Clark, Montgomery, and Preble counties, Ohio
F. Adams County, Indiana

G. Elkhart and La Grange counties, Indiana
H. Stevenson County, Illinois
I. Adams County, Illinois
J. Washington and Ozaukee counties, Wisconsin
K. Lincoln and Marathon counties, Wisconsin
L. Johnson and Washington counties, Iowa

Figure 4.1. Half-open-forebay standard barn, circa 1870, in Shenandoah County, Virginia, in the southwestern extension of the Pennsylvania barn's domain. The drop front configuration of the door on the forebay front wall indicates that the mows on either side of the threshing floor are raised. Horizontal wooden barn siding is common in Virginia and on later barns elsewhere. (Photo 1988.)

servers. In some cases, their reports have been backed up with photographs; in many other cases, I have followed up by personally checking out the accuracy of the reports. So far, not one of these observers has misidentified a Pennsylvania barn. References for sightings I have not personally surveyed are listed in Appendix A of this book.

The Pennsylvania barn core represents an area which was settled and essentially filled by the middle of the eighteenth century. Germanic immigrants, including the farmers from Switzerland who introduced the forebay bank barn, began to arrive in 1682 and occupied generally the more easterly and fertile limestone regions (Wenger 1966, 57–68). The Scotch-Irish began to arrive after 1717. Both groups moved west, completing settlement of the core (Leyburn 1962, 184–200). They carried forebay bank barns to the Cumberland Valley in Pennsylvania and south into the Hagerstown Valley in Maryland. The initial diffusion involved direct contact, farmer to farmer, a transfer of those practices which had proved successful: German and Scotch-Irish farmers used Swiss forebay bank barns and carried them to new areas of settlement. Thus, imitation and short distance relocation diffusion were the processes that carried the forebay bank barn throughout the core.

The boundaries of the core were influenced by various forces: to the

Figure 4.2. Open-forebay standard barn in Knox County just north of Knoxville, Tennessee. This is the southernmost Pennsylvania barn within the barn's sphere known to me. (Photo 1988.)

north and west by the physical presence of the Blue Mountain and the Indian territories beyond, and on the east and south by the English counties around Philadelphia and the political boundaries of New Jersey, Delaware, and Maryland.

Migration from the core began before 1730, when lands in the northern part of the Valley of Virginia were made available (185–89). The scarcity and high prices of land in Pennsylvania deflected new pioneers to the Shenandoah Valley in Virginia and farther south. Pennsylvania Germans settled in the north while Scotch-Irish were predominant farther south. Both groups carried Pennsylvania barns into the new territory. South of Roanoke, Virginia, the valley narrows and Pennsylvania barns disappear, although pioneer settlement continued into northwestern North Carolina and the Great Valley in east Tennessee. This outpouring to the southwest by people coming from or through Pennsylvania produced the distinct lobe on the southern end of the Pennsylvania barn's domain.

Beyond the domain, scattered barns in southwestern Virginia and northeastern Tennessee extend the barn's sphere to its southern-most point. Disjunct examples in eastern Maryland and southern New Jersey deflect the boundary of the sphere eastward in opposition to the main streams of migration. These were largely the result of moves by individual families.

After the end of the French and Indian War, in 1763, Indian problems

Figure 4.3. The Helb barn, dated 1881, is an open-forebay standard barn located in Calvert Cliffs State Park, Calvert County, Maryland, one mile from the Chesapeake Bay. (Photo 1972.)

gradually declined beyond the Blue Mountain, which forms the northern boundary of Pennsylvania's Great Valley. Pennsylvania-German and Scotch-Irish pioneers moved up the rivers into fertile valleys and extended the domain of the Pennsylvania barn north and west to the base of the Appalachian Plateau.

Migration and relocation diffusion were also responsible for the broader distribution of Pennsylvania barns across Canada and the United States. Maps, particularly of the Midwest, that show migration from Pennsylvania reveal that migration patterns correlate closely with the distribution of Pennsylvania barns. (Later in the chapter, Ohio will be used as a case study to illustrate this.) Even better correlations emerge if select groups of Pennsylvania Germans are examined. The settlements of the Amish, Mennonites, and Brethren all seem to correlate with Pennsylvania barn locations in and beyond Pennsylvania. Other factors were also operating. In many midwestern locations, ethnic Germans who had come directly from the Old World settled along with the Pennsylvania Germans, obviously attracted by the similarity of culture and language. They also built Pennsylvania barns. In some locations, local barn builders appear to have promoted Pennsylvania barns.

The path of westward movement of early settlers was often influenced by the routes and means of transportation available to them. Although some

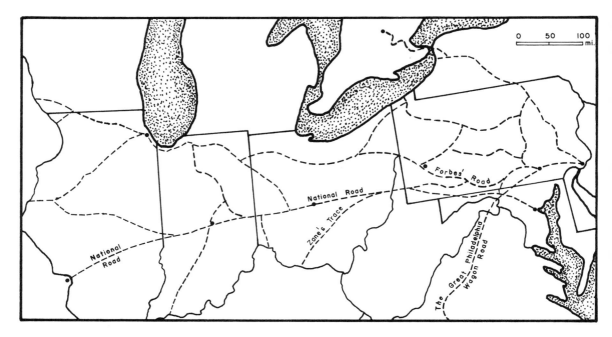

Map 4.2. Major roads out of Pennsylvania in 1834. A comparison to the Pennsylvania barn distribution map (Map 4.1) reveals that access by road at an early date was an important factor influencing Pennsylvania barn distribution patterns. These early routes continue to function today as important arteries in the national highway network. For example, the Great Philadelphia Wagon Road has become Interstate 81. Forbes' Road is now the Pennsylvania Turnpike, and the National Road has grown into Interstate 70.

pioneers used the Ohio River and later immigrants from Europe utilized the Erie Canal and Great Lakes network, most from Pennsylvania relied upon the early roads (see Map 4.2).[1] The earliest of these, the Great Philadelphia Wagon Road, provided access throughout the 1700s from Philadelphia west through the core and southwest through the Valley of Virginia, permitting an extension of the barn's domain far beyond Pennsylvania. After the French and Indian War, travel along Forbes' Road enabled Pennsylvania-German and Scotch-Irish pioneers to settle across the southern Pennsylvania portion of the Appalachian Plateau. Pennsylvania barns are frequent along this corridor to Pittsburgh. Although the occurrences are not dense enough for the area to be included in the domain, the corridor along Forbes' Road constitutes the third most important Pennsylvania barn region in the state. It includes concentrations in heavily Germanic Somerset County, which was initially settled by Amish and Mennonite pioneers, and in the Pennsylvania part of the Monongahela Valley, farther west.

Southwestern Pennsylvania was also served by the National Road, which brought settlers west from Maryland and connected western Pennsylvania to the fertile plains of Ohio and lands farther west. This route and

1. Leyburn 1962, pp. 195, 202, 219–222; *The Brethren Encyclopedia* 1984, 3:1440; Fink 1987, 81; Reaman 1957, map on front inside cover; Mitchell 1832; 1834.

Figure 4.4. The Newmeyer barn, circa 1796, near Pennsville, Fayette County, Pennsylvania, is a rare and early western Pennsylvania example of a classic stone Sweitzer barn. (Photo 1988.)

others developed into a network, offering access to many parts of Ohio, Indiana, and Illinois. A comparison of these roads and Pennsylvania barn distributions in the Midwest shows a strong correlation.

Pennsylvania Barns in Ohio

The largest and densest concentrations of Pennsylvania barns beyond the domain occur in Ohio, which lies almost completely within the barn's sphere (see Map 4.1). Following the Revolutionary War, Ohio was the first focus of rapid settlement in the Old Northwest, attracting settlers from New England, the Middle Atlantic region, and the South. Ohio borders Pennsylvania and is traversed by roads that originate there. Migration to Ohio from Pennsylvania was greatest before 1850. The locations of Pennsylvania barns in Ohio coincide almost perfectly with the migration routes used by Pennsylvania settlers and the counties where they settled in highest proportion. Hubert Wilhelm, who earlier studied Pennsylvania barns in southeastern Ohio, has just completed new studies of barns and settlements in Ohio (1974, 155–62; 1982; 1989a; 1989b, 29–37). His works are a main source of information for this section.

As Map 4.1 illustrates, Ohio has four major concentrations of Pennsylvania barns, while additional significant scatterings can be found over all but the southernmost portion of the state. The largest and most concentrated

Figure 4.5. The Smith barn, circa 1850, near Jeromesville, Ashland County, Ohio. Mortising forebay beams into the forebay sill is a technique frequently used throughout the Midwest. (Photo 1972.)

area is in the northeastern quadrant. It stretches from Mahoning and Columbiana counties on the Pennsylvania border, across Stark, Wayne, Holmes, Ashland, and Richland counties, forming a broad belt generally along old U.S. Route 30. In 1850, 75 percent or more of the settlers in these counties came from Pennsylvania (Wilhelm 1989a, 10–11). The area also includes adjacent parts of Carroll, Tuscarawas, Portage, Summit, and Medina counties. Taken together, these counties form the largest region of Pennsylvania barns not only in Ohio but anywhere beyond the domain.

The second major concentration of Pennsylvania barns centers on fertile Fairfield County and incorporates parts of adjacent counties. This is another region of heavy Pennsylvania-German settlement astride a major route of access—Zane's Trace, which leaves the National Road at Zanesville, Ohio, and arcs southwest to the Ohio River (Wilhelm 1982, 19–20). Lancaster, the county seat of Fairfield County, Ohio, was named after Lancaster, Pennsylvania, and was settled by Pennsylvania Germans from that area. Significant concentrations of Pennsylvania barns in Ohio coincide with other routes of migration west, including the Mennonite regions of Allen and Putnam counties, along old U.S. Route 30 in northwestern Ohio, and Clark, Montgomery,

Figures 4.6 and 4.7. The Rauskop farmstead (*above*), north of Somerset, Perry County, Ohio, includes a log Sweitzer barn built in 1837. Figure 4.7 (*left*), showing the interior of the Rauskop barn, reveals a forebay framed into a V-notched log crib. Identical technology is found in log Sweitzer barns throughout the Pennsylvania barn core. (Photos 1988.)

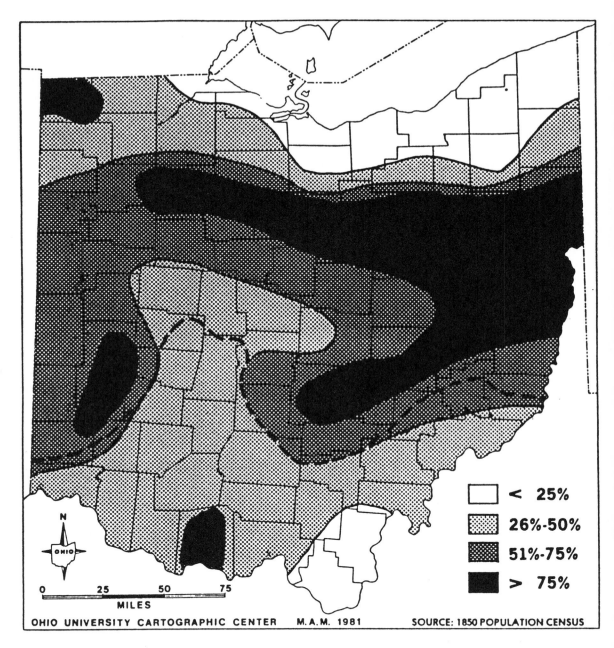

Map 4.3. Distribution of migrants to Ohio from the Middle Atlantic states as of 1850. Percentages are of all immigrants to the state. (Map prepared by Hubert Wilhelm and used by his permission.)

Southern boundary of Pennsylvania barn in Ohio

Figures 4.8 and 4.9. The Stanley Mertz frame Sweitzer barn (*left*), dated 1831, near Pleasantville, Fairfield County, Ohio. The heavy hand-hewn bent with tie beam–over–plate and post joint and "double connection" is identical to the framing of earlier barns in the Pennsylvania barn core. Figure 4.9 (*right*) shows a bent in the Thompson barn, circa 1860, near Springfield, Clark County, western Ohio. The "double connection" is retained, but the tie beam is mortised into the end posts 6 inches below the roof plate, which is a later bent form. (Photos 1988.)

Preble, and parts of adjacent counties, which lie along the National Road in western Ohio. The north-south axis of the Miami Valley, in southwestern Ohio, intersects the National Road, and also channeled into that area settlers who built Pennsylvania barns.

A map produced by Hubert Wilhelm to show the influence of Middle Atlantic settlement in Ohio shows the southern boundary of the Pennsylvania barn in Ohio. The area south of Wilhelm's boundary line, which in part follows Zane's Trace, has no significant occurrence of Pennsylvania barns (Wilhelm 1982, 46). The area is rolling plateau country with poor soils and was settled, in part, by pioneers from Appalachian Virginia, who imported the culture and architecture of the Upland South. The south-central lobe of Ohio, included in this area, occupies what was originally the Virginia Military District, set aside specifically for homesteading by Virginia war veterans, to satisfy colonial claims by Virginia to this part of Ohio: land warrants issued in Richmond could be exchanged for land titles in Ohio when veterans arrived and had their claims surveyed. Since many Pennsylvania

Figure 4.10. The Bricker barn, circa 1850, in the village of Doon, Waterloo County, Ontario, Canada, is a posted-forebay standard barn typical of the area. (Photo 1987.)

Germans belonged to conservative and pacifist churches and sects (Amish, Mennonite, Brethren), they had not served in the military and were unable to obtain land warrants in this and other military districts (Wilhelm 1989a, 14–15, 19). Except for the Connecticut Western Reserve of extreme northeastern Ohio, which was settled primarily by New Englanders, much of the remaining territory in congressional tracts was available to all settlers (Wilhelm 1982, 18). The Middle Atlantic migrants whose settlement patterns Wilhelm mapped came mostly from Pennsylvania. A comparison of this map and the Pennsylvania barn distribution map shows that Ohio is a good example with which to illustrate the various factors that have influenced the diffusion of Pennsylvania barns.

Pennsylvania Barns in Ontario

The landscape of southern Ontario also has a strong Pennsylvania flavor. Pennsylvania-German names are found on business signs, tombstones, and in the telephone directory. The antique country furniture of the area is identical to the dry sinks, bucket benches, and corner cupboards found in southeastern Pennsylvania. Mennonite plain churches, farmsteads, and horse drawn vehicles accentuate a rural landscape that is the setting for numerous Pennsylvania barns.

The area in and around Waterloo County, Ontario, was settled largely by Mennonites from southeastern Pennsylvania. It provides an excellent example of a disjunct outlier of Pennsylvania-German culture, and it has a dense distribution of Pennsylvania barns. These were mapped in 1972 by Peter

Figure 4.11. Interior of the Bricker barn, showing single-tie-beam, H-pattern framing bent. This bent is typically found in middle and late nineteenth-century Pennsylvania barns, the most common beyond Pennsylvania. (Photo 1987.)

Ennals, and the boundary he described has been incorporated in Map 4.1 (1972, 256–70). The history of the settlement and development of this area can be found in Graeff's article "The Pennsylvania Germans in Ontario, Canada" and in Reaman's book *The Trail of the Black Walnut* (Graeff 1948, 1–80; Reaman 1957, pref., intro., chaps. 3 and 4). Migration from Pennsylvania to Ontario started soon after the Revolution and continued until after the War of 1812. Waterloo County was the last area to receive settlers from Pennsylvania but the only area to retain the ethnic characteristics of the early settlers, thanks largely to the conservative nature of the Mennonites (Reaman 1957, 108).

Early log and stone Sweitzer barns are found in Ontario. They are survivors of the styles that prevailed in eastern Pennsylvania at the time of emigration. The majority of barns in Waterloo County are later. The Bricker barn (Figure 4.10) is a representative example. It is located south of Kitchner, in the village of Doon, which is now a historic preserve. This barn is a frame structure with stone basement walls. Its deep, 15-foot forebay is supported by beams that cantilever under the barn frame but require the extra support provided by posts under the forebay cross beam. The sym-

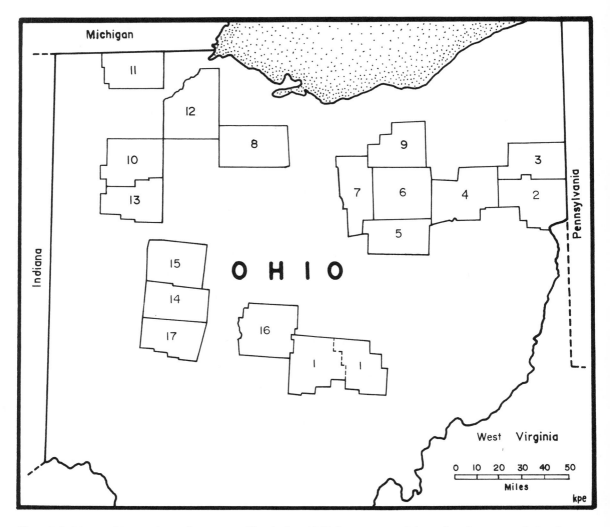

Map 4.4. Pioneer Mennonite settlements in Ohio before 1850, by county and date of settlement. Includes those of the Old Order Amish, who later merged with the Mennonite church.

1. Fairfield and Perry, 1799

2. Columbiana, 1801

3. Mahoning, 1806

4. Stark, 1810

5. Holmes, 1812

6. Wayne, 1815

7. Ashland, 1820

8. Seneca, 1820

9. Medina, 1825

10. Putnam, 1830

11. Fulton, 1834

12. Wood, 1835

13. Allen, 1841

14. Champaign, 1834

15. Logan, 1845

16. Franklin, 1848

17. Clark, 1848

metrical gable end qualifies this structure as a standard Pennsylvania barn. The upper level of the Bricker barn has a simple bent consisting of four vertical posts and a single tie beam mortised into the end posts 2 feet below the roof plate—the H-bent. These characteristics define a posted-forebay standard barn. With its H-bent, it is similar to later standard barns in the Pennsylvania barn's domain and regions beyond. However conservative the Ontario Pennsylvania German farmers were in most aspects of their lives, they were progressive when it came to farming, and this included building barns. Since most existing Pennsylvania barns were built after 1840, they represent what was then modern technology (Ensminger 1988, 69).

Plain People and Pennsylvania Barns

Pennsylvania pioneers represented various ethnic and religious groups that had resided in the core or domain for a period then moved on to new territories. These included Quakers, Scotch-Irish, and various Germanic groups, such as Lutherans, Calvinists, Catholics, Amish, Mennonites, and Brethren. While all contributed to the diffusion of the Pennsylvania barn, Mennonites were particularly effective agents in relocating the Pennsylvania barn to Ontario. Were the conservative Protestant sectarians—the Plain People, Mennonites, Amish, and Brethren—effective "barn carriers" in other places throughout the sphere?

Ohio again will serve as an excellent model on which to base a comparative study of the settlement patterns of Plain People and the distribution of Pennsylvania barns. Abundant data are available on early Mennonite settlement throughout the state (Alderfer 1986, 14–15; Wenger 1966, 98–104; Stoltzfus 1969, 42–81). A map based on these data shows the counties where Mennonites settled before 1850. There is a strong correlation to the Pennsylvania barn distribution in Ohio (see Map 4.1). Most striking is the coincidence of Ohio's four significant Pennsylvania barn regions with groupings of counties reporting early Mennonite settlement. As in Ontario, Mennonite settlers have proven to be an excellent index group for predicting the occurrence of Pennsylvania barns.

Numerous other barns across the Midwest can be attributed to Mennonite settlers who came either directly from Pennsylvania or, more frequently, from secondary centers of Mennonite settlement in Virginia, Ontario, and Ohio (Wenger 1966, 104–20). Adams County, cited in Chapter 2, was the first area of Mennonite settlement in Indiana (settled in 1838). Its immigrants came directly from Canton Bern, Switzerland, and included both Amish and Mennonite groups (108). The Pennsylvania barns here were probably introduced later by settlers from Ohio. They remain today and constitute one of the significant barn regions in the state.

Are the Amish as reliable a predictor of Pennsylvania barn occurrence as the Mennonites? In 1693, Jacob Ammann led a schism from the Mennonite Church of Canton Bern, Switzerland, in a dispute over the practice of shunning. Ammann believed in strict observation of this practice, and his fol-

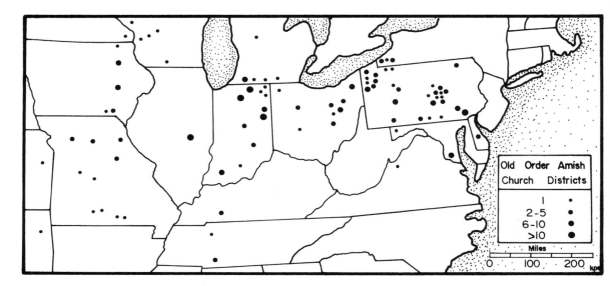

Map 4.5. Old Order Amish settlements surviving in 1976, based on number of church districts. (Map adapted from Crowley 1978, 262.)

lowers eventually became known as Amish. They were exiled from Bern, and they dispersed widely over Germanic Europe. Some merged with various Mennonite groups there. For many Amish, migration to America, with its almost limitless land and expanding frontier, insured their survival. The first wave, approximately 500, came from the Palatinate and Switzerland to Pennsylvania between 1717 and 1750 (Crowley 1978, 249–51). They eventually became established in Lancaster County, from where the founding of new colonies proceeded in a westward progression. At the end of the eighteenth century, they established colonies in Mifflin and Somerset counties, in central Pennsylvania, and adjacent Garrett County, in western Maryland. By 1809, they had spread into Holmes and Tuscarawas counties, Ohio (252). This is now the largest concentrated area of Amish settlement in North America. Between 1817 and 1861, colonies were established in western Ohio, northeastern Indiana, central Illinois, and eastern Iowa as Amish farmers moved west with the frontier. After the Civil War, expansion occurred on the High Plains and into the South. This pattern continued throughout the twentieth century, with new colonies being established in literally all directions, fed by rapid population increases in the older colonies. Newer settlements in southwestern and northern New York State exemplify this trend.

By 1972, more than 85,000 Old Order Amish were living in North America, 75 percent of them in Ohio, Pennsylvania, and Indiana. The Holmes and Tuscarawas counties area of north-central Ohio had grown to outrank the original Lancaster County, Pennsylvania, settlement, while the Elkhart and La Grange counties area of northeastern Indiana had become the third largest area of Amish settlement in North America (Hostetler 1980,

Figure 4.12. Gable-forebay standard barn near Leon, Cattaragus County, in western New York State, was built by an Amish farmer who had migrated from Carroll County, Ohio. (Photo 1987.)

94–100). A mapping of Old Order Amish settlements in the United States in 1976 (Map 4.5) reflects this pattern and will serve to test the correlation between Amish settlements and Pennsylvania barns. Amish settlements surviving in 1976 generally were ones dating back to the nineteenth century, when most Pennsylvania barns were built.

Amish settled in the same general regions as did Mennonites, but not close to one another. Conservative Old Order Amish differ significantly from the main body of Mennonites. Their use of selected technology is prescribed by their local churches. They do not educate children beyond the eighth grade. They worship in private homes and organize their churches around local family groups, rather than hierarchical church conferences, as do the Mennonites. The correlation of Pennsylvania barns and Amish settlement is strong in pioneer Amish settlement areas, such as Holmes County, Ohio, and Elkhart County, Indiana. The dense concentration of Pennsylvania barns in the northeastern quadrant of Ohio, which includes Holmes County, has been reported by Wilhelm and other scholars and has been verified by field counts.

No prior studies have focused specifically on Pennsylvania barns in northeastern Indiana, an excellent testing ground for the hypothesis that there is a correlation between Amish settlement and the presence of Pennsylvania barns. Although I had observed several forebay barns in the southwestern part of the region, I had not carried out a definitive field count. The available data showed a large Old Order Amish population and early Mennonite settlement, and I expected to find a significant concentration of Pennsylvania barns in Elkhart County and adjacent La Grange County. An inquiry made to the Mennonite Library at Goshen, Indiana, provided names of several local inhabitants, who verified the existence of Pennsylvania barns in the area. One of these people, LeRoy Troyer, was raised by an Amish family and later joined the Mennonite Church. He is an engineer and builder who is interested in local barns. He stated that there are at least two hundred surviving Pennsylvania barns in Elkhart and La Grange counties and that many more existed in the past. Terry Herschberger, photographer and barn enthusiast from Middlebury, Indiana, in Elkhart County, stated that his own observations support the barn count of LeRoy Troyer. Based on this evidence, it is clear that northeastern Indiana ranks as one of the most important Pennsylvania barn regions west of Ohio. The expected correlation between combined Amish and Mennonite regions and Pennsylvania barn distributions can be readily documented.

Members of various Germanic Baptist Brethren churches, called Dunkards or Brethren, were also part of the population of Pennsylvania-German settlers who moved beyond the Pennsylvania hearth. One could expect that Brethren pioneers also participated in the diffusion of the Pennsylvania barn. In 1987, I came across several Pennsylvania barns while traveling through Carroll County, in northwestern Illinois. A few miles down the road from the barns, I encountered an old Brethren Church. Later, Wayne Price, who has done extensive barn research in Illinois, recounted to me similar occurrences of Pennsylvania barns within Brethren settlements throughout the state. In order to examine the broader implications of these examples, a comparison of the locations of Pennsylvania barns and Brethren population over a larger region was necessary. The *Brethren Encyclopedia* includes maps showing membership in German Baptist Brethren churches by county across the United States; Map 4.6 illustrates this information for the Pennsylvania barn domain and the eastern Midwest. This population is the cumulative result of original settlement and expansion in colonial Pennsylvania, eighteenth- and nineteenth-century migration across Pennsylvania and to the south and west, and twentieth-century growth in all areas. Its distribution correlates closely with Pennsylvania barn locations as well as with Amish and Mennonite settlements. The lesson to be learned is that, while the Amish, Mennonites, and Brethren constituted a minority of the pioneers and migrants carrying Pennsylvania culture across the country, they serve as excellent markers by which to identify areas of Pennsylvania settlement and Pennsylvania barn construction.

Pennsylvania Barns in Illinois

Pennsylvania barn distributions in Illinois also conform to established patterns. For example, Wayne Price has identified a cluster of ten or twelve Pennsylvania barns on the Macon-Piatt county line east of Decatur, which were built by members of the Church of the Brethren.

In Illinois the largest and densest concentration of Pennsylvania barns is in Stephenson County, one hundred miles northwest of Chicago. The area

Figure 4.13. Posted-forebay standard barn north of Syracuse, Elkhart County, Indiana. The shadow line on the upper gable wall reveals the position of the gable-wall tie team and indicates the use of an H-bent in this barn frame. (Photo by Terry Herschberger, used by his permission.)

Figure 4.14. Closed-forebay standard barn in Stephenson County, in northwestern Illinois. (Photo by H. Wayne Price, used by his permission.)

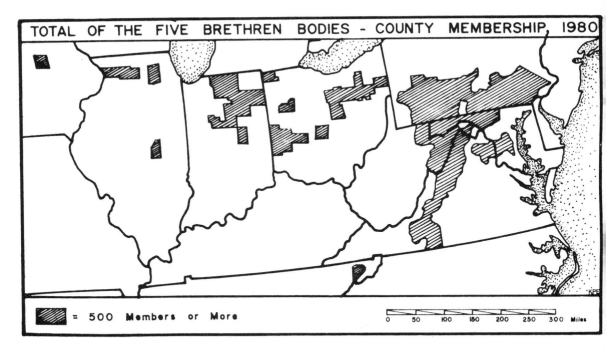

Map 4.6. Counties with five hundred or more members of five German Baptist Brethren or Dunkard church bodies, based on congregation membership in 1980. (Map based on data drawn from map in *The Brethren Encyclopedia* 1984, vol. 3, 1457.)

was originally settled by Mennonites who came from Pennsylvania and Ohio in the early 1840s (Alderfer 1986, 16; Wenger 1966, 107–8; Price 1988, 12). Wayne Price and Keith Sculle have surveyed these barns (Price and Sculle 1985, 45–53). At least 136 have been identified. Most are in townships that had a high percentage of Pennsylvania-German settlers. Since the barns were built after the 1840s, they should reflect the styles that prevailed during that period. It is not surprising, then, that the barns described by Price and Sculle are all standard barns, mostly of the closed-forebay type. Several open and half-open-forebay standard barns were also identified. All of these types were being built in Pennsylvania and the Midwest during this period.

Price and Sculle described two methods of forebay sill articulation. Forebay beams can be butted directly onto, and mortised into, the forebay sill. This method, used in Stephenson County and in western Ohio and Wisconsin, is less common in Pennsylvania. A simpler and stronger way is to rest the forebay sill and front wall frame directly on top of the ends of the forebay beams. This, the most common method in Pennsylvania, is also used in many barns in Stephenson County. In some cases, the ends of these beams are beveled. A similar beveling of forebay beam ends occurs in Centre, Clinton, and Clearfield counties in central Pennsylvania. Minor style variations such as this could be the result of local barn builders favoring and promoting a particular form.

Figures 4.15 and 4.16. This posted-forebay standard barn with shallow closed fore-bay is typical of many found in Adams County, Illinois. Slatted ventilating sections (*bottom*) in the upper part of the stable wall are used instead of windows on many Adams County barns. They are found in all regions in some later barns that have frame stable front walls. (Photos by H. Wayne Price, used by his permission.)

Figure 4.17. This unusual shedlike gable forebay is found on several barns in Sangamon County, Illinois. (Photo by H. Wayne Price, used by his permission.)

Wayne Price has reported a second significant Pennsylvania barn region in Illinois, in Adams County, along the Mississippi River (1987, 29–35). Seventy-six barns were surveyed in 1986, and more, undoubtedly, had previously existed. Adams County was originally part of the military tract set aside by the federal government for soldiers of the War of 1812. This may account for the lack of early settlement here by the Amish, Mennonites, or Brethren. Some other settlers did come from Pennsylvania and Indiana, along with migrants from New England, the South, and Europe.

Price's descriptions indicate that all of the Adams County barns are posted-forebay standard barns. They display a mixture of open, half-open, and closed forebays, and all use four or more original support posts to reinforce the forebay sill. With forebay depths of only 6 feet and forebay beams cantilevered under the barn frame, support posts would not have been necessary; their use in this barn design remains a mystery. The use of posts in extended supported-forebay barns in Pennsylvania to Wisconsin is necessary, to hold up the enlarged forebay straw sheds of those barns.

Another distinguishing feature of the Adams County barns was the use of meshing, slatted ventilating sections in the upper stable wall beneath the forebay. These could be opened and closed to control ventilation and were an alternative to the windows that are usually found in this location. Although similar devices are occasionally found in later barns in all regions, they were used on over 30 percent of the barns in Adams County.

Figure 4.18. The Votsis barn, circa 1870, near Sullivan, Jefferson County, in southern Wisconsin, is similar in form to other upcountry posted-forebay barns with gabled dormer in southeastern and central Wisconsin. (Photo 1982.)

Price also noted that the stabling layout in many barns was originally oriented lengthwise with stalls for horses and cows divided by a feeding aisle running from gable end to gable end. This center aisle plan was usually found in later barns, or in old barns in which the stable had been remodeled to accommodate a larger herd. Post-to-purlin framing bents were noted in about 15 percent of the barns surveyed. The range of variations found in the Pennsylvania barns of Adams County suggests that while the later settlers, who built most of these barns, perceived the functional advantages of the Pennsylvania barn, they also knew of a variety of new forms, which they incorporated into their version of the barn.

Pennsylvania Barns in Wisconsin

The migration and diffusion processes that distributed Pennsylvania barns across Ohio, Indiana, and Illinois, continued into Wisconsin (Ensminger 1983, 98–114). The southern two tiers of counties received significant numbers of settlers directly from Pennsylvania plus additional Pennsylvania Germans from secondary centers of Pennsylvania culture in Ohio, Indiana, and Illinois (Dundore 1955, 59, 78, 80). Settlers from New England and New York State and immigrants directly from Europe added to the growing population. Many of the pioneers formed nationality-oriented settlements

Figure 4.19. Schlittler barn, circa 1880, near Monticello, Green County, Wisconsin. High ramp at rear leads to upper threshing bridge of this double-decker barn. (Photo 1982.)

Figure 4.20. Winskell barn, circa 1857, near New Diggings, Lafayette County, in southwestern Wisconsin. This is the only Chester County stone-posted-forebay barn known to me in the Midwest. (Photo 1987.)

and built structures that reflected their national and ethnic origins. A representative assemblage of vernacular structures built in Wisconsin, which reveal these origins, has been preserved in an outdoor museum called Old World Wisconsin, located west of Milwaukee. The Pennsylvania barn distribution map indicates a scattering of barns across the southern counties of Wisconsin, where they are found among New York State banked basement barns and various other types.

The Votsis barn, near Sullivan, in Jefferson County, is a good example of a Wisconsin upcountry posted-forebay barn. The Schlittler barn (circa 1880), located near Monticello, in Green County, is a posted-forebay standard barn with shallow 4-foot forebay. Although the forebay beams cantilever beneath the barn frame and provide ample support, forebay posts are part of the original design. In this respect, the barn resembles those reported in Adams County, Illinois, and may indicate a widespread acceptance of this type in the Midwest. The Schlittler barn is a three-level barn; this is revealed by the presence of a high bank bridge to the upper level.

The Winskell barn (Figure 4.20), in southwestern Lafayette County, is an all-stone structure, which is rare in the Midwest. The most unusual feature, however, is the use of conical stone support columns for the large extended forebay. In this and other aspects of its morphology, the Winskell barn is virtually an exact copy of a Chester County, Pennsylvania, stone-posted-forebay barn (Figure 2.29). Although no direct connections have yet been established, it seems highly unlikely that its presence could result from spontaneous and independent evolution. Research into the background of the Winskell barn was carried out by the Galena–Jo Daviess County (Illinois) Historical Society and Museum.[2] The barn was built by Samuel Scales around 1857. Scales was a prosperous miner and farmer, who lived on the property from 1836 until his death in 1877. Born in North Carolina in 1805, he migrated to the area in 1830 and was first involved in lead mining and smelting. When mining became unprofitable, during the 1850s, he turned to farming. The coming of the railroads, during this period, permitted the export and marketing of wheat, which had become the main money crop. Scales also raised and raced horses. The demands of expanding agriculture, along with his position as a respected citizen and businessman, may have influenced him to build a stone barn of impressive proportions. Pennsylvania-German settlers coming into the area could have provided him with information about their barn styles. Whatever the reasons, the barn he built remains today and is unique among Pennsylvania barns in the Midwest.

The Pennsylvania barn distribution map shows a significant region of Pennsylvania barns in southeastern Wisconsin, just north of Milwaukee. These barns were first surveyed by Charles Calkins and Martin Perkins, who, in addition to serving as my field guides, provided me with valuable

2. Daryl Watson, executive director of the Galena-Jo Daviess County Historical Society and Museum, provided background information about the local region, and researcher Marge Smith supplied the details concerning the Winskell barn and its owners.

Figure 4.21. Closed-forebay standard barn, circa 1880, north of Milwaukee in Washington County, Wisconsin. (Photo 1982.)

data about the area and its barns. Approximately 150 Pennsylvania barns, making up 15 percent of the barn structures, are distributed over a 300-square-mile area in Washington and Ozaukee counties. A majority are closed-forebay standard barns almost identical to those found in southeastern Pennsylvania. One barn, with a date stone inscribed 1881, is representative of the earlier barns of the area. Another has an outside stairway leading from the front of the stable area up into the forebay. This feature, while common in southeastern Pennsylvania, is rare in the Midwest. The location of stable doors under the forebay and the presence of a traditional Pennsylvania stable plan are indicative of an earlier barn. Stable doors being centered on the gable walls signifies a longitudinal, center-aisle stable plan and a later barn. A group of 27 barns located in eastern Ozaukee County are upcountry posted-forebay barns. Several have the gabled dormer frequently found in Wisconsin barns of this type.

These Pennsylvania barns in southeastern Wisconsin represent a continuation of the distribution of Pennsylvania barns across the Midwest. A major difference emerges when the ethnic and national origins of the population are checked. The region around Milwaukee was settled largely by people from northern Germany who arrived after 1850. Few settlers from Pennsylvania came to Washington and Ozaukee counties (Dundore 1955, 78, 87–89; *Wisconsin's Changing Population* 1942). The diffusion of Pennsylvania barns into this area did not result from the in-migration of barn carriers. It resulted from the conscious choice of a versatile, multiple-purpose barn by ethnic Germans who were aware of its use by their Pennsylvania-German cousins throughout the Midwest.

Figure 4.22. Upcountry posted-forebay barn, circa 1900, with gabled dormer, north of Milwaukee in Ozaukee County, Wisconsin. (Photo by Charles Calkins, used by his permission.)

Figure 4.23. The Krausie barn, circa 1900, west of Wausau, Marathon County, Wisconsin, is typical of the earlier, gable-roof upcountry posted-forebay barns of central Wisconsin. (Photo 1982.)

Figure 4.24. This posted-forebay standard barn, circa 1880, in Holt County, in northwestern Missouri, is similar to examples in Adams County, in western Illinois. The sheds on the gable ends have been added on, and the original stable walls were revised to increase the stabling capacity. (Photo by Emily Yoder Roberts, used by her permission.)

A significant region of Pennsylvania barns can be found 140 miles northwest of Milwaukee near the northern limit of agriculture in Wisconsin. This outlier, in Lincoln and Marathon counties, includes 150 structures that are quite uniform in morphology. All are large (80 feet or more in length) frame structures on stone basement walls and have deep extended forebays supported by wooden posts. They are upcountry posted-forebay barns and are identical to similar examples in southeastern and southern Wisconsin. Except for the simple H-bent of the main barn frame and the mortising of forebay beams into a plank sill above the stone stable front wall, they are virtually identical to their prototypes in Pennsylvania.

Most of the central Wisconsin Pennsylvania barns were built after 1900. They represent the last large group to be built in Canada and the United States. It has been suggested that they are the result of independent but parallel development (Bastian 1975, 200–204). When one compares them to similar barns in southern Wisconsin and back through the Midwest to Pennsylvania, the morphological continuity clearly defines them as Pennsylvania barns, however spatially disjunct they may be from their closest neighbors (Ensminger 1983).

Valuable insights concerning the barns in central Wisconsin were provided me by Edmund Schield, a retired barn builder, who was 78 years old when I interviewed him in 1981. He pointed out that the barns in the area were built under the supervision of professional barn builders, like Robert Hackbarth (who built Schield's brother's barn in 1908) who frequently promoted a favored barn style. These builders were knowledgeable businessmen who read the agricultural journals of the period, which regularly featured Pennsylvania barns. Many of the pioneers who settled the area came directly from northern Germany during the middle of the nineteenth century. Their sudden conversion to the Pennsylvania barn fifty years later was not due to in-migrating barn carriers. The diffusion of the Pennsylvania barn into central Wisconsin resulted from the spread of knowledge, rather than the spread of people. The agricultural literature certainly influenced individual farmers, but it more effectively influenced barn builders, who actively served as agents of diffusion. Wayne Price has documented the success of this process in the case of the progressive farmers and barn builders in Illinois who promoted and built round barns (1988, 16–21). The application of the Pennsylvania barn to large-scale dairying in central Wisconsin into the early twentieth century demonstrates its functional versatility.

Pennsylvania Barns in Missouri, Iowa, Nebraska, and Texas

As settlement pushed west beyond the Mississippi River in the middle nineteenth century, pioneers from the East, the South, and the Midwest were joined by immigrants from Europe. Included in this population were groups familiar with the Pennsylvania barn, who served as barn carriers. In central Missouri is a rare bank-into-forebay type located in the Germanic area of Morgan County; it was built by Mennonite farmers in 1875 (Ravensway 1977, 268–69). Other Pennsylvania barns have been documented in scattered locations across Missouri (Colville and Curran 1990). Emily Yoder Roberts, a barn researcher from Iowa, identified a Pennsylvania barn in Holt County, in northwestern Missouri (Figure 4.24). Its location near the state's western boundary suggests that Pennsylvania barns were carried into Kansas. Mennonite settlers reached northeastern Kansas in 1879 (Alderfer 1986, 19). I do not yet have documentation of Pennsylvania barns in Kansas, but if they do exist, they will eventually be reported.

The most significant cluster of Pennsylvania barns west of the Mississippi River is in southeastern Iowa, in Washington and Johnson counties, near the town of Kalona. Amish settlers from Pennsylvania and Ohio arrived in the area in 1846 (Wenger 1966, 117). Wooded valleys provided oak and walnut timbers suitable for the construction of heavy timber frame bents, and forebay bank barns were constructed by these barn carriers (Zielinski 1989, 135–39). The Old Order Amish in Iowa, who in 1972 had a population of over 2,000, have maintained a traditional agricultural landscape (Hostetler 1980, 100). The numerous Pennsylvania barns they have preserved represent the last serious stand in the barn's westward diffusion.

In determining the size of the Pennsylvania barn population in southeastern Iowa, I was assisted by Emily Yoder Roberts, who lives in Iowa City. She and several other barn enthusiasts did a partial field survey and accounted for sixty Pennsylvania barns in Johnson County and parts of adjacent Washington County. The survey did not include a comprehensive examination of the numerous Pennsylvania barns in the Amish areas around Kalona, in Washington County, that have been reported by John Zielinski (1989, 44, 135–37) or the Pennsylvania barns in northern Johnson County. Based on these data, it can be inferred that Johnson and Washington counties and environs contain at least 150 Pennsylvania barns. The area therefore ranks as the most significant Pennsylvania barn region west of the Mississippi River.

The most common barn in this population is the upcountry posted-forebay type of the extended Pennsylvania barn. The Iowan examples closely resemble those in southern and central Wisconsin. Balanced-gable standard barns also occur. This mix of middle and late nineteenth-century barn types is similar to the assemblage of structures found in many other Pennsylvania barn regions in the Midwest.

A scattering of Pennsylvania barns has been documented one county to the east, in Cedar County (*Cedar County Historical Review* 1980, 9, 16, 23, 33, 51, 75–76, 88–89). This group consists of at least eight structures, most of which are open- or closed-forebay standard types. One posted-forebay standard barn is much like those in Adams County, in western Illinois.

The presence of so many Pennsylvania barns in southeastern Iowa should come as no surprise. This area, which is far enough east to permit mixed livestock and grain farming, also lies directly in the path of pioneer movement west. The pattern of scattered small clusters plus larger and denser groupings of Pennsylvania barns that is found farther east occurs also in this westernmost region of significant barn frequency.

The diffusion west of the Pennsylvania barn did not stop abruptly in southeastern Iowa. Sightings have been reported near Des Moines, in the center of the state, and beyond, in eastern Nebraska. Professor Walter Kollmorgen recalled seeing them there as a youngster.[3] Morell Toelle, the owner of a barn near Beemer, Nebraska, told me that the barn had been built by his great-grandfather in the 1860s, after he migrated from Wisconsin. It was a timber frame structure with an original forebay, which he had called a shed (similar terminology is still used in Wisconsin). As is so frequently the case, this barn has been modified by complete enclosure of the under-forebay area and removal of the old front stable wall.

Terry Jordan documented a gable-ramp bank barn in Erath County, in central Texas, that has a forebaylike overhang on one eave side. He has

---

3. Letter from Johanna Kollmorgen, sister of Walter, dated March 18, 1984. According to Johanna, Walter remembered several Pennsylvania barns near Beemer, Cuming County, Nebraska, northwest of Omaha. He stated that more existed years ago, but most had disappeared. The names of several farmers who still had intact Pennsylvania barns were provided.

Figures 4.25 and 4.26. Two barns in southern Johnson County, in southeastern Iowa. The Sleichter barn (*top*) is a posted-forebay standard barn with closed forebay end walls. The stable front wall has been removed and the basement revised to provide pens for cattle and pigs. According to Emily Yoder Roberts, timbers for its frame were floated down the Mississippi River to Burlington, Iowa, and hauled overland by horse teams. Figure 4.26 (*bottom*) shows the Maas barn, circa 1880, an upcountry posted-forebay barn. This barn has two ramps on the rear side, for access to the upper level. Local lore says that it once served as an overnight stop for a circus en route to Iowa City. (Photos by Emily Yoder Roberts, used by her permission.)

Figure 4.27. The Wehmeyer barn, circa 1900, near Winthrop, Okanogan County, Washington, is one of the few known Pennsylvania barns in the Far West. (Photo, 1988, by Robert E. Walls, used by his permission.)

identified two barns with similar morphology in Bell County, Texas, and is aware of one other potential example in that area (1980–81, 72–77; 1983).

Pennsylvania Barns in the Far West

The diffusion of the Pennsylvania barn across the Central and Great Plains generally followed the westward advance of the agricultural frontier. Initially, the lack of irrigation and the dry farming technology on the semi-arid High Plains plus the early installation there of livestock ranching served as barriers to the continuation of agriculture as it was practiced farther east. There was no need for Pennsylvania barns on the cattle ranches and wheat farms of the High Plains.

The Oregon Trail directed pioneers from the East and Midwest across the western mountains and arid intermontane plateaus to the more humid Pacific ranges and valleys. Included in this group would have been many farmers who knew about Pennsylvania barns. Did these farmers carry their barns to the Far West? A recent article in the newsletter of the Washington State Folklore Council was sent to me by Terry Jordan (Walls 1989, 1). Clearly pictured in it is an all-frame forebay bank barn—a Pennsylvania barn in Washington State! I immediately contacted the author of the article, Robert E. Walls, to obtain more information. He supplied the following data and the photograph, which appears as Figure 4.27.

The barn is on the south side of Highway 20, eight miles northwest of

Figure 4.28. The Ivan Kropf barn near Hubbard, in the northern Willamette Valley, Oregon, is the westernmost Pennsylvania barn in North America known to me. (Photo by John Fraser Hart, used by his permission.)

Winthrop, in Okanogan County on the eastern slope of the northern Cascades, north of Lake Chelan. According to Walls, the barn has all the characteristic Pennsylvania features, including stalls in the basement and a possible granary enclosure in the forebay, which faces south. The barn was built around 1900, and the original farmstead included a blacksmith shop, carpenter shop, and milkhouse. The farmhouse still remains, but the barn is scheduled for demolition. William Wehmeyer, who built the barn, came from Goshen, Indiana, but was born in Philadelphia, in 1850. So the answer is yes, pioneers from the East and Midwest did successfully relocate the Pennsylvania barn to the Far West.

Is a Pennsylvania barn in northern Washington State an isolated occurrence, or could others exist in the region? All of the evidence presented in this chapter points strongly to the existence of Pennsylvania barns in areas of the Far West where settlers from the East and Midwest were able to transplant the agricultural practices with which they were familiar. The Willamette Valley of Oregon, with its variable marine climate, mixed forest and grassland vegetation, and deep fertile soils, would come close to replicating the homeland environment of many of these settlers. It was also the destination of the Oregon Trail. Aurora, fifteen miles south of the terminus of the Oregon Trail, was established in 1856 as a communal colony by settlers from Pennsylvania. The Old Aurora Colony Museum has preserved an original farmstead, including a Pennsylvania log farmhouse and a timber frame Pennsylvania Grundscheier.

The nearby community of Hubbard was settled by Mennonites in the 1870s and includes a Pennsylvania barn possibly built by them.[4] According to Philip Dole, of the University of Oregon in Eugene, this is the only surviving Pennsylvania barn in Oregon. It has a cantilevered forebay that faces north, away from local "south-storm" winds.[5] Its extended endwall and balanced gable silhouette (see Figure 4.28) qualify this structure as a half-open-forebay standard barn. A seam in the vertical siding, like the one visible on the gable wall of this barn, usually shows the location of the tie beam, on which the siding is nailed. Location of the tie beam below the eaves nearly always indicates that H-bents have been used for the barn frame. These characteristics, plus the cupola on the roof, are consistent with a barn built in the later nineteenth century. The current owner, Ivan Kropf, recently verified that the barn was built in 1889 by a brother of his mother. In a phone conversation with me he described the hewn-timber frame construction and the forebay, which he called the overshoot. In this structure we have evidence of the Pennsylvania barn's diffusion and distribution across the entire United States.

Conclusion

The vigor of the Pennsylvania barn tradition is demonstrated by its survival through 250 years of movement and change in Canada and the United States. If its origins in Graubünden, Switzerland, are added to the chronicle, the forebay bank barn can be traced for 7,000 miles and 400 years. This is an amazing record indeed. Barns, in general, are practical, functional structures, and they resist the influence of changing styles. In the case of the Pennsylvania barn, loyalty to the forebay tradition was deeply embedded in the minds of Pennsylvania-German culture groups. In addition, the barn's versatility helped preserve its fundamental form even while it underwent functional changes. Will the factors and conditions that have served to maintain the presence of the Pennsylvania barn for 250 years continue to operate in the future?

4. Phone conversation with Allen Epp of Portland Community College, Portland, Oregon, October 1989. Dr. Epp identified the family name of the barn's owners as Kropf, a local Mennonite name.

5. Phone conversations with Philip Dole, of the University of Oregon, and Alan Yoder, of the Old Aurora Colony Museum, in October 1989. Both scholars verified the barn's characteristics.

5

THE FUTURE OF THE PENNSYLVANIA BARN

For more than two hundred years, Pennsylvania barns have enriched agricultural landscapes across a broad region of the United States and Canada. What does the future hold for these magnificent vernacular structures? Suburban expansion continues to consume open spaces and to encroach upon farms within commuting distance of urban areas. Farm houses, barns, and outbuildings continue to fall to the blades of bulldozers in most urban zones. Comprehensive land use planning is frequently lacking, especially in rural areas, and historic preservation groups usually lack the political and financial clout to counteract financial and development interests. The Pennsylvania barn core lies within and adjacent to the rapidly urbanizing northeastern corridor, known as Megalopolis East. With its concentration of significant and early farm structures, the core is susceptible to a particularly important loss.

Developments in agricultural technology have rendered obsolete some of the original functions of many farm structures, including barns. Mechanization and farm consolidation continue to shrink the number of farms and farmers, while the cost of maintaining old farm buildings escalates.

Can this wave of change be managed, to protect the vernacular landscapes that connect us with our past and help us to define our national origins? There are some hopeful signs. Historical preservation in urban areas has become an active force in protecting and recycling historic structures and neighborhoods. With the support of both public funds and private investments, new uses are being made of the old areas of many cities. Similar strategies could be employed in rural areas. Local grass-roots organizations to preserve farmland as well as historic structures are attempting to counteract the subdivide-and-develop mentality.

An important way to preserve farmland and farm buildings is to maintain family farms. The vast majority of Pennsylvania barns still standing are privately owned by individual farmers. Most owners appreciate their barns, many of which have been in their families for several generations. They continue to use, and therefore maintain, their farm buildings. Usage is the key to preservation. Farmers realize that the replacement cost of a Pennsylvania barn could reach close to a million dollars for an all-stone structure.

Family farms may range from large agribusiness operations to small, intensive specialty farms. A growing interest in organic and alternative farming practices, yielding high-quality chemical-free products, may help preserve some smaller farms. High population growth rates among Amish and Mennonite groups, who are bound to agricultural traditions, result in maintenance of farms and barns and expansion of traditional agriculture into new regions.

Farmers must keep up with agricultural changes if they are to stay in business. This requires the enlargement and modification of existing farm buildings. Many Pennsylvania barns on functioning farms have, therefore, been enlarged and amended. While some purists might not approve, the bottom line is that the basic original structure of the barns is usually fairly well preserved.

Many small and part-time farmers raise crops and animals as a hobby or for supplemental income. This type of farming does not require extensive farm modification and, frequently, results in preservation of an original barn. This is particularly true of the upper level of Pennsylvania barns: even the hay and straw "packages" produced by modern baling machines can be accommodated in the original mows. Threshed grains, as in the past, can be stored in Pennsylvania barn granaries. The threshing floor of even a small barn is large enough to house most modern tractors and combines. Revisions of the basement stable are more likely to occur. Concrete and metal pens and stanchions usually replace the original wooden stalls and mangers. If hand-feeding and cleaning is practiced, the original basement layout may be retained.

The rarest type of barn preservation is restoration for historic and aesthetic purposes. In some cases, individual barn lovers have become involved in such projects for purely personal reasons. In other cases, efforts by local historical societies or county or state agencies have led to restoration. These restorations are usually part of museums or historic preservation sites. They are open to the public for educational and recreational purposes.

Distinctive results can occur when barns are renovated and recycled for totally new, nonagricultural functions. The conversion of barns to offices or stores may involve drastic interior remodeling to accommodate the new uses. Decorators and architects may participate in such projects, which, if planned properly, can result in aesthetically pleasing structures that maintain the integrity of the exterior barn form.

A more personal form of barn recycling is conversion to private residential use. An expensive undertaking, barn-to-house conversion can produce architectural showplaces that preserve the stonework or hand-hewn timber

Figure 5.1. Barn and pigsty with forebaylike overhang on the Walter Reidenhour farm near Kutztown, Berks County, Pennsylvania. (Photo 1989.)

frames and blend them artistically with the interior decor and arrangement of space. Some might feel that the simple functional honesty of the original barn structure is compromised by efforts such as these, but, be that as it may, if the basic barn structure is saved, this may not be too high a price to pay.

Small Traditional Farms

Small-scale and part-time farmers operate many of today's farms. The limited requirements of these operations have permitted on-going use of existing farm structures without drastic modification. Barns have remained intact and continue to function much as they did fifty to one hundred years ago. The example that follows is typical and will illustrate how this type of farming helps to preserve Pennsylvania barns.

Walter Reidenhour has been a farmer for forty-four years. During most of those years, he also worked full-time at a local foundry. His small thirty-five-acre farm is near Kutztown, Berks County, Pennsylvania. Having retired from the foundry, he now operates the farm full-time, but in a manner similar to that practiced fifty years ago. His farmstead is, therefore, simple and unchanged. It consists of a circa 1860 frame farmhouse and a small frame closed-forebay standard barn from the same period. There is a shed attached to one end of the barn, a garage, a chicken house, and a pigsty. Walter is currently raising twenty pigs, eight steers, assorted chickens, and ducks. Some of the animals scavenge about the barnyard, and he grows oats, barley, corn, and hay to use as feed. Some surplus corn is sold for cash, as are most of the pigs and steers. One steer and three pigs are butchered every winter for personal use.

The barn is largely unchanged, except for the later addition of a shed to the lower gable-end wall. The barn's upper level is completely original, but the stable has been modified. It has been opened into two pens for steers, eliminating the original stalls and part of the feeding aisle. The end of the basement that was originally a wagon shed now serves as a pen for cattle.

Much of the farm machinery, which is old and was purchased secondhand, and includes a tractor, combine, mower, baler, plow, drill, cultivator, harrow, and hay rake, is stored on a neighboring farm, where Walter provides some labor and other services. The old-fashioned style of operation of this farm allows for the preservation of its Pennsylvania barn with very few alterations.

Modern Farms

Large-scale farming is big business; it necessitates heavy investment in modern machinery and farm buildings and cultivation of a large acreage. These needs are often met by the incremental enlargement of a smaller farm through the purchase of more land, plus the rental of additional acreage, and a corresponding increase in the size and number of farm structures to house machinery, store products, and maintain livestock.

The usual first step in barn enlargement is to increase the area of the stable. This can be accomplished by enclosing the space under the forebay and eliminating the original front wall of the stable. The larger stable can then be revised to accommodate more livestock. In dairy farms, a gable-access center-aisle stable plan generally replaces the original front-access plan. This permits efficient feeding and mechanical removal of manure. If beef cattle are being raised, the stable may be converted to open pens where large numbers of animals can be maintained.

Adding to the barn is the second step in barn modification. It is readily accomplished by adding to the forebay side of the barn, thus increasing stabling and storage capacity. In spite of these modifications and amendments, the foundation and framework of the original barn are usually preserved. The assimilation of the original forebay into the additions may drastically change the appearance of the barn, but this is one of the costs of maintaining its agricultural functions.

The final stage of barn alteration is usually the addition and connection of complete buildings, sheds, or silos, which results in a rambling barn complex. The expenses incurred by large farming operations require intensive cultivation and the use of the latest production techniques. In many fertile areas, such as Lancaster County, Pennsylvania, or Holmes County,

Figures 5.2 and 5.3. The Dietrich barn (*top*), Klinesville, Berks County, Pennsylvania, has an enclosed forebay, added-on milkhouse, front shed, and loafing shed. The center feeding aisle (*bottom*) leads directly from a mixing room built around the base of the feed storage silos. (Photo 1990.)

Figure 5.4. Elwood Long's restored barn, circa 1790, Oley village, Berks County, Pennsylvania. Rectangular louvered openings provide light and ventilation for both mow and stable areas. (Photo 1990.)

Ohio, the extensive farmstead modification required by modern farming has made it difficult to identify the numerous Pennsylvania barns that occupy the countryside.

The Dietrich farm near Klinesville, in Berks County, Pennsylvania, is an excellent example of a modern family dairy farm that grew from a smaller farm in the way just described. This farm has been in the family since the early 1800s and is operated by William Dietrich and his wife, their son and his wife, plus two teenage grandchildren. These three generations share the 1859 stone farmhouse and provide all the labor necessary to operate the farm.

The farm has been enlarged to 190 acres, including 40 rented acres, providing a total of 175 acres of tillable land and 15 acres of woodland and pasture. This land produces all the feed grains and haylage necessary to maintain a herd of fifty milking cows. Crops include corn, wheat, soybeans, alfalfa, clover, and timothy, which can be stored in their one concrete stave silo and two steel Harvestore silos.

In the course of various farmstead enlargements, the Dietrichs have constructed several barn amendments and numerous outbuildings. In addition to the original blacksmith shop, butcher house, and wagon shed, the farm now has a pigsty, chicken house, woodshed, potato cellar, and several equipment sheds. Thus, storage is provided for eight tractors, a combine, plow, disc, corn planter, drill, cutter, rake, baler, and various wagons. A large truck shed houses three milk trucks, which are used to service twenty-nine local dairy farmers by transporting milk to the wholesale dairy in Allentown, Pennsylvania, thus generating additional income.

The original barn is a mid-nineteenth-century, stone closed-forebay standard barn that has been enlarged in four stages. An outshed was added on either side of the bank in the late 1800s. One of these housed a horse treadmill, which provided power for threshing. A two-level front shed was added to one corner of the forebay around 1900, giving the barn a three-gable configuration. The upper level of this wing provides storage for hay and straw, while the lower level provides open stabling space.

In 1952, the under-forebay space was enclosed, and two rows of stanchions were installed facing a center feeding aisle. Manure and the bedding of shredded newspaper and sawdust are removed mechanically from gutters behind each aisle, out of the barn, and into a spreader.

The feeding aisle leads directly from a feed-mixing shed adjacent to one gable wall. This shed encloses the bases of three silos, which store and dispense corn silage (green chopped cornstalks and ears), haylage (fermented alfalfa, clover and grasses), and high moisture shelled corn. Roasted soybeans are added to the blended feed, which is put into carts and wheeled into the stable. The milkhouse, located at the other gable end of the barn, was also built in 1952. Automatic milking equipment was installed in 1977.

The final amendment to the barn was a "loafing shed," which was attached to one end of the front shed in 1959. This is a large, covered pen in which the cows can stay, particularly in winter, when weather prohibits their going to the barnyard meadow between milkings.

The basic barn structure is still the functional center of the farmstead. When one talks with a farm family like the Dietrichs one senses their love of farm life. Functioning farms like theirs are among thousands on which Pennsylvania barns, however modified, have been preserved by continued use (Little 1988).

Barn Restorations by Individuals

Individual owners sometimes restore or maintain barns for personal reasons. Some are highly motivated barn lovers who gain satisfaction from the preservation of historic vernacular structures, in spite of the costs involved. Elwood Long of Oley, Berks County, Pennsylvania, exemplifies this type of personal dedication. In 1986, he purchased the property next to his residence, which included a classic stone Sweitzer barn in need of considerable restoration. His goal was to return it to its original eighteenth-century form. Mr. Long planned no special uses for this structure, only historic preservation consistent with the objectives of the Oley Heritage Association, which encourages similar projects throughout Oley Township.

This project has been in progress for over three years and the basic restoration has been completed. The first step was to repair the barn frame and roof support system. The original summer beam could be used, but all the forebay floor beams were replaced with red oak timbers from a nearby 200-year-old dismantled barn. Other beams from this barn were used to rebuild the two main inner bents, which were articulated by mortising and fastened with new hand-split wood pins.

After support was insured, the roof was repaired. Original rafters were retained, but new lath strips to hold shingles were needed. Hand-split cedar shakes, available only from Canada, were used to cover the roof, achieving the look of early barns.

The upper barn floor was completely replaced with 2-inch-thick, random-width yellow pine planks, which were nailed to the floor beams with hand-forged spikes ordered from a foundry in Tremont, Massachusetts. Because of the hardness of the supporting beams, predrilling was necessary to permit penetration of the spikes. Custom-cut, 12-inch white pine boards were used to cover the forebay frame and were fastened with old square-cut nails.

The barn's stone rear and gable walls have been pointed, but the stable has not yet been restored. Mr. Long has rebuilt the split stable doors and the large threshing floor doors. Original hand-forged hardware and hinges have been used throughout. The framing work, roofing, and pointing were done by a local contractor, while most of the remaining work will be completed by the owner. Mr. Long estimates that the total restoration costs will reach $35,000. His willingness to incur these expenses is a measure of his commitment. As he told me recently, he just loves doing it.

The Polak barn at New Smithville, in Lehigh County, Pennsylvania, is a fine example of a closed-forebay standard barn that has been perfectly maintained for personal and aesthetic reasons. Its elaborate barn decorations were repainted in 1960 and again in 1982. They provide one of the finest examples of barn decorative art in the country. Barn signs such as these are found only in a restricted area centering on Lehigh, Berks, and Lebanon counties. They were originally applied, beginning in the mid-nineteenth century, largely for decorative purposes and are maintained today as part of on-going efforts to preserve and promote Pennsylvania-German culture. A recent publication by Don Yoder and Thomas Graves (1989) provides detailed information about the decoration of Pennsylvania barns.

Preservation of Historic Structures and Open Land by Citizens' Organizations

Elwood Long's barn is in the Oley Valley, in Berks County, Pennsylvania. This valley is a small limestone valley very like the ones well known to settlers from the Palatinate. It lies between Philadelphia and the Great Valley and is drained by the Manatawny Creek system, which is tributary to the Schuylkill River. These streams provided routes to the Oley Valley from early settlements in and around Philadelphia.

Figure 5.5. The elaborately decorated Polak barn, circa 1850, near New Smithville, Lehigh County, Pennsylvania. (Photo 1990.)

The rich soil and easy accessibility of the valley led to its early settlement, as the frontier moved inland away from the tidewater region. The name Oley was derived either from an Indian word *oleka,* meaning kettle (for the shape of the valley), or from the German word *olich,* meaning oily, which could have referred to the oily texture of the rich black soil (Bertolet 1980 [1860], 1). Many tracts in the valley had already been surveyed by 1682, when William Penn took title to his colony (2). Although exploration by Swedes from the lower Delaware River occurred earlier, settlement surged after 1700, in response to the promotional strategies of William Penn. By the mid-eighteenth century, local family names were a mix of German, Swiss, French, and English. ("Oley Valley Heritage Festival" 1983, 4).

This diverse heritage has produced a varied group of vernacular structures with a strong Germanic component, and many remain today. There are very few rural locations in the United States where so rich an assemblage of early structures can be found in so compact an area. In 1980, an agreement was entered into between the National Trust for Historic Preservation and the Township of Oley. It was designed as a three-year, experimental, rural conservation project. Professional consultants and local citizens conducted studies of water resources, geology, and soils. Additional volunteers carried out agricultural and historic surveys. At the conclusion of the project in 1983, the entire township was admitted to the National Register of Historic

Figures 5.6, 5.7, and 5.8. Barns in Oley Valley, Berks County, Pennsylvania: Side-by-side Bertolet barns (*top left*), owned by Jim and Kathy Coker, permit comparison of a 1787 classic Sweitzer barn (*middle ground*) and an 1837 closed-forebay standard barn (*background*). The Maul barn (*bottom left*) is a later stone Grundscheier dated 1791 with one of two surviving pent roofs. The Shelley barn (*above*), the original date stone of which reads, "1793/GF" (George Focht). The distinctive brick arches over the stable doors and large draft door are found in other Oley Valley structures. The absence of a forebay is a trait also of many English Lake District bank barns in the counties adjacent to Philadelphia. (Photos 1990.)

Places, thus becoming the first rural national historic district in the United States (5–6).

In 1983, the Oley Valley Heritage Association was incorporated to continue conservation and historic preservation efforts (14). The association is dedicated to the maintenance of open land, retention of agricultural functions, and preservation of colonial heritage in the Oley Valley. It promotes educational activities, including lectures, tours, festivals, and exhibits. It sponsors scholarly research of original local deeds and documents and supports the Historic Oley Buildings and Archives Survey. This is an on-going project in which key examples of eighteenth-century farm outbuildings and small barns are being documented through measured drawings, photographs, and written analysis. This record will be available for future publication and for deposition in the Library of Congress.

The association has had its greatest success in stimulating community awareness and participation in preservation activities. Up to one hundred historic structures in Oley Valley have been preserved or restored. In the hamlet of Spangsville, which as a whole has been designated as historic, an ordinance requires property owners to get approval from an architectural review board before changing the exterior of any structure.

The local citizens' committee that formed the Oley Valley Heritage Association actively lobbied farmers in Oley Township to support Pennsylvania Act 43, the Agricultural Security Law; and, as a result, more than ninety landowners, owning nearly ten thousand acres, indicated an intent to keep their land in agricultural uses for seven years (12). In 1988, Pennsylvania Act 149 amended the original legislation, allowing additional acreage to be added to the agricultural security areas established under Act 43 and resulting in the inclusion of almost six hundred additional acres. More significantly, mechanisms and procedures were established for a statewide program to purchase agricultural conservation easements from landowners in agricultural security areas. Farmers willing to sell conservation easements to the state would be compensated for a portion of the development value of the land without having to take it out of production.

The association actively supports participation in these programs and is promoting effective agricultural zoning regulations to control suburban development and preserve agricultural land. The people of Oley Township have demonstrated that citizen involvement and grass-roots organizational efforts can be successful in preserving open space and historic structures (Stokes 1989, 51–57).

Historic Preservation by the Public Park System

Federal, state, and county parks, many of which contain structures of historic significance, have maintained and restored Pennsylvania barns as part of preservation complexes. The Daniel Boone Homestead, in Amity Township in the Oley Valley, is a good example. The Pennsylvania state park system has restored the historically significant circa 1750 farmhouse located on the homestead. A closed-forebay standard Pennsylvania barn has also been restored, although it is not the farmstead's original barn.

The colonial iron charcoal furnace at Hopewell Village, in southern Berks County, is an example of historic preservation by the National Park Service, and it also involves a Pennsylvania barn. The ironmaster's farmstead, which is part of this complex, includes an early nineteenth-century stone classic Sweitzer barn. This structure has been completely rebuilt with traditional framing and authentically restored to original specifications. Parks such as this guarantee public access to vernacular structures and insure their long-term preservation.

An example of public preservation that focuses directly on agricultural landscapes is provided by Springton Manor Farm, which is operated by the Chester County Parks and Recreation Department. It is in northwestern Chester County on three hundred acres that had originally been set aside by William Penn for his own use. The property passed through many owners and was last purchased in 1886 by George Bartol. Upon the death of Bartol's

Figure 5.9. This circa 1840 closed-forebay standard barn is part of the Daniel Boone Homestead Park, in the Oley Valley, Berks County, Pennsylvania. (Photo 1989.)

Figure 5.10. This restored classic Sweitzer barn, circa 1820, belongs to the ironmaster's big house at Hopewell Furnace National Historic Site in southern Berks County, Pennsylvania. (Photo 1990.)

Figures 5.11 and 5.12. Interior view of the upper level of Springton Manor barn, circa 1875, Chester County, Pennsylvania, shows mow and post-to-purlin bent. The open upper section of this bent permitted easy loading of the mow using the hay fork and track. Exterior view shows the conical stone forebay-support posts typical of Chester County barns and is evidence of their construction into the late nineteenth century. (Photos 1990.)

daughter, the property became part of a conservation trust, and it was placed on the National Register of Historic Places in 1979. In 1980, Springton Manor Farm was acquired by Chester County, which is developing it as an educational and recreational facility.

The land is being farmed as a model of conservation practices. Vegetable gardens, an orchard, and farm animals are maintained at the farmstead, which centers on the 1833 manor house and the large Pennsylvania barn. The barn maintains its agricultural functions and utilizes the barnyard as a petting zoo of farm animals. A museum depicting the development of farming in Chester County from 1800 to 1850 is housed in the upper level.

Springton Manor barn is a stone structure, and its post-to-purling framing, original hay track, and circular sawn timbers all indicate construction in the late nineteenth century. The deep forebay supported by conical stone columns provides an excellent example of the Chester County Pennsylvania barn described in Chapters 2 and 3 and demonstrates that its popularity continued for almost a century.

Recycling Pennsylvania Barns

The increasing urbanization of the United States can be expected to continue. Expanding suburbs and rural residential development will encroach upon agricultural land even around small cities. Farmsteads and barns will be swallowed up by this process.

Old buildings in areas of development can sometimes be saved by modification for new functions. The "adaptive reuse" of Pennsylvania barns is becoming increasingly popular throughout southeastern Pennsylvania.[1] Farms along major roads near urban areas are frequently engulfed by business sprawl. While the farm buildings are usually destroyed, occasionally some are converted and adapted to new functions. Because of their large size, barns are usually recycled into stores and offices. In spite of drastic remodeling, the forebays are frequently retained, preserving the building's original identity as a Pennsylvania barn. One example of adaptation for commercial use, Murdough's Christmas Barn, is on U.S. Route 422 near Womelsdorf, in Berks County. It has been in continuous use as a retail store since the 1950s.

The conversion of barns into homes is part of this growing trend in southeastern Pennsylvania. As the costs of constructing large, high-quality houses escalate, remodeling or even relocating barns for residential use is becoming more attractive. Dale Ahlum of Springtown, in Bucks County, is in the business of designing renovations of old farm buildings for alternative uses.[2] The Kerridge home in Williams Township, south of Easton, is an example of a Pennsylvania barn that has been relocated, redesigned, and remodeled into a unique and spacious residence by Mr. Ahlum. The cost of this type of conversion can be as much as $400,000 for a large barn. An all new home of equivalent size could cost as much but would lack the charm and handmade quality of a recycled barn.

A final example of barn preservation by adaptive reuse involved moving the structure one thousand miles. This project, conceived by Harold and Patti Campton, required the relocation of an early Ohio classical revival house and a Pennsylvania barn, from Wadsworth, Ohio, to central Florida. Both structures were dismantled, trucked to Citra, Florida, and then reassembled. The barn, a frame standard Pennsylvania type measuring 40 by 72 feet, was originally built in 1864. It has been set on a cement block foundation in its new location and serves several functions. The upper level houses an antique shop and apartment, while Harold Campton's photography studio and office occupy the stable area. Although this barn came to its location by an abnormal process, this structure is, to my knowledge, the southernmost Pennsylvania barn in the United States.

---

1. I first heard the term *adaptive reuse* from Samuel Cantrell, superintendent of Springton Manor Farm, in Chester County, Pennsylvania.

2. Snyder 1988 provides excellent pictures and details of a restoration designed by Dale Ahlum for a stone Pennsylvania barn.

Figure 5.13. This 1837 closed-forebay standard barn, located along Route 512 north of Bethlehem, in Northampton County, Pennsylvania, has been converted to a modern office building. Porthole ventilating openings like those seen here are found on numerous barns in the area. (Photo 1990.)

Figure 5.14. Murdough's Christmas Barn, near Womelsdorf, Berks County, Pennsylvania, is a retail store. (Photo 1990.)

Figure 5.15. The Ker-ridge home, near Easton, in Northampton County, Pennsylvania, has been expertly recycled from a mid-nineteenth-century closed-forebay standard barn. The dining room, shown here, is on what was originally the barn's central threshing floor. (Photo 1990.)

Figure 5.16. The Harold Campton barn, Citra, Florida, was relocated from Wadsworth, Ohio, and restored with combined business and residential functions. (Photo by Harold Campton, used by his permission.)

Contemporary Pennsylvania Barns

The need for new structures on functioning farms can be satisfied today by construction of simple ground-level buildings, such as pole barns. The cost of replicating a full-size Pennsylvania barn would be prohibitive, except where labor costs can be virtually eliminated, as they are in Amish and Mennonite communities. Large barns of heavy timber frame construction are still occasionally built in these communities by large crews of volunteers under the supervision of professional barn builders. Ivan Shirk, a Mennonite barn builder from Kutztown, Pennsylvania, is still putting up barns, but most of them utilize prefabricated trusses and frames made of commercial lumber. His last traditional barn, utilizing heavy oak mortise-and-tenoned timber frame bents, was constructed upon an early stone basement foundation in 1985. He hopes he will have the chance to build several more before retiring.

Amish builders from Lancaster County, Pennsylvania, are still constructing barns in the traditional way. Joseph Glass has observed several of their barn raisings and discussed the procedures with them. He provided the information that follows. A typical Amish builder uses a small hired crew that is reinforced by more than one hundred volunteer Amish laborers. The crew assembles traditional framing bents on the barn's upper floor, using commercial lumber. Builder and crew then supervise and help the volunteers, who raise and connect the bents in traditional fashion.

Sometimes, both Amish and other farmers will have old Pennsylvania barns disassembled and their frames moved and erected on new basement foundations. If volunteer labor is available for the disassembly phase, this procedure may be somewhat less expensive than using all new framing lumber, even though new roofing and siding are required to finish the barn.

One builder stated that the barns he has built for Amish farmers did not retain the forebay, even when using old Pennsylvania barn frames. By including the under-forebay space in a new basement, increased stable area is gained. The need for space has, therefore, displaced the traditional forebay form in most contemporary two-level barns in Amish areas and beyond. The same builder revealed that, in a few of the barns that he has constructed using old frames, specific instructions to retain the forebay were given. These involved non-Amish clients, who were not practicing commercial agriculture. They demonstrate that the forebay tradition is maintained today, if only in a small number of cases.

New structures modeled after Pennsylvania barns are occasionally built. A good example is the Jack Dolly barn near Lenhartsville, in Berks County. Built in 1977 to stable horses, it is a frame structure set on cement block stable walls. The upper level is cantilevered 6 feet over the stable front wall, producing a forebay, which is reinforced with wooden support posts. When asked about the barn's design, the owner said that he wanted to retain the style of the large Pennsylvania barn on the farm where he was raised, near Gettysburg.

Figure 5.17. The Jack Dolly barn near Lenhartsville, Berks County, Pennsylvania, was built in 1977 as a small posted-forebay standard barn. (Photo 1990.)

Figure 5.18. The Tworkoski barn, built in 1979, is in Berks County, Pennsylvania, near New Smithville (which is in Lehigh County). It is a unique posted-forebay bank barn, in that its upper level is made from a prefabricated, steel quonset hut. (Photo 1988.)

A unique example of a new Pennsylvania-type barn, located nearby at New Smithville, is the Tworkoski barn, built for horses and a few steers in 1979. The upper level consists of a prefabricated, steel quonset hut set on a cement stable built into a hillside. The quonset hut overhangs the stable by 10 feet, forming a rounded forebay supported by wooden posts. When asked why a Polish farmer would build a forebay barn, Mrs. Tworkoski answered that it was her idea. She is Pennsylvania-German and was raised a few miles away on a farm with a Pennsylvania barn. She also pointed out that the forebay overhang provided protection for tools and during manure removal. Here we see both the well-known influence of a farmer's wife and the strength of the forebay tradition, which has endured for more than four hundred years.

Conclusion

The completion of this book represents the fulfillment of my long-time dream to do a comprehensive study of the Pennsylvania barn. In addition to reviewing, evaluating, and summarizing the pertinent literature on this subject, it presents a new body of information, developed during fifteen years of research and fieldwork. I hope it will provide a record for other scholars of vernacular architecture, historical and settlement geography, and Pennsylvania-German culture to examine, refine, or revise, and that it will contribute to the development of more knowledge.

For me, a Pennsylvania German who has spent his entire life in south-eastern Pennsylvania, it has been a labor of love and an exercise in discovery. Like many native Pennsylvania Germans, I took for granted many of the unique elements of Pennsylvania-German culture. The joy of exploring this heritage led to the desire to share it with others. Thus it is with the Pennsylvania barn. This structure serves not only to symbolize but also to define the Pennsylvania-German region (Glass 1986, 21–38). The passage of time in America has not been kind to old buildings, including Pennsylvania barns. Fortunately, rural agricultural landscapes change more slowly than urban ones. Thousands of Pennsylvania barns have survived and continue to be used for agricultural purposes. I hope this book will lead to an even greater appreciation of these magnificent vernacular barns and contribute to their long-term survival on the American landscape.

APPENDIX A
Supplemental Sightings of Pennsylvania Barns

Documentation of Sightings by Observers Other Than the Author

1. Apps and Allen 1977, 21, 23, 36: pictures of Pennsylvania barns in Wisconsin.

2. Bastian 1975, 200–204: Pennsylvania barns in Lincoln and Marathon counties, Wisconsin.

3. Bennett 1977, 112: stone-arch-forebay barn near New Castle, Delaware.

4. Bertland 1974, 18, 24–25, 80: Pennsylvania barns in Warren County, New Jersey.

5. *Cedar County Historical Review* 1980, 9, 16, 23, 33, 51, 75–76, 88–89: Pennsylvania barns in Cedar County, Iowa.

6. Coffee 1978, 55: Pennsylvania barns in Geauga County, Ohio.

7. Colville and Curran 1990, 22, 28: pictures of Pennsylvania barns in Missouri.

8. Conlyn 1983, 70–73: Pennsylvania barns in Erie County, New York.

9. Cooper 1982, 294–95: Pennsylvania barns in Iowa.

10. Ennals 1972, 265–69: Pennsylvania barns in southern Ontario.

11. Glass 1971: first map of Pennsylvania barn region; maps of Pennsylvania barn types.

12. Glassie 1965a, 27–29: Pennsylvania barns in the South from Maryland to Tennessee.

13. Glassie 1965b, 9, n. 2: Pennsylvania barns in Franklin and Green counties, Ohio.

14. Glassie 1966, 12–25: more Pennsylvania barns in the South from Maryland to Tennessee.

15. Harper and Smith 1988, 73–81: Pennsylvania barns in Adams County, Indiana.

16. Hutslar 1977, 50: log Sweitzer Pennsylvania barn in Ohio.

17. Jordan 1980–81, 73: map showing distribution of forebay barns in eastern United States and southeastern Canada.

18. Kiefer 1972, 494–503: Pennsylvania barns in Marshall and St. Joseph counties, Indiana.

19. Kreider et al. 1988, 45: picture of the Neuenschwander barn near Bluffton, Ohio.

20. Leestma 1951, 99: Pennsylvania barn in Clare County, Michigan.

21. Ludwig 1947, 29: map showing region west of Pennsylvania with strong Pennsylvania-German settlement and influence.

22. Ludwig 1964, 42–54: Pennsylvania barns in Johnson County, Iowa, and scattered occurrences in Nebraska.

23. Noble 1977, 62–79: Pennsylvania barns in Ohio.

24. "Old Picturesque Barns Are Fast Becoming Endangered Species" 1964, (June 3), 6: picture of Pennsylvania barn near Astoria, Illinois.

25. Perrin 1981, 57–58: Pennsylvania barns in Green and Rock Counties, Wisconsin.

26. Price 1987, 29–35: summary of Pennsylvania barns in Adams County, Illinois.

27. Price 1988, 9–12: statewide summary of Pennsylvania barns in Illinois.

28. Price and Sculle 1985, 45–53: Pennsylvania barns in Stephenson County, Illinois.

29. Ravensway 1977, 269: Pennsylvania barn in Morgan County, Missouri.

30. Rawson 1979, 56–60: Pennsylvania barn in Butler County, Pennsylvania.

31. Ridlen 1972, 25–43: twenty-two Pennsylvania barns in Cass County, Indiana, including one stone barn, one double-decker barn, and one unusual gable-ramp barn with 15-foot gable forebay supported by conical stone columns.

32. Schreiber 1967, 25–43: Pennsylvania barns in Ohio.

33. Stotz 1966, 78, 146–48: Pennsylvania barns in western Pennsylvania.

34. Sutton 1980, 9–22: Pennsylvania barn near Helvetia, West Virginia.

35. Wacker 1974, 173–74: Pennsylvania barns in New Jersey.

36. Wells 1976: possible log forebay barn pictured at Defiance, Missouri; gable-forebay Pennsylvania barn pictured at Janesville, Iowa.

37. Wilhelm 1974, 155–62: Pennsylvania barns in southeastern Ohio.

38. Wilhelm 1989a: Pennsylvania barns in southeastern Ohio.

39. Wilhelm 1989b, 29–37: Pennsylvania double-overhang barns in southeastern Ohio.

40. Zielinski 1982: Pennsylvania barns in Iowa.

41. Zielinski 1989: Amish Pennsylvania barns across America.

Sightings Reported Directly to the Author

1. James Darlington of Queens University, Kingston, Ontario, and Randy Nash, Canasota, New York, have photographically documented a group of Pennsylvania barns between Plainville and Fulton, New York. At least one of these barns has a double overhang.

2. Terry Donnelly displayed a photo of a Pennsylvania barn in Bureau County, in northwestern Illinois, at Western Illinois University, Macomb, during the Pioneer America Society meetings, 7 October 1983.

3. Loren Gannon of the Ohio Preservation Office, Wright State University, Dayton, verified a Pennsylvania barn count of at least 75 per county in the region paralleling the National Road in Clark, Montgomery, and Preble counties, and extending into Miami, Darke, and Green counties in western Ohio.

4. Steve Gordon of the Ohio Preservation Office, Columbus, surveyed the Garver barn near Hamilton, in southwestern Ohio. This is a rare Sweitzer type with a stone foundation but a log plank front stable wall.

5. Steve Gordon identified a cluster of several stone Pennsylvania barns along the corridor of U.S. Route 23 in Delaware County, Ohio.

6. A significant region of at least 75 Pennsylvania barns has been identified in northwestern Ohio by Glenn Harper of the Ohio Preservation Office, Bowling Green. They are located in the boundary area of Putnam and Allen counties. Herman Hilty and Darvin Luginbuhl of the Swiss Community Historical Society of Bluffton-Pandora, Ohio, verified this barn region. Mr. Hilty also mentioned 2 double-gable ramp bank barns with drive-through threshing floors near Bluffton. One, the Schumacher barn, had been in his family since its construction in 1843. It now belongs to the Swiss Historical Society of Bluffton. The other, the Neuenschwander barn, built in 1864, is a double-eave-forebay barn. These rare types have been reported in only a few locations.

7. John Fraser Hart of the University of Minnesota, Minneapolis, photographically documented a Pennsylvania barn west of Indianapolis.

8. Forebay barns occur in Greene and Fayette counties, in southwestern Pennsylvania. Their presence was first reported to me by Marguerite Keeler, curator of the Folkcraft Center, at Witmer, Pennsylvania, and verified by LeRoy Schultz of the University of West Virginia, who surveyed barns in West Virginia, and southwestern Pennsylvania. Ms. Keeler also identified several forebay barns in Monongalia County, West Virginia, which may represent diffusion up the Monongahela Valley from Pennsylvania.

9. A letter from Johanna Kollmorgen, March 1984, to Dr. Walter Kollmorgen, verified 2 Pennsylvania barns near Beamer, Nebraska, and 1 near Humphrey, in Platte County.

10. William G. Laatsch of the University of Wisconsin at Green Bay reported a group of forebay barns in those sections of Kewaunee and Manitowoc counties, Wisconsin, that were settled by Bohemian and Czech pioneers.

11. William Laatsch, Allen Noble, and John Fraser Hart identified a Pennsylvania barn on the Door Peninsula, in Wisconsin.

12. Marian Moffett and Lawrence Wodenhouse of the University of Tennessee, identified a Pennsylvania barn in the northern outskirts of Knoxville, Tennessee.

13. Dr. Greg Moore of Weedville, Pennsylvania, identified several Pennsylvania barns near Frenchville, Pennsylvania.

14. Allen Noble, of the University of Akron, in a conversation in October 1981, reported a large forebay barn south of Des Moines, in Madison County, Iowa, and another in central Marshall County, northeast of Des Moines.

15. Allen Noble, in a phone conversation on 29 November 1989, verified the barn count that qualifies the northeastern Ohio quadrant as a significant Pennsylvania barn region. He personally counted more than 100 Pennsylvania barns in Columbiana County and estimates that the following counties easily meet the 75-barn per county criterion: Stark, Tuscarawas, Holmes, Wayne, Ashland, and Richland.

16. Allen Noble sighted Pennsylvania barns along U.S. Route 224 in northwestern Ohio and farther west in Wabash County, Indiana.

17. Allen Noble provided a photo, taken in 1977, of a log Sweitzer barn near Boswell, Pennsylvania.

18. A letter from Wayne Price of the Pioneer America Society, in August 1989, provided photographs of 2 unusual gable-forebay barns in Sangamon County, Illinois.

19. Wayne Price reported to the Pioneer America Society, in fall of 1986, a group of 75 to 100 Pennsylvania barns in Adams County, Illinois. He reported the following additional sightings directly to me: a group of Pennsylvania barns in the western part of Owen County, Indiana, including several with a double overhang; some along the Macon-Piatt county line, east of Decatur, Illinois, where settlement was made by members of the Church of the Brethren (German Baptist) around 1870, one family of which can be traced back through Indiana, Ohio, and Lancaster County, Pennsylvania, to Switzerland; and west of Jacksonville, in Scott County, Illinois; near Astoria, in Fulton County, Illinois; in Sangamon, Winnebago, Lee, and Ogle counties, Illinois; and near Plainfield, in Will County, Illinois. Wayne Price noted that Brethren families in the Midwest frequently built Pennsylvania barns.

20. A survey in 1984 by Wayne Price and Keith Sculley of the Illinois Department of Conservation, identified 136 Pennsylvania barns in Stephenson County, in northern Illinois.

21. Herbert Richardson of Glassboro State College, Glassboro, New Jersey, identified several forebay barns in Salem and Gloucester counties, New Jersey.

22. Orlando Ridout of the Maryland Historical Trust, Annapolis, identified forebay barns on the Eastern Shore of Maryland.

23. Emily Yoder Roberts of Iowa City, Iowa, in October 1989, verified that there are more than 75 Pennsylvania barns in Johnson County and Washington County, Iowa, combined, and scattered occurrences in Iowa County just to the west. In a conversation in August 1991, she reported a Pennsylvania barn in Holt County, Missouri, that she had previously photographed.

24. Lynn Sprankle of Kutztown University, Kutztown, Pennsylvania, sighted a Pennsylvania barn near Rochester, Indiana.

25. Bill Tishler and Jane Eisley of the University of Wisconsin, Madison, Wisconsin, documented the Tobler barn, a Pennsylvania barn in Sauk County, Wisconsin.

26. LeRoy Troyer of Mishawaka, Indiana, and Terry Herschberger of Middlebury, Indiana, both verified the existence of several hundred Pennsylvania barns in Elkhart and La Grange counties, in northeastern Indiana.

27. Willard Wichers of the Netherlands Museum, Holland, Michigan, in a letter of 22 September 1983, documented a Pennsylvania barn in St. Joseph County, in southern Michigan.

28. Hubert Wilhelm of Ohio University, Athens, identified a cluster of 30 or more Pennsylvania barns in Monroe County, in southeastern Ohio.

29. Hubert Wilhelm, in a letter in March 1990, reported a Pennsylvania barn in central Brown County, in southwestern Ohio.

30. Hubert Wilhelm, in December 1991, verified a previous estimate that Perry and Lancaster counties, Ohio, each have at least 75 Pennsylvania barns.

Sightings beyond the Limits of Map 4.1

1. Arthur and Witney 1972, 123–24, 132: scattered forebay barns in eastern Quebec.

2. The Harold Campton barn, now near Citra, Florida, was reassembled and restored after being relocated from Wadsworth, Ohio.

3. Jordan 1980–81, 72–77: gable-ramp forebay bank barn in Erath County, in central Texas.

4. Montell and Morse (1976, 78) state that some bank barns that occur

in north-central Kentucky may have forebays, but they provide no specific locations.

5. Walls 1989, 1: Pennsylvania barn near Mazama, Washington.

6. Alan Yoder of the Old Aurora Colony Museum, Aurora, Oregon, verified the existence of a Pennsylvania barn near Hubbard, Oregon, in a region of early Pennsylvania settlement. Philip Dole of the University of Oregon, Eugene, examined the barn, and his description to me suggested a late nineteenth-century standard Pennsylvania barn.

APPENDIX B
Classification of Pennsylvania Barns by Charles Dornbusch*

*Dornbusch and Heyl 1958. Reprinted by permission of the Pennsylvania German Society.

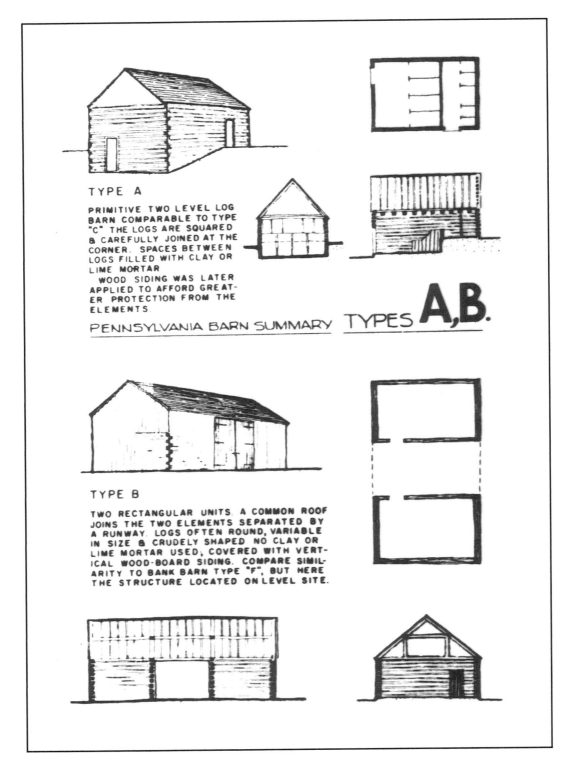

TYPE A

PRIMITIVE TWO LEVEL LOG
BARN COMPARABLE TO TYPE
"C" THE LOGS ARE SQUARED
& CAREFULLY JOINED AT THE
CORNER. SPACES BETWEEN
LOGS FILLED WITH CLAY OR
LIME MORTAR
   WOOD SIDING WAS LATER
APPLIED TO AFFORD GREAT-
ER PROTECTION FROM THE
ELEMENTS.

PENNSYLVANIA BARN SUMMARY TYPES **A,B.**

TYPE B

TWO RECTANGULAR UNITS. A COMMON ROOF
JOINS THE TWO ELEMENTS SEPARATED BY
A RUNWAY. LOGS OFTEN ROUND, VARIABLE
IN SIZE & CRUDELY SHAPED NO CLAY OR
LIME MORTAR USED; COVERED WITH VERT-
ICAL WOOD-BOARD SIDING. COMPARE SIMIL-
ARITY TO BANK BARN TYPE "F", BUT HERE
THE STRUCTURE LOCATED ON LEVEL SITE.

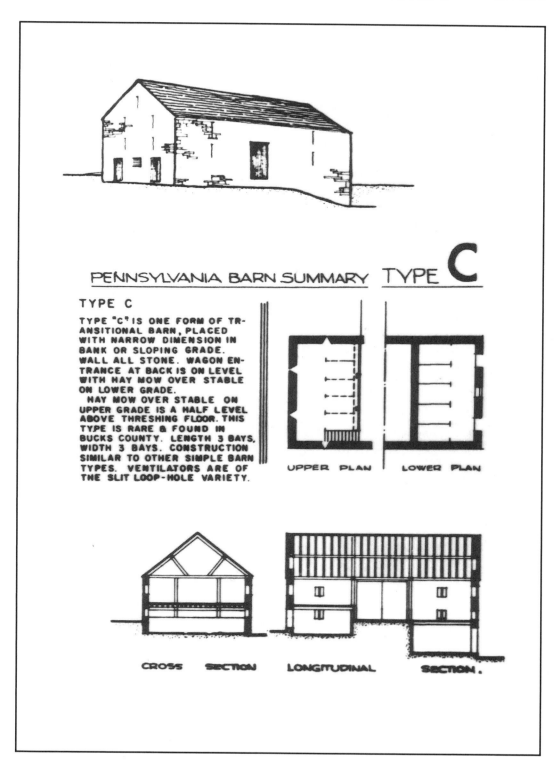

PENNSYLVANIA BARN SUMMARY   TYPE C

TYPE C

TYPE "C" IS ONE FORM OF TR-
ANSITIONAL BARN, PLACED
WITH NARROW DIMENSION IN
BANK OR SLOPING GRADE.
WALL ALL STONE. WAGON EN-
TRANCE AT BACK IS ON LEVEL
WITH HAY MOW OVER STABLE
ON LOWER GRADE.
  HAY MOW OVER STABLE ON
UPPER GRADE IS A HALF LEVEL
ABOVE THRESHING FLOOR. THIS
TYPE IS RARE & FOUND IN
BUCKS COUNTY. LENGTH 3 BAYS,
WIDTH 3 BAYS. CONSTRUCTION
SIMILAR TO OTHER SIMPLE BARN
TYPES. VENTILATORS ARE OF
THE SLIT LOOP-HOLE VARIETY.

UPPER PLAN   LOWER PLAN

CROSS   SECTION   LONGITUDINAL   SECTION.

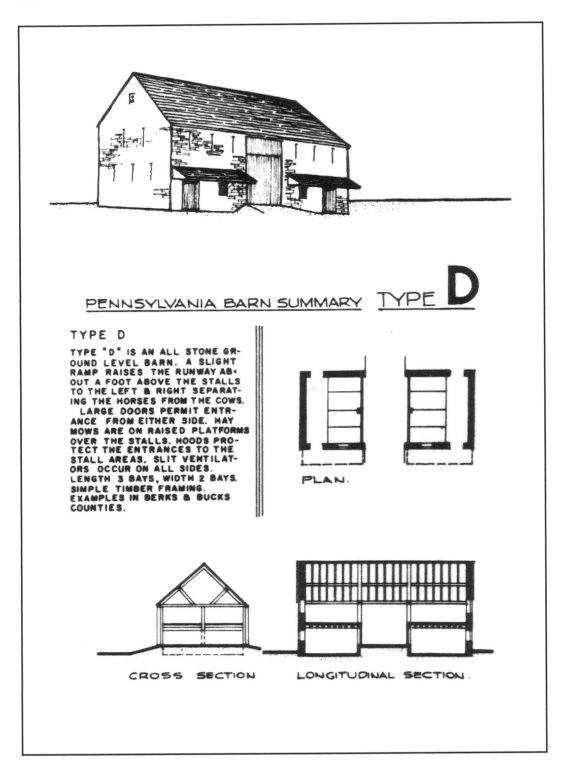

PENNSYLVANIA BARN SUMMARY TYPE **D**

TYPE D

TYPE "D" IS AN ALL STONE GROUND LEVEL BARN. A SLIGHT RAMP RAISES THE RUNWAY ABOUT A FOOT ABOVE THE STALLS TO THE LEFT & RIGHT SEPARATING THE HORSES FROM THE COWS.
  LARGE DOORS PERMIT ENTRANCE FROM EITHER SIDE. HAY MOWS ARE ON RAISED PLATFORMS OVER THE STALLS. HOODS PROTECT THE ENTRANCES TO THE STALL AREAS. SLIT VENTILATORS OCCUR ON ALL SIDES. LENGTH 3 BAYS, WIDTH 2 BAYS. SIMPLE TIMBER FRAMING. EXAMPLES IN BERKS & BUCKS COUNTIES.

PLAN.

CROSS SECTION

LONGITUDINAL SECTION.

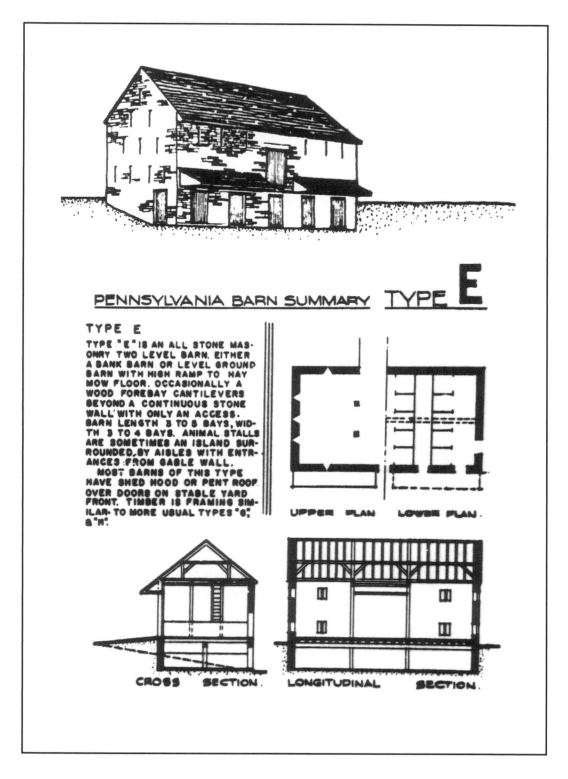

PENNSYLVANIA BARN SUMMARY   TYPE E

TYPE E

TYPE "E" IS AN ALL STONE MAS-
ONRY TWO LEVEL BARN, EITHER
A BANK BARN OR LEVEL GROUND
BARN WITH HIGH RAMP TO HAY
MOW FLOOR. OCCASIONALLY A
WOOD FOREBAY CANTILEVERS
BEYOND A CONTINUOUS STONE
WALL WITH ONLY AN ACCESS.
BARN LENGTH 3 TO 5 BAYS, WID-
TH 3 TO 4 BAYS. ANIMAL STALLS
ARE SOMETIMES AN ISLAND SUR-
ROUNDED BY AISLES WITH ENTR-
ANCES FROM GABLE WALL.

MOST BARNS OF THIS TYPE
HAVE SHED HOOD OR PENT ROOF
OVER DOORS ON STABLE YARD
FRONT. TIMBER IS FRAMING SIM-
ILAR TO MORE USUAL TYPES "G",
& "H".

UPPER PLAN   LOWER PLAN.

CROSS   SECTION.   LONGITUDINAL   SECTION.

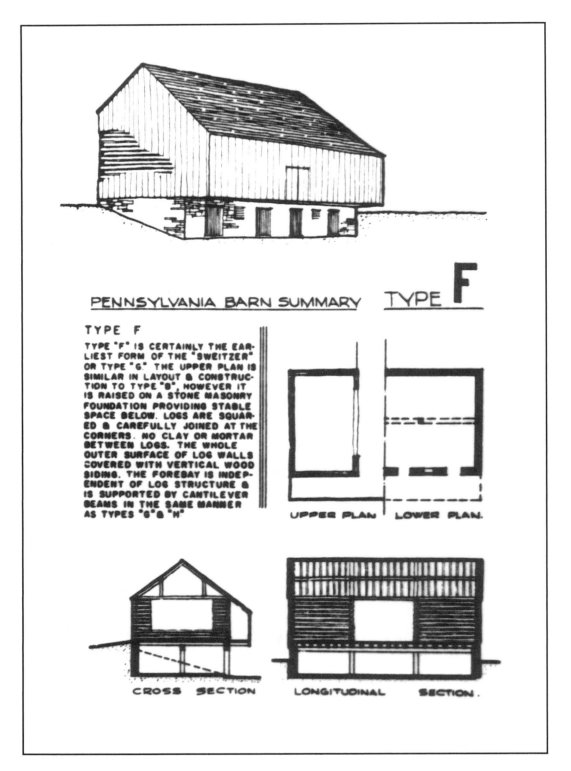

PENNSYLVANIA BARN SUMMARY   TYPE F

TYPE F

TYPE "F" IS CERTAINLY THE EAR-
LIEST FORM OF THE "SWEITZER"
OR TYPE "G". THE UPPER PLAN IS
SIMILAR IN LAYOUT & CONSTRUC-
TION TO TYPE "B", HOWEVER IT
IS RAISED ON A STONE MASONRY
FOUNDATION PROVIDING STABLE
SPACE BELOW. LOGS ARE SQUAR-
ED & CAREFULLY JOINED AT THE
CORNERS. NO CLAY OR MORTAR
BETWEEN LOGS. THE WHOLE
OUTER SURFACE OF LOG WALLS
COVERED WITH VERTICAL WOOD
SIDING. THE FOREBAY IS INDEP-
ENDENT OF LOG STRUCTURE &
IS SUPPORTED BY CANTILEVER
BEAMS IN THE SAME MANNER
AS TYPES "G" & "H"

UPPER PLAN   LOWER PLAN.

CROSS SECTION   LONGITUDINAL   SECTION.

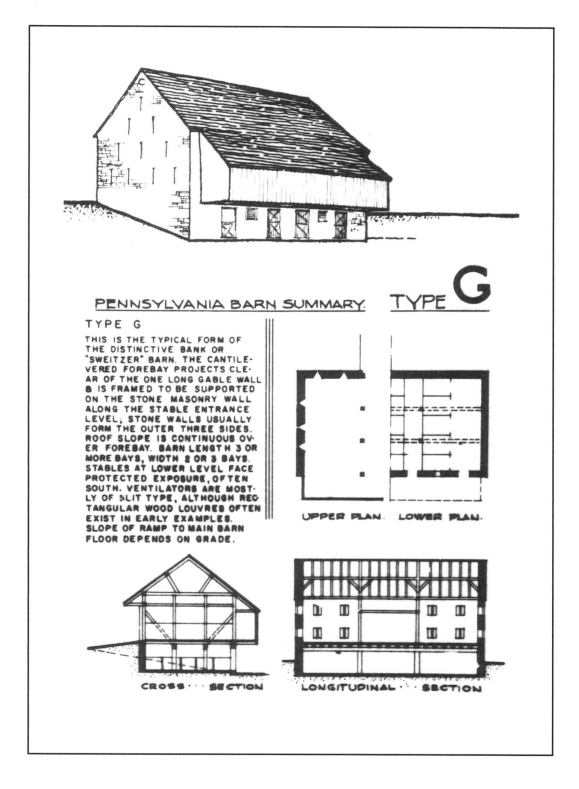

PENNSYLVANIA BARN SUMMARY. TYPE **G**

TYPE G

THIS IS THE TYPICAL FORM OF THE DISTINCTIVE BANK OR "SWEITZER" BARN. THE CANTILEVERED FOREBAY PROJECTS CLEAR OF THE ONE LONG GABLE WALL & IS FRAMED TO BE SUPPORTED ON THE STONE MASONRY WALL ALONG THE STABLE ENTRANCE LEVEL; STONE WALLS USUALLY FORM THE OUTER THREE SIDES. ROOF SLOPE IS CONTINUOUS OVER FOREBAY. BARN LENGTH 3 OR MORE BAYS, WIDTH 2 OR 3 BAYS. STABLES AT LOWER LEVEL FACE PROTECTED EXPOSURE, OFTEN SOUTH. VENTILATORS ARE MOSTLY OF SLIT TYPE, ALTHOUGH RECTANGULAR WOOD LOUVRES OFTEN EXIST IN EARLY EXAMPLES. SLOPE OF RAMP TO MAIN BARN FLOOR DEPENDS ON GRADE.

UPPER PLAN. LOWER PLAN.

CROSS SECTION   LONGITUDINAL SECTION

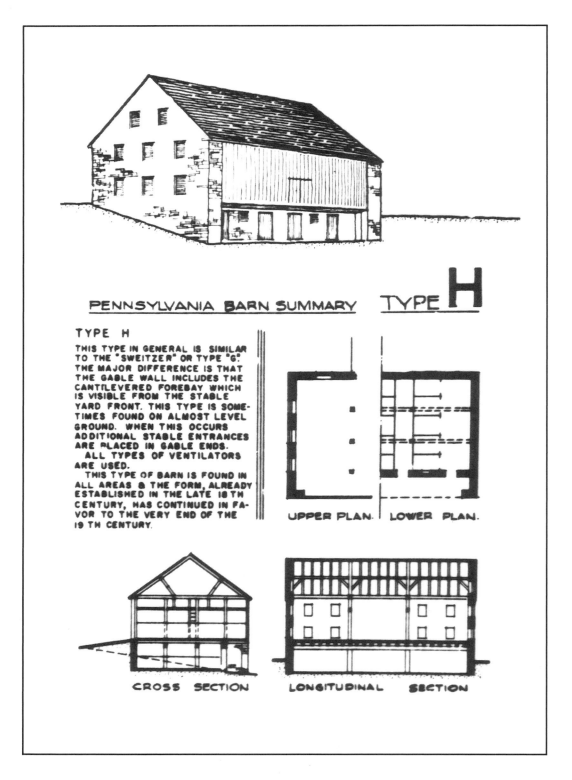

PENNSYLVANIA BARN SUMMARY   TYPE H

TYPE H

THIS TYPE IN GENERAL IS SIMILAR
TO THE "SWEITZER" OR TYPE "G".
THE MAJOR DIFFERENCE IS THAT
THE GABLE WALL INCLUDES THE
CANTILEVERED FOREBAY WHICH
IS VISIBLE FROM THE STABLE
YARD FRONT. THIS TYPE IS SOME-
TIMES FOUND ON ALMOST LEVEL
GROUND. WHEN THIS OCCURS
ADDITIONAL STABLE ENTRANCES
ARE PLACED IN GABLE ENDS.
    ALL TYPES OF VENTILATORS
ARE USED.
    THIS TYPE OF BARN IS FOUND IN
ALL AREAS & THE FORM, ALREADY
ESTABLISHED IN THE LATE 18 TH
CENTURY, HAS CONTINUED IN FA-
VOR TO THE VERY END OF THE
19 TH CENTURY.

UPPER PLAN.   LOWER PLAN.

CROSS SECTION   LONGITUDINAL SECTION

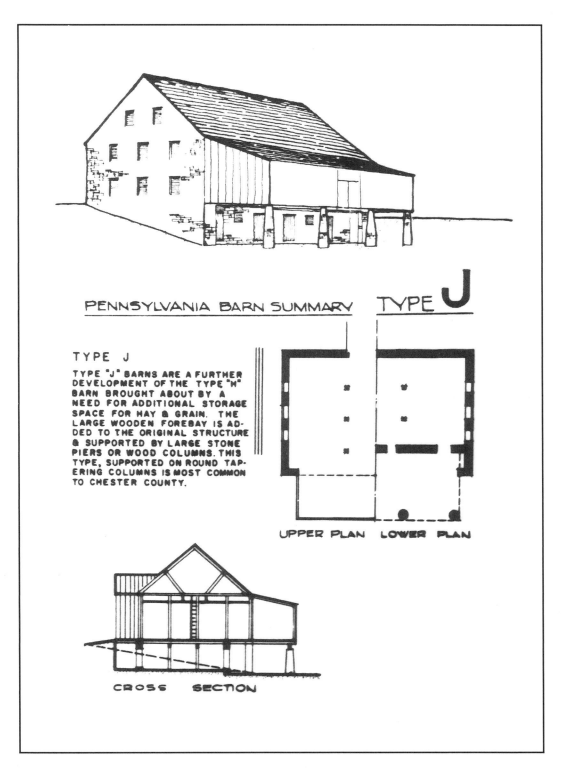

PENNSYLVANIA BARN SUMMARY   TYPE **J**

TYPE J

TYPE "J" BARNS ARE A FURTHER DEVELOPMENT OF THE TYPE "H" BARN BROUGHT ABOUT BY A NEED FOR ADDITIONAL STORAGE SPACE FOR HAY & GRAIN. THE LARGE WOODEN FOREBAY IS ADDED TO THE ORIGINAL STRUCTURE & SUPPORTED BY LARGE STONE PIERS OR WOOD COLUMNS. THIS TYPE, SUPPORTED ON ROUND TAPERING COLUMNS IS MOST COMMON TO CHESTER COUNTY.

UPPER PLAN   LOWER PLAN

CROSS   SECTION

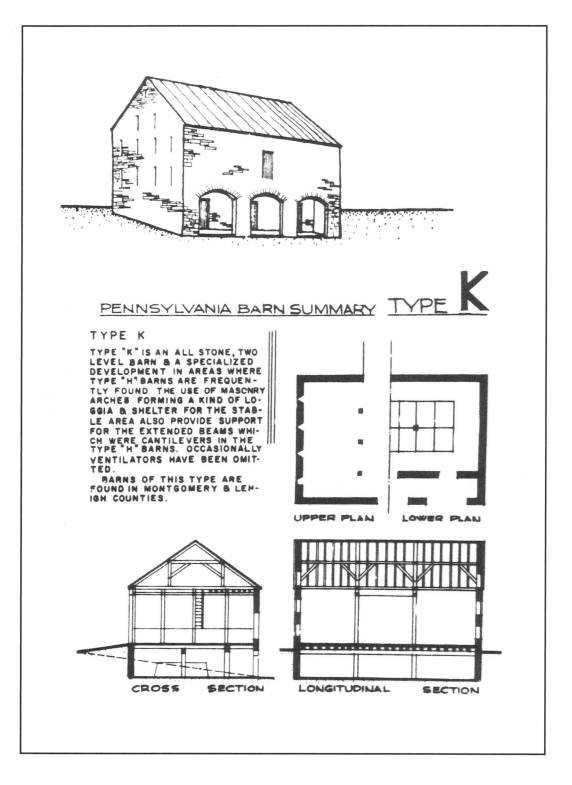

PENNSYLVANIA BARN SUMMARY TYPE K

TYPE K

TYPE "K" IS AN ALL STONE, TWO
LEVEL BARN & A SPECIALIZED
DEVELOPMENT IN AREAS WHERE
TYPE "H" BARNS ARE FREQUEN-
TLY FOUND. THE USE OF MASONRY
ARCHES FORMING A KIND OF LO-
GGIA & SHELTER FOR THE STAB-
LE AREA ALSO PROVIDE SUPPORT
FOR THE EXTENDED BEAMS WHI-
CH WERE CANTILEVERS IN THE
TYPE "H" BARNS. OCCASIONALLY
VENTILATORS HAVE BEEN OMIT-
TED.
   BARNS OF THIS TYPE ARE
FOUND IN MONTGOMERY & LEH-
IGH COUNTIES.

UPPER PLAN   LOWER PLAN

CROSS SECTION   LONGITUDINAL SECTION

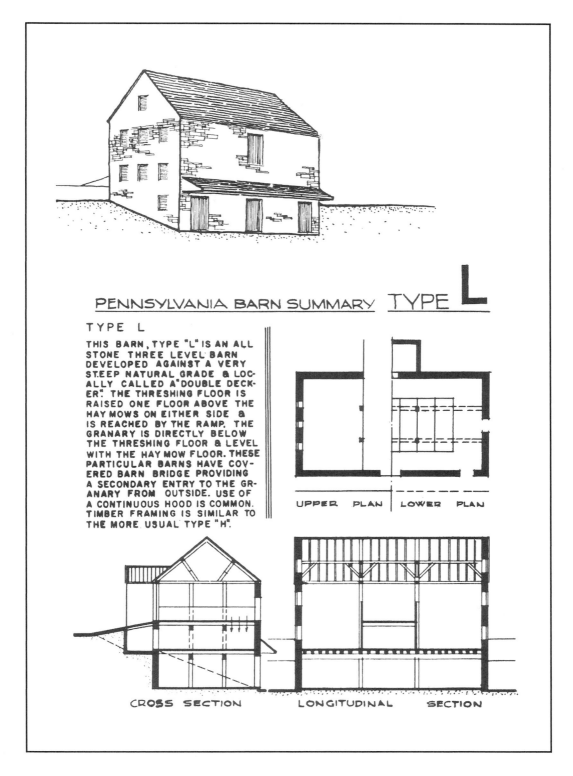

PENNSYLVANIA BARN SUMMARY TYPE L

TYPE L

THIS BARN, TYPE "L" IS AN ALL STONE THREE LEVEL BARN DEVELOPED AGAINST A VERY STEEP NATURAL GRADE & LOCALLY CALLED A "DOUBLE DECKER". THE THRESHING FLOOR IS RAISED ONE FLOOR ABOVE THE HAY MOWS ON EITHER SIDE & IS REACHED BY THE RAMP. THE GRANARY IS DIRECTLY BELOW THE THRESHING FLOOR & LEVEL WITH THE HAY MOW FLOOR. THESE PARTICULAR BARNS HAVE COVERED BARN BRIDGE PROVIDING A SECONDARY ENTRY TO THE GRANARY FROM OUTSIDE. USE OF A CONTINUOUS HOOD IS COMMON. TIMBER FRAMING IS SIMILAR TO THE MORE USUAL TYPE "H".

UPPER PLAN | LOWER PLAN

CROSS SECTION

LONGITUDINAL SECTION

GLOSSARY

Added-on forebay. Forebay built on to a nonforebay barn or added to an existing forebay.

Added-on outshed. Shed added adjacent to ramp on rear side of a barn.

Alemanni. Ancient Germanic people who occupied the Alpine areas of central Europe.

Bank barn. Two-level barn whose upper level is entered from a bank or hillside or by a ramp constructed against the barn.

Basement barn. Nonforebay, two-level bank barn with stables on first level (basement) and hay, straw, and grain storage on upper level.

Basement drive-through standard barn. Standard Pennsylvania barn with machinery bay in lower level that opens on both forebay and bank sides of barn.

Bay. Area of a building, physically defined and used for specific functions.

Bent. Heavy timber framework section of barn's superstructure which is connected to similar sections to complete the barn frame.

Bent configuration. Pattern produced by posts, tie beams, and braces of an assembled bent.

Bent typology. Study and comparison of variations in bent configuration.

Breton barn. Typical long ground barn from Brittany, in France.

Brickender. Pennsylvania barn of brick construction with prominent, brick gable-end walls.

Cantilevered. Supported by beams which extend from the supported feature (e.g., a forebay) back beneath the superstructure of a building.

Canton. Any of the states in the Swiss confederation.

Chinked. Filled with mud, moss, or the like to provide insulation, as the interstices in a log wall.

Chischner. Large, freestanding, grain-drying rack found in Romansch settlements in the Swiss Alps. *See* Talina

Classic Sweitzer barn. Early Pennsylvania barn type, characterized by asymmetrical gable ends and an unposted cantilevered forebay.

Closed-forebay standard barn. Standard Pennsylvania barn type in which gable-end walls extend to end of forebay front wall, closing the under-forebay space at the ends.

Collar beam. The horizontal member that connects and stiffens opposing principal rafters, thus stabilizing the roof truss.

Crib. Log wall compartment, or pen, in barn serving both stable and mow functions.

Cross beam. Heavy member of bent, reaching from end post to end post, positioned below tie beam.

Cupola. Small, towerlike structure on roof providing additional light and ventilation.

Diamond. Common pattern of brick ventilating openings in gable walls of masonry barns.

Double-decker barn. Bank barn with a two-level storage loft above a basement stable.

Double-outshed barn. Type of Pennsylvania barn with two rear storage sheds flanking the rear ramp or bank.

Eave. Lower overhanging edge of a sloping roof.

Eave-forebay barn. Barn whose forebay is positioned on eave wall of barn.

End post. Heavy outer post of a bent.

English Lake District barn. Two-level bank barn that developed in north-eastern England; lacks forebay but frequently has a pentroof over stable doors.

Extended Pennsylvania Barn. Pennsylvania barn which has been enlarged by the inclusion of front, rear, or vertical extensions.

Extended supported-forebay barn. Extended Pennsylvania barn which has been enlarged by the inclusion of a deep forebay reinforced with support posts.

Extra-overhang barn. Standard Pennsylvania barn with upper-level over-hangs in addition to a forebay.

False Sweitzer standard barn. Open-forebay standard Pennsylvania barn with unposted cantilevered forebay.

Flared post. End post enlarged at upper end to increase strength and support for tie beams.

Forebay. Eave side overhang of upper level of Pennsylvania barn (*Vorbau* or *Vorschuss* in Pennsylvania German).

Forebay bank barn. Two-level barn with bank and forebay; correctly called a Pennsylvania barn in Canada and the United States.

Forebay beam. Heavy beam that extends beneath forebay back to stable front wall and on beneath frame of upper barn.

Forebay cross beam. Heavy beam that runs under and supports outer ends of forebay beams.

Forebay sill. Bottom member of forebay front wall frame which rests on and is supported by outer forebay beam ends.

Fraktur art. European and early Pennsylvanian illuminated script and decoration, usually found on birth certificates and other personal documents.

Front-shed barn. Extended Pennsylvania barn with two-level storage wing projecting at right angle from forebay.

Fudergang. Pennsylvania-German term for the feeding alley that runs adjacent to cattle pens in stable of barn.

Gable. Triangular upper wall space extending from the eaves to the roof ridge.

Gable-forebay barn. Barn with forebay on gable rather than eave side of barn.

Gable roof. A ridged roof terminating at ends in a gable.

Gambrel roof. A ridged roof each side of which has two slopes.

Gin pole. Tall, sturdy vertical post with pulley on top, used to help raise heavy bents during barn raising.

Girt. Horizontal framing member connecting end posts below roof plate.

Grundscheier. Pennsylvania-German term for single-story (ground level) multiple-purpose barn.

Hay hole. Opening in mow floor through which hay and straw are lowered to basement stable.

Haylage. Cattle feed consisting of fermented alfalfa, clover, and grasses plus shelled corn, stored in a silo.

Hay track and fork. Pulley and fork mounted on track below roof ridge, used to carry hay or straw into mow.

Hewn bents. Bent made of framing members which have been cut and shaped using hand tools.

Hex sign. Colorful, usually circular, decoration found on outside forebay front wall of Pennsylvania barns.

High Alemannic or Swiss-German house. Folkhouse of central European uplands, usually a two- or three-level, combined house-barn.

Hof. Barnyard area adjacent to stable doors.

House-barn. Basic European farm structure with dwelling and barn combined under one roof.

Kick-in-the-roof. European roof style in which overhanging edge of sloping roof changes to more gentle angle as it projects beyond the outer wall as the eave.

Kornhist. German term for freestanding grain-drying rack of high Alpine regions (*Chischner* in Romansch).

Laube. Upper level overhanging open gallery or porch, commonly found on Alpine-Alemannic folkhouses and barns.

Liegender Stuhl. Germanic roof framework utilizing a heavy, truncated principal rafter and braced double collar beam truss to support purlins.

Loafing shed. Large, open shed adjacent to stable, used to accommodate dairy cows during bad weather.

Loft. Hay and straw storage area above stable; upper level storage area of a Pennsylvania barn.

Log Sweitzer barn. Earliest type of Pennsylvania forebay bank barn.

Loophole. Narrow, vertical opening in masonry barn wall which lets in air and light while retarding penetration of rain and snow.

Louvered ventilator. Window-sized ventilating opening in masonry walls of Pennsylvania barns, using horizontal, tilted, wooden slats to retard penetration of rain and snow.

Material culture. Visible, tangible elements of a cultural environment (houses, barns, tools, etc.), which may distinguish one culture group from another.

Mortise. In a mortise-and-tenon joint, the slot or hole cut into one member, into which is inserted the tenon from another member.

Mow. Space in barn reserved for hay and straw storage.

Multiple-overhang standard barn. Standard Pennsylvania barn which has one or more projecting upper-level walls in addition to the forebay.

New York Dutch barn. New York version of north German and Dutch ground-level barn, with primary access on gable end.

Open-forebay standard barn. Standard Pennsylvania barn without extended end wall forebay support.

Outshed. Wing of rear-extension Pennsylvania barn, on ramp or bank side.

Outshut. Ramp-side storage shed found on some English Lake District barns in Great Britain.

Overhanging, extended, framed bay. Shallowly overhanging upper level of many medieval European structures.

Overshoot (overshot, overhang). Commonly used terms for forebay of Pennsylvania barn.

Peiler. Masonry pier or pillar that strengthens barn wall or helps to support forebay.

Peilereck (pillar corner). Pennsylvania-German name for alcove between Peiler and stable front wall of closed forebay standard barn.

Pennsylvania barn core. Region of early settlement and of dense concentration of Sweitzer barns, in southeastern Pennsylvania.

Pentroof. Shallow, sloping roof above lower floor of house or barn.

Pike. Long pole with metallic point, used to push up bents when raising a barn.

Pomeranian stable. Small two-level unbanked forebay stable that originated in northern Germany and is found in southeastern Wisconsin.

Porch. Name used for forebay in central Wisconsin.

Porch barn. Name given to up-country, posted-forebay Pennsylvania barns in central Wisconsin.

Post-to-purlin. Barn bent in which interior posts reach to purlin, eliminating the need for queen posts.

Prätigau barn. Log forebay bank barn abundant in Prätigau region of Canton Graubünden, Switzerland.

Principal rafter. Heavy rafter which is larger at the bent than common rafters are between the bents.

Purlin. Timber placed under and horizontal to rafters to provide their support.

Quebec barn. French-Canadian version of long, ground-level barn found in Brittany, France.

Queen post. Vertical or canted roof framework member supporting purlin and resting on the tie beam.

Quoins. Interlocking, alternating stone blocks laid at wall corners to add strength to the corner.

Raising the barn. Building a barn frame using teams of workers who erect and connect the bents.

Ramp shed. Rear enlargement shed that covers entire back wall of Pennsylvania barn.

Ramp shed barn. Rear-extension Pennsylvania barn with ramp shed.

Reading Prong. Line of low crystalline hills which extend from New England into Pennsylvania south of the Great Valley, ending southwest of Reading.

Rear-extension barn. Extended Pennsylvania barn with enlargement on ramp or rear side.

Ridge board. Board connecting rafter ends at peak of gable roof.

Romansch. Ethnic and language group living in southern Switzerland and deriving from the ancient Raetian people, later Romanized.

Roof framework. Arrangement of queen posts, struts, and braces which supports the purlins and roof rafters.

Roof plate. Heavy frame member connecting tops of end posts and supporting lower ends of rafters.

Root cellar. Storage cellar for root crop and cattle feed, usually built beneath barn bank.

Schweizer Scheier (also Schweitzer Scheier). Pennsylvania-German term for Swiss, Swisser, or Sweitzer Pennsylvania barn.

Sheaf of wheat pattern. Common pattern of brick ventilating openings in gable walls of masonry barns.

Sill. Heavy frame member resting on foundation and supporting posts and braces of outer wall frame.

Special form standard barn. Consists of several subtypes of standard Pennsylvania barns with unusual morphology but limited population.

Speicher. Separate granary on farmsteads in Germanic Europe.

Split doors. Stable doors divided into separately hinged upper and lower sections.

Stable front wall. Wall below forebay of Pennsylvania barn with stable doors.

Stadel. Walser high Alpine structure combining grain drying, threshing, and storage functions.

Standard Pennsylvania barn. Class of Pennsylvania barns characterized by balanced bent and symmetrical gable silhouette.

Strut. Light roof framework bracing member that connects queen post and tie beam.

Summer beam. Heavy main horizontal beam, anchored in gable foundation walls, that supports forebay beams and barn frame above.

Talina. Romansch term for upper-level drying gallery of barn in eastern Graubünden and deep separate forebay of barn in Prätigau, Graubünden, Switzerland. *See* Chischner

Tenon. In mortise and tenon joints, the short shaft projecting from one member which is fitted into mortise in other joint member.

Three-level barn. *See* Double-decker barn.

Threshing floor. Floor space between mows, on which grains were hand-threshed by flailing.

Tie beam. Uppermost cross beam, which connects end posts of bent.

Transition Sweitzer barn. Sweitzer Pennsylvania barn with extended forebay-end walls providing additional forebay support.

Truss. Triangular arrangement of beams, braces, and ties to form a rigid framework.

Uncantilevered forebay beams. Forebay beams that are supported by front stable wall and do not extend back and under barn frame.

Ventilating slits. *See* Loophole.

Vernacular architecture. Houses and barns derived from traditions of a culture group rather than from formal architectural plans.

Vorschub. German term for forebay.

Vürschutz. Swiss term for deep separate forebay of barn. While this type of forebay is found elsewhere, use of the term is confined to Prätigau, Graubünden, Switzerland.

Walser. Name of a Germanic language and of an ethnic group who settled the upper Rhone Valley (Goms) in Canton Wallis, Switzerland, and then spread westward into Canton Graubünden, and Vorarlberg, Austria, and beyond.

Yankee barn. New England version of English hay and grain ground barn, modified to house cattle also.

REFERENCES AND SELECTED BIBLIOGRAPHY

Alderfer, Joel D. 1986. *Mennonite Migration from Southeastern Pennsylvania*. Souderton, Pa.: Mennonite Historians of Eastern Pennsylvania.

Apps, Jerry, and Allen Strang. 1977. *Barns of Wisconsin*. Madison, Wis.: Tamarack Press.

Arthur, Eric, and Dudley Witney. 1972. *The Barn: A Vanishing Landmark in North America*. Toronto: M. F. Feheley Arts Co.

Ball, Bernice M. 1974. *Barns of Chester County, Pennsylvania*. Kennett Square, Pa.: KNA.

Bastian, Robert W. 1975. "Southeastern Pennsylvania and Central Wisconsin Barns: Examples of Independent Parallel Development?" *Professional Geographer* 27 (May): 200–204.

Baumgartner, Roland, and Esther Woerdehoff. 1988. "The Great Walser Route." *Switzerland*. Zurich: Swiss National Tourist Office 7.

Bennett, George Fletcher. 1977. *The Perennial Apprentice, 60-Year Scrapbook: Architecture 1916–1976*. Wilmington, Del.: Tri Mark Publishing.

Bertland, Dennis N. 1974. *Early Architecture of Warren County*. Belvedere, N.J.: Warren County Board of Chosen Freeholders.

Bertolet, Peter G. 1980 [1860]. *Fragments of the Past: Historical Sketches of Oley and Vicinity*. Oley, Pa.: Woman's Club of Oley Valley.

Billigmeier, Robert H. 1979. *A Crisis in Swiss Pluralism*. New York: Mouton Publications.

The Brethren Encyclopedia. 1984. 3 vols. Philadelphia: Brethren Encyclopedia.

Brockmann, Jerosch. 1933. *Schweizer Bauernhaus*. Bern: Verlag Hans Huber.

Brunskill, Ronald W. 1971. *Illustrated Handbook of Vernacular Architecture*. London: Faber and Faber.

———. 1974. *Vernacular Architecture of the Lake Counties*. London: Faber and Faber.

———. 1987. *Traditional Farm Buildings of Britain*. London: Victor Gollancz.

Bucher, Robert C., and Alan G. Keyser. 1982. "Thatching in Pennsylvania." *Der Reggeboge* (journal of the Pennsylvania German Society) 16:1–23.

Calkins, Charles F., and Martin C. Perkins. 1980. "The Pomerian Stable of Southeastern Wisconsin." *Concordia Historical Institute Quarterly* 53, no. 3:121–25.

Carter, Edward C., John C. Van Horne, and Charles E. Brownell, eds. 1985. *Latrobe's*

View of America 1795–1820: Selections from the Watercolors and Sketches. New Haven: Yale University Press.

Cedar County Historical Review. 1980. Tipton, Iowa: Cedar County Historical Society (July).

"Chester County Pennsylvania Barn Plan." 1838. *The Farmers Cabinet* (February 15): 195–97.

Coffee, Brian. 1978. "Nineteenth-Century Barns of Geauga County, Ohio." *Pioneer America* 10, no. 2 (December): 53–63.

Colville, Darrel, and Donna Curran. 1990. *Do Barns Go to Heaven?* Parkville, Mo.: Arrow Press.

Conlyn, John. 1983. "Barns of Erie County." In *Erie County's Architectural Legacy,* edited by Austin Fox. Erie County, N.Y.: Erie County Preservation Board.

Cooper, Tom. 1982. *Iowa's Natural Heritage.* Des Moines: Iowa National Heritage Foundation and the Iowa Academy of Natural Sciences.

Crowley, William K. 1978. "Old Order Amish Settlement: Diffusion and Growth." *Annals of the Association of American Geographers* 68:249–64.

Dornbusch, Charles H., and John D. Heyl. 1958. "Pennsylvania German Barns." *The Pennsylvania German Folklore Society* (vol. 21, 1956). Allentown, Pa.: Schlechter's.

Dundore, M. Walter. 1955. "The Saga of the Pennsylvania Germans in Wisconsin." *The Pennsylvania German Folklore Society* (vol. 19, 1954). Allentown, Pa.: Schlechter's.

Ennals, Peter. 1972. "Nineteenth-Century Barns in Southern Ontario, Canada." *Canadian Geographer* 16, no. 3:256–70.

Ensminger, Robert F. 1980–81. "A Search for the Origin of the Pennsylvania Barn." *Pennsylvania Folklife* 30, no. 2:50–71.

———. 1983. "A Comparative Study of Pennsylvania and Wisconsin Forebay Barns." *Pennsylvania Folklife.* 32, no. 3:98–114.

———. 1988. "Pennsylvania in Canada." *Pioneer American Society Transactions* 11:63–72.

Evans, E. Estyn. 1974. "Folk Housing in the British Isles in Materials other than Timber." In *Geoscience and Man.* Vol. 5, *Man and Cultural Heritage,* edited by Bob F. Perkins, 53–64. Baton-Rouge: Louisiana State University.

Faust, Albert B., and Gaius M. Brumbaugh. 1968. *Lists of Swiss Emigrants in the Eighteenth Century to the American Colonies.* Baltimore: Genealogical Publishing Company.

Fegley, H. Winslow. 1987. "Farming, Always Farming." *The Pennsylvania German Society* (vol. 20, 1986). Birdsboro, Pa.: Pennsylvania German Society.

Fink, Daniel. 1987. *Barns of the Genesee County: 1790–1915.* Geneseo, N.Y.: James Brunner.

Fitchen, John. 1968. *The New World Dutch Barn.* Syracuse: Syracuse University Press.

Fletcher, Stevenson W. 1950. *Pennsylvania Agriculture and Country Life, 1640–1840.* Harrisburg: Pennsylvania Historical and Museum Commission.

Gephard, Torsten. 1977. *Alte Bauernhäuser.* Munich: Georg D. W. Callwey.

Glass, Joseph W. 1971. *The Pennsylvania Culture Region: A Geographical Interpretation of Barns and Farmhouses,* Ph.D. thesis, Department of Geography, State College, Pennsylvania State University.

———. 1986. *Pennsylvania Culture Region: A View from the Barn.* Ann Arbor, Mich.: UMI Research Press.

Glassie, Henry. 1965a. "The Old Barns of Appalachia." *Mountain Life and Work* 41, no. 2 (Summer): 21–30.

———. 1965b. "The Pennsylvania Barn in the South." Part 1. *Pennsylvania Folklife* 15, no. 2:8–19.

———. 1966. "The Pennsylvania Barn in the South." Part 2. *Pennsylvania Folklife* 15, no. 4:12–25.

———. 1968. *Pattern in the Material Folk Culture of the Eastern United States.* Philadelphia: University of Pennsylvania Press.

———. 1970. "The Double-Crib Barn in South-Central Pennsylvania." Part 4. *Pioneer America* 2, no. 2 (July): 23–34.

———. 1974. "The Variation of Concepts within Tradition: Barn Building in Otsego County, New York." In *Geoscience and Man.* Vol. 5, *Man and Cultural Heritage,* edited by Bob F. Perkins, 177–235. Baton Rouge: Louisiana State University.

———. 1975. "Barns across Southern England: A Note on Transatlantic Comparison and Architectural Meanings." *Pioneer America* 7, no. 1 (January): 9–19.

Graeff, Arthur D. 1948. "The Pennsylvania Germans in Ontario, Canada." *The Pennsylvania German Folklore Society* (vol. 11, 1946). Allentown, Pa.: Schlecter's.

Grieser, Orlando R., and Ervin Beck, Jr. 1960. *Out of the Wilderness.* Grand Rapids, Mich.: Dean-Hicks Company.

Gschwend, Max. 1965. "Bäuerlich Haus-und Hofformen." In *Atlas der Schweiz,* Eduard Imhoff, director, plates 36 and 36a. Wabern-Bern, Switzerland: Verlag der Eidgenössischen Landestopographie.

Harper, Glenn A., and Leslie H. Smith. 1988. "They Chose Land Wisely: Settlement Patterns and Land Use among Mennonite Settlers in Southern Adams County, Indiana." *Pioneer America Society Transactions* 11:73–81.

Herman, Stewart W. 1978. *Daniel's Line.* Shelter Island Heights, N.Y.: privately published.

Hostetler, John A. 1980. *Amish Society.* Baltimore: Johns Hopkins University Press.

Hunziker, Jacob. 1900. *Das Schweizerhaus.* Vol. 1, *Das Wallis.* Aarau, Switzerland: H. R. Sauerländer.

———. 1905. *Das Schweizerhaus.* Vol. 3, *Graübunden.* Aarau, Switzerland: H. R. Sauerländer.

Hutslar, Donald A. 1977. *The Log Architecture of Ohio.* Columbus: Ohio State Historical Society.

Jordan, Terry G. 1980. "Alpine Alemannic, and American Log Architecture." *Annals of the Association of American Geographers* 70, no. 2:154–80.

———. 1980–81. "A Forebay Bank Barn in Texas." *Pennsylvania Folklife* 30, no. 2:72–77.

———. 1983. Letter to author, 6 July.

———. 1985. *American Log Buildings.* Chapel Hill: University of North Carolina Press.

———. 1987–88. "Some Neglected Swiss Literature on the Forebay Bank Barn." *Pennsylvania Folklife* 37, no. 2:75–80.

———. 1989. "Preadaption and European Colonization in Rural North America." *Annals of the Association of American Geographers* 79, no. 4:489–500.

Jordan, Terry G., and Matti Kaups. 1989. *The American Backwoods Frontier: An Ethnic and Ecological Interpretation.* Baltimore: John Hopkins University Press.

Kauffman, Henry J. 1954. "Pennsylvania Barns." *Farm Quarterly* 9, no. 3:58–61, 80–82.

Keyser, Alan G., and William P. Stein. 1975. "The Pennsylvania German Tri-Level Ground Barn." *Der Reggeboge: Quarterly of the Pennsylvania German Society* 9, no. 3, 4:1–25.

Kiefer, Wayne. 1972. "An Agricultural Settlement Complex in Indiana." *Annals of the Association of American Geographers* 62:487–506.

Kniffen, Fred B. 1965. "Folk Housing: Key to Diffusion." *Annals of the Association of American Geographers* 55, no. 1:549–77.

Krieder, Robert, Carol Diller, Herman Hilty, and Darvin Luginbuhl. 1988. "The Swiss Settlement at the Turn of the Century: A Photographic Essay." *Mennonite Life* 43, no. 4:20–47.

Kuhns, Oscar. 1901. *The German and Swiss Settlements of Colonial Pennsylvania: A Study of the So-called Pennsylvania Dutch.* New York: Henry Holt.

Laedrach, Walter. 1954. *Das Bernische Speicher: Berner Heimatbücher.* Vol. 57/58. Bern: Verlag Paul Haupt.

Laedrach, Walter, and Christian Rubi. 1948. *Das Simmentaler Bauernhaus: Berner Heimatbücher.* Vol. 35/36. Bern: Verlag Paul Haupt.

Learned, Marion D. 1915. "The German Barn in America." In *University of Pennsylvania Lectures Delivered by Members of the Faculty in the Free Public Lecture Course,* pp. 338–49. Philadelphia: University of Pennsylvania.

Leestma, Roger A. 1951. *The Muskegan River Basin.* Ph.D. dissertation, University of Michigan.

Leyburn, James G. 1962. *The Scotch Irish: A Social History.* Chapel Hill: University of North Carolina Press.

Little, Charles E., ed. 1988. *Louis Bromfield at Malabar: Writings on Farming and Country Life.* Baltimore: Johns Hopkins University Press.

Long, Amos, Jr. 1972a. *Farmsteads and Their Buildings.* Lebanon, Pa.: Applied Arts Publishers.

———. 1972b. "The Pennsylvania German Family Farm," *The Pennsylvania German Society* (vol. 6, 1972). Breinigsville, Pa.: Pennsylvania German Society.

———. 1989. "An Overview of Travel and Transportation in Pennsylvania." *Pennsylvania Folklife* 39, no. 1:2–26.

Ludwig, George M. 1947. "The Influence of the Pennsylvania Dutch in the Middle West." *The Pennsylvania German Folklore Society* (vol. 10, 1945). Allentown, Pa.: Schlechters.

———. 1964. "The Pennsylvania Dutch Barn in Iowa." *Iowan* 12, no. 3:42–54.

Mitchell, S. Agustus. 1832. *The Tourist Pocket Map of Pennsylvania.* Philadelphia: n.p.

———. 1834. *Map of the States of Ohio, Indiana, and Illinois.* Philadelphia: n.p.

Montell, William, and Michael Morse. 1976. *Kentucky Folk Architecture.* Lexington: University of Kentucky Press.

Noble, Allen G. 1977. "Barns as Elements of the Settlement Landscape." *Pioneer America* 9, no. 1 (July): 62–79.

———. 1984. *Wood, Brick, and Stone: The North American Settlement Landscape.* Vol. 2, *Barns and Farm Structures.* Amherst: University of Massachusetts Press.

Noble, Allen G., and Gayle A. Seymour. 1982. "Distribution of Barn Types in Northeastern United States." *Geographical Review* 72:155–70.

"Old Picturesque Barns Are Fast Becoming Endangered Species." 1984. *The Youngstown Vindicator,* June 3, p. 6.

"Oley Valley Heritage Festival." 1983. Oley, Pa.: Oley Valley Heritage Association.

Perrin, Richard W. E. 1981. 2nd ed., rev. *A Survey in Pioneer Architecture 1835–1870.* Milwaukee: Milwaukee Public Museum.

Phleps, Hermann. 1942. *Holzbaukunst: Der Blockbau*. Karlsruhe, Germany: Fachblattverlag Dr. Albert Bruder.

———. 1982. *The Craft of Log Building*. Ottawa: Lee Valley Tools.

Price, H. Wayne. 1987. "The Pennsylvania Barn in Adams County, Illinois: A Study in Variations." *Pioneer America Society Transactions* 10:29–35.

———. 1988. "The Barns of Illinois." *Bulletin of the Illinois Geographical Society* 30, no. 1:3–22.

Price, H. Wayne, and Keith A. Sculle. 1985. "Observations on the Pennsylvania German Barns in Stephenson County, Illinois." *Pioneer America Society Transactions* 8:45–53.

Ravensway, Charles van. 1977. *The Arts and Architecture of German Settlements in Missouri: A Survey of a Vanishing Culture*. Columbia: University of Missouri Press.

Rawson, Richard. 1979. *Old Barn Plans*. New York: Bonanza Books.

Raymond, Eleanor. 1977. *Early Domestic Architecture of Pennsylvania*. Exton, Pa.: Schiffer.

Reaman, G. Elmore. 1957. *The Trail of the Black Walnut*. Toronto: McClellen and Stewart.

Ridlen, Susanne S. 1972. "Bank Barns in Cass County, Indiana." *Pioneer America* 4, no. 2 (July): 25–43.

Schäfer, Dietrich. 1906. *Das Bauernhaus im Deutchen Reiche und in Seinen Granzgebieten*. Vols. 1 and 2. Dresden: Gerhard Kühtmann.

Schilli, Hermann, and Helmut Richter. n.d. *Vogtsbauernhof in Gutach in the Black Forest: English Guide*. Published by Ortenaukreis Offenburg.

Schreiber, William I. 1967. "The Pennsylvania Dutch Barn in Ohio." *Journal of the Ohio Folklore Society* 2:15–28.

Schultz, LeRoy G. 1986. *Barns, Stables, and Outbuildings: A World Bibliography in English, 1700–1983*. Jefferson, N.C.: McFarland.

Shoemaker, Alfred L. 1953. *Hex, No!* Lancaster: Pennsylvania Dutch Folklore Center, Franklin and Marshall College.

———. Ed. 1959 [1955]. *The Pennsylvania Barn*. Lancaster: Pennsylvania Dutch Folklore Center, Franklin and Marshall College. Reprint, Kutztown: Pennsylvania Folklife Society.

Simonett, Christopher, and J. U. Könz. 1968. *Die Bauernhaüser des Kantons Graubünden*. Vol. 2. Basel, Switzerland: Verlag Schweizerische Gesellshaft für Volkskunde.

Snyder, Tim. 1988. "Dutch Reformed." *Harrowsmith* 17 (October): 62–71.

Sobon, Jack, and Roger Schroeder. 1984. *Timber Frame Construction*. Pownal, Vt.: Garden Way Publishing.

Stokes, Samuel N., A. Elizabeth Watson, Genevieve P. Keller, and J. Timothy Keller. 1989. *Saving America's Countryside: A Guide to Rural Conservation*. Baltimore: Johns Hopkins University Press.

Stoltzfus, Grant M. 1969. *Mennonites of the Ohio and Eastern Conference*. Scottsdale, Pa.: Herald Press.

Stotz, Charles S. 1966. *The Architectural Heritage of Early Western Pennsylvania: A Record of Building before 1860*. Pittsburgh: University of Pittsburgh Press.

Sutton, David. 1980. "A West Virginia Swiss Community: The Aegerter Photographers of Helvetia, Randolph County." *Goldenseal* 6, no. 2:9–22.

Thiede, Klaus. 1955. *Deutche Bauernhäuser*. Stuttgart, Germany: J. E. Steinkopf.

Wacker, Peter O. 1974. "Traditional House and Barn Types in New Jersey: Keys to

Acculturation." In *Geoscience and Man.* Vol. 5, *Man and Cultural Heritage,* edited by Bob F. Perkins, 163–76. Baton Rouge: Louisiana State University.

Walls, Robert E. 1989. "Ethnicity and Architecture in Eastern Washington." *The Washboard: The Newsletter of the Washington State Folklife Council* 5, no. 1:1.

Weiss, Richard. 1943. "Stallbauten und Heutraggeräte Graubündens in sach-geographisher Betrachtung." *Sach, Ort und Wort: Jakob Jud zum sechzigsten Geburtstag, 12 Januar 1942, Romantica Helvetica,* vol. 20. Geneva: Libraire E. Droz; and Zürich-Erlenbach: Eugen Rentsch Verlag.

———. 1959. *Haüser und Landschaften der Schweiz.* Zürich: Eugen Rentsch Verlag.

Wells, Wilson. 1976. *Barns of the U.S.A.* San Diego: Acme Printing.

Wenger, J. C. 1966. *The Mennonite Church in America.* Scottsdale, Pa.: Herald Press.

Wertenbaker, Thomas J. 1938. *The Founding of American Civilization: The Middle Colonies.* New York: Charles Scribners Sons.

Weyer, Jim. 1988. *Red Walls, Black Hats.* Toledo: Weyer International Book Division.

Wilhelm, Hubert G. H. 1974. "The Pennsylvania Dutch Barn in Southeastern Ohio." In *Geoscience and Man.* Vol. 5, *Man and Cultural Heritage,* edited by Bob F. Perkins, 155–64. Baton Rouge: Louisiana State University.

———. 1982. *The Origin and Distribution of Settlement Groups: Ohio, 1850.* Athens: Ohio University.

———. 1989a. *The Barn Builders: Pennsylvania Settlers in Ohio: A Study Guide.* Athens: Ohio University.

———. 1989b. "Double-Overhang Barns in the Pennsylvania Settlement Region of Southeastern Ohio." *Pioneer America Society Transactions* 12:29–37. Paper presented at PAS meetings, November 1988, Mobile, Ala.

Williams, David G. 1950. *The Lower Jordan Valley Pennsylvania German Settlement.* Vol. 18. Allentown, Pa.: Lehigh County Historical Society.

Wisconsin's Changing Population. October 1942. "The People of Wisconsin According to Ethnic Stock, 1940." Map insert. *Bulletin of the University of Wisconsin,* no. 2642, general series no. 2426.

Yoder, Donald H. 1965. "The Domestic Encyclopaedia of 1803–1804." *Pennsylvania Folklife* 14, no. 3:10–27.

Yoder, Donald H., and Thomas E. Graves. 1989. *Hex Signs: Pennsylvania's Dutch Barn Symbols and Their Meaning.* New York: E. P. Dutton.

Zeller, Willy. 1972. *Kunst und Kultur in Graubünden.* Bern, Switzerland: Paul Haupt.

Zielinski, John M. 1982. *Iowa Barns, No. 1.* Iowa City: privately published.

———. 1989. *Amish Barns across America.* Iowa City: Amish Heritage Publications.

Zinsli, Paul. 1986. *Walser Volkstum.* Chur, Switzerland: Terra-Grischuna Buch-verlag.

INDEX